Psallité

Sacred Song for Liturgy and Life

Year C

Music by
The Collegeville Composers Group

LITURGICAL PRESS
Collegeville, Minnesota

www.litpress.org
800.858.5450

ACKNOWLEDGMENTS

Imprimatur: ✠ Most Reverend John F. Kinney, Diocese of Saint Cloud in Minnesota, April 21, 2006.

Music from *Psallité: Sacred Song for Liturgy and Life,* © 2005, 2006 by The Collegeville Composers Group (Carol Browning, Catherine Christmas, Cyprian Consiglio, O.S.B. Cam., Paul F. Ford, Ph.D., Paul Inwood). All rights reserved. Published and administered by Liturgical Press, Collegeville, Minnesota 56321.

The Psalm texts from The Grail (England), © 1963, 1986, 1993, 2000, The Grail. The Canticle texts from the Grail (England), © 1967, The Grail. All rights reserved. Licensed for *Psallité* and reprinted by permission of GIA Publications, Inc., 7404 South Mason Avenue, Chicago, IL 60638, North American agent for The Grail. *Imprimatur:* ✠ Most Reverend William Keeler, President, National Conference of Catholic Bishops, September 12, 1993.

The Canticle texts from the New Revised Standard Version (NRSV) Bible, © 1989, Division of Christian Education of the National Council of the Churches of Christ in the United States of America. All rights reserved. Used with permission. *Imprimatur:* ✠ Most Reverend Daniel E. Pilarczyk, President, National Conference of Catholic Bishops, September 12, 1991.

The cover design is by James Rhoades; photograph by Rob Fiocca, Botanica Images.

ISBN 13: 978-0-8146-3065-5

ISBN 10: 0-8146-3065-0

Contents

INTRODUCTORY NOTES

A new collection of liturgical songs inspired by the antiphons and psalms of the *Roman Missal, Psallité: Sacred Song for Liturgy and Life* includes music for each Sunday, Solemnity, and major feast day of the liturgical year.

For each liturgy, *Psallité* provides biblically based options for the entrance/opening song (the SONG FOR THE WEEK/DAY); the response song during the Liturgy of the Word (the SONG FOR THE WORD); and the song during the Communion procession (the SONG FOR THE TABLE). This collection contains a wealth of biblically based liturgical songs. While the music in this collection suggests specific Sundays or celebrations for its use, they have various, repeatable uses throughout the liturgical year.

The name *Psallité* (SAH-lee-tay) comes from the Latin version of Psalm 47:8, *psallite sapienter*, "sing praise with all your skill."

Psallité's music connects liturgy and life, church and home. The SONG FOR THE WEEK may be your theme tune for the entire week. The SONG FOR THE WORD may echo in your mind and keep the Word alive in your heart all day. The SONG FOR THE TABLE may be the one that you sing around your own dining table. All this is achieved by means of memorable music that will transform your life. Once this music gets under your skin, there's no turning back.

The **SONG FOR THE WEEK** opens the celebration, intensifies the unity of the assembly, leads their thoughts to the mystery of the liturgical season or festivity, and accompanies the procession of the presider and ministers. Another option is to use the SONG FOR THE WEEK at the end of the liturgy (with the addition of a doxology) to send forth the assembly into the world.

The **SONG FOR THE WORD**, an entirely new repertory of short, memorable antiphons, serves as the golden thread of the Liturgy of the Word.

The **SONG FOR THE TABLE**, which is the heart of *Psallité*, takes its texts and themes from the Liturgy of the Word, especially from the gospel of the day, transformed into processional music. People will now experience that the promises God made in his Word are fulfilled in the body and blood of Christ.

Psallité's music provides flexibility and allows leaders of music ministry to adapt the music for their assemblies. On the one hand, *Psallité* was designed for those parishes with the most limited musical resources: one well-trained cantor, no accompanist, but an assembly eager to sing the Mass. On the other hand, satisfying vocal, keyboard, and guitar arrangements will win the hearts of the most accomplished choirs and instrumentalists. Many of the descants not marked for a specific voice part may be sung in the alto/tenor range as well as the soprano range.

The style of music is eclectic—with influences ranging from chant to Afro-Caribbean to folk song but in all cases essentially vocal. The cantor calls to the assembly and the assembly responds. And every word they sing is biblically based.

The verse tones of *Psallité* can be used with any translation of the psalms, especially any Grail-based translation. Because *Psallité* models the use of moderately inclusive, horizontally inclusive language, it employs the 1993 Grail revision sponsored by the United States Conference of Catholic Bishops with the *imprimatur* of then-Bishop now Cardinal William H. Keeler, who was president at that time. The biblical canticles are mostly taken from the New Revised Standard Version, with some original translations for good measure.

Singing the antiphons and psalms of *Psallité* restores psalm-singing as our primary prayer language. Singing this kind of music helps our assemblies find their voices so that we all can sing the Mass, not just sing at Mass. Singing the same antiphons that our sisters and brothers sang at least a thousand years ago, and in some cases nearly two thousand years ago, connects us spiritually to the great communion of saints, a procession in which we are only the most recent walkers. Singing the various styles of music in *Psallité* will also help break down the cultural barriers that keep us from being "one body, one spirit, in Christ."

ABOUT THE COMPOSERS

The Collegeville Composers Group, a team of international musicians working collaboratively to create the collection, composed the music of *Psallité*. The composers group includes:

Carol Browning, the Director of Liturgy and Music at Saint Mary Magdalen Catholic Community in Camarillo, California and a music minister for almost twenty years. A member of the Religious Society of Friends (Quakers), Carol is a liturgical composer and an independently published inspirational songwriter.

Catherine Christmas, an accomplished organist and former cathedral director of music, currently working as Pastoral Coordinator for a group of parishes based in Winchester, England, and studying for a Master's in Pastoral Liturgy at Heythrop College, University of London.

Cyprian Consiglio, O.S.B. Cam., a musician, composer, author, and teacher who is a monk of the Camaldolese Congregation. He spends about half his time at home, writing and composing, and the other half of his time on the road, performing and teaching.

Paul F. Ford, Ph.D., a professor of systematic theology and liturgy, Saint John's Seminary, Camarillo, California. He is the author of *By Flowing Waters: Chant for the Liturgy,* published by Liturgical Press.

Paul Inwood, the Director of Liturgy and Director of Music for the Diocese of Portsmouth, England. He is an internationally known liturgist, composer, organist, choir director, and clinician. His liturgical music appears in numerous hymnals worldwide.

ADDITIONAL RESOURCES

Psallité: Sacred Song for Liturgy and Life

Published in three volumes, these editions include the full accompaniment and cantor/schola verses for all Sundays, Solemnities and major feast days of the liturgical cycle. Plastic coil binding, 8½" x 10⅞", over 320 pp.

Individual volumes: 1–4 copies, $24.95 each; 5 or more copies, $19.95* net each; please inquire for bulk purchases.

0-8146-3064-2 Year A
0-8146-3059-6 Year B
0-8146-3065-0 Year C

Complete three-volume set (Years ABC): 1–4 sets, $59.95 per set; 5 or more sets, $49.95* net per set; please inquire for bulk purchases.

0-8146-3060-X Years ABC

Psallité Antiphons on CD-ROM

Easy-to-use graphic files of all Psallité assembly antiphons (Years ABC) that can be used to select and insert music into desktop publishing documents, PowerPoint presentations, or other custom worship aids and programs. The parish or institution must purchase an annual reprint license in order to legally reproduce the antiphons.

0-8146-7961-7 $39.95 CD-ROM
0-8146-3061-8 $35.00 Annual license

Walk in My Ways

A collection of twenty-seven titles taken from Psallité: Sacred Song for Liturgy and Life (Year B). Titles include: To You, O Lord, I Lift My Soul • Rejoice in the Lord, Again, Rejoice • We Receive from Your Fullness • Here Is My Servant, Here Is My Son • Give, Your Father Sees • Those Who Love Me, I Will Deliver • My Shepherd Is the Lord • There Is Mercy in the Lord • This Is My Body • Send Out Your Spirit • Christ, Our Pasch • Live on In My Love • I Will See You Again • Walk in My Ways • Venite, adoremus • God Heals the Broken • Lead Me, Guide Me • Here in Your Presence • All You Nations • Don't Be Afraid • Those Who Do Justice • Let the Word Make a Home in Your Heart • I Loved Wisdom More than Health or Beauty • Courage! Get Up! • My Plans for You Are Peace • Rejoice in the Lord on This Feast of the Saints • May God Grant Us Joy of Heart

The music collection includes full accompaniment for cantor, schola, keyboard, and guitar plus reprintable antiphon graphics for assembly use. A CD recording of the collection is also available.

Music collection: 0-8146-3058-8 • $11.95;
5 or more copies $9.95* each
CD recording: 0-8146-7960-9 • $16.95

We Will Follow You, Lord

A collection of twenty-eight titles taken from Psallité: Sacred Song for Liturgy and Life (Year C). Titles include: The Days Are Coming, Surely Coming • My Soul Rejoices in God • God's Love Is Revealed to Us • Not on Bread Alone Are We Nourished • You Are My Hiding-Place, O Lord • Lord, Cleanse My Heart, Make Me New • People of God, Flock of the Lord • A New Commandment • Joyfully You Will Draw Water • All Who Labor, Come to Me • This Day Is Holy to the Lord Our God • Love Bears All Things • Cast Out into the Deep • Forgive, and You Will Be Forgiven • Speak Your Word, O Lord, and We Shall Be Healed • For You My Soul Is Thirsting, O God, My God • We Will Follow You, Lord • Listen: I Stand at the Door and Knock • Do Not Store Up Earthly Treasures • From the East and West, from the North and South • In Every Age, O Lord, You Have Been Our Refuge • I Am Your Savior, My People • Seek the Lord! Long for the Lord! • Take Hold of Eternal Life • Worthy Is the Lamb Who Was Slain • Let Us Go Rejoicing to the House of the Lord • I Will Praise You, I Will Thank You • I Will Dwell with You, My House a House of Prayer

The music collection includes full accompaniment for cantor, schola, keyboard, and guitar plus reprintable antiphon graphics for assembly use. A CD recording of the collection is also available.

Music collection: 0-8146-3075-8 • $11.95;
5 or more copies $9.95* each
CD recording: 0-8146-7964-1 • $16.95

To order or for further information contact:

Liturgical Press • www.litpress.org • 800.858.5450

*Asterisk indicates discount price available only on "no-returns" basis.

The Days Are Coming, Surely Coming

First Sunday of Advent, Song for the Week
Thirty-third Sunday in Ordinary Time, Song for the Word

Verse Tone

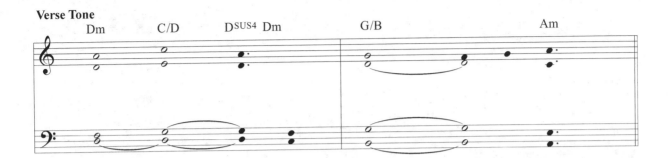

Verses for the First Sunday of Advent *Jeremiah 31:10-14*

1. Hear the word of the LORD, O nations,
   and declare it in the coastlands far away;
   say, "He who scattered Israel will gather him,
   and will keep him as a shepherd a flock."

2. For the LORD has ransomed Jacob,
   and has redeemed him from hands too strong for him.

3. They shall come and sing aloud on the height of Zion,
   and they shall be radiant over the goodness of the LORD,
   over the grain, the wine, and the oil,
   and over the young of the flock and the herd;
   their life shall become like a watered garden,
   and they shall never languish again.

4. Then shall the young women rejoice in the
     dance,
   and the young men and the old shall be merry.
   I will turn their mourning into joy,
   I will comfort them and give them gladness
     for sorrow.
   I will give the priests their fill of fatness,
   and my people shall be satisfied with my
     bounty, says the LORD.

Verses for the Thirty-third Sunday in Ordinary Time *Psalm 98:5-9*

1. Sing psalms to the LORD with the harp
   with the sound of music.
   With trumpets and the sound of the horn
   acclaim the King, the LORD.

2. Let the sea and all within it, thunder;
   the world and all its peoples.

   Let the rivers clap their hands
     and the hills ring out their joy
   at the presence of the LORD.

3. The LORD comes, comes to rule the earth.
   God will rule the world with justice
     and the peoples with fairness.

Performance Notes

The Antiphon is sung twice through each time. The Verse Tone is repeated as necessary.
The descants may be sung by any voice; the voice indications are only suggestions.

To You, O Lord, I Lift My Soul

First Sunday of Advent, Song for the Word

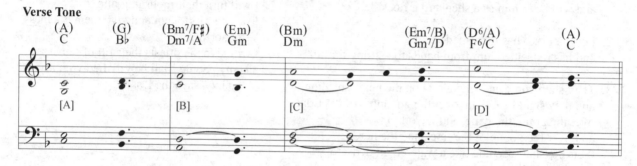

Psalm 25:2-21   [The Lectionary selections for the day are indicated by an asterisk.]

1. My God, I trust in you, let me not be disap<u>point</u>ed;
   do not let my enemies <u>tri</u>umph.
   Those who hope in you shall not be <u>disappoint</u>ed,
   but only those who wantonly <u>break</u> faith.

2. * LORD, make me know your <u>ways</u>.
   * LORD, teach me your <u>paths</u>.
   * Make me walk in your <u>truth</u>, and teach me,
   * for you are God <u>my</u> savior.

3. In you I hope all the day <u>long</u>
   because of your goodness, O <u>LORD</u>.
   Remember your <u>mer</u>cy, LORD,
   and the love you have shown from <u>of</u> old.
   [repeat C-D)
   Do not remember the sins <u>of</u> my youth.
   In your love <u>remem</u>ber me.

4. * The LORD is good and <u>up</u>right,
   * showing the path to those who <u>stray</u>,
   * guiding the humble <u>in</u> the right path,
   * and teaching the way to <u>the</u> poor.

5. * God's ways are steadfastness and <u>truth</u>
   * for those faithful to the covenant de<u>crees</u>.
   LORD, for the sake <u>of</u> your name
   forgive my guilt, for it <u>is</u> great.

6. Those who revere the <u>LORD</u>
   will be shown the path they should <u>choose</u>.
   Their souls will <u>live</u> in happiness
   and their children will possess <u>the</u> land.
   [repeat C-D)
   * The LORD's friendship is <u>for</u> the God-fearing;
   * and the covenant is revealed <u>to</u> them.

Verse Tone

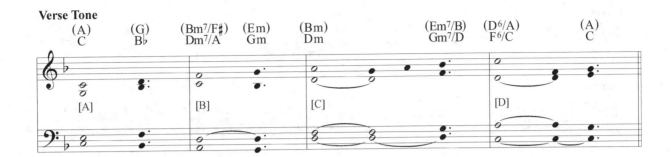

7. My eyes are always on the LORD,
   who will rescue my feet from the snare.
   Turn to me and have mercy
   for I am lonely and poor.

8. Relieve the anguish of my heart
   and set me free from my distress.
   See my affliction and my toil
   and take all my sins away.

9. See how many are my foes,
   how violent their hatred for me.
   Preserve my life and rescue me.
   Do not disappoint me, you are my refuge.
   [repeat C-D)
   May innocence and uprightness protect me,
   for my hope is in you, O LORD.

Lift Up Your Heads, Stand and Believe

First Sunday of Advent, Song for the Table

Verses Superimposed tone

stand and be-lieve;   free-dom   is near.

Luke 21:9a, 10a, 18, 17, 19-20a, 22b, 23b, 24c-25a, 27a, 28a, 31b, 33, 36ac

1. When you hear of wars and insur<u>rec</u>tions,   *stand and believe;*
   do not be <u>ter</u>rified: *freedom is near.*

2. Nation will rise against <u>na</u>tion,   *stand and believe;*
   but not a hair of your head will <u>per</u>ish: *freedom is near.*

3. You will be hated by all because of my <u>name</u>;   *(simile)*
   By your endurance you will gain your <u>souls</u>:

4. When you see Jerusalem surrounded by <u>ar</u>mies,
   as a fulfillment of all that is <u>writ</u>ten;

5. There will be great distress upon the <u>earth</u>,
   until the times of the Gentiles are ful<u>filled</u>;

6. There will be signs in the sun and the <u>moon</u>;
   Then you will see the Son of Man coming in a <u>cloud</u>;

7. When you see these things taking <u>place</u>,
   know that the kingdom of God is <u>near</u>:

8. Heaven and earth will pass a<u>way</u>;
   my words will not pass a<u>way</u>:

9. Be alert at all <u>times</u>,
   to stand before the Son of <u>Man</u>.

Performance Notes
As the cantor sings the verses, the other voices may vocalize to 'oo' under measures 1 and 3 of the
superimposed tone instead of singing the words.

Arise, Jerusalem, Stand on the Height

Second Sunday of Advent, Song for the Week

Baruch 5:1-2, 5-7, 9; Isaiah 12:3-6

1. Jerusalem, take off your robe of mourning and misery,
   put on forever the beauty of glory!

2. Wrapped in the robe of your justice and righteousness,
   put on your head the miter of majesty!

3. Jerusalem, arise, and look east from the highest heights!
   Your children are gathered at the word of your holy one.

4. Even though you went, led away by your enemies,
   God brings them back, borne aloft as if royalty.

5. God has ordered valleys and hills made into level ground
   so you can march safely in the light of God's glory.

6. God himself in joy will be the leader of Israel
   in glory, with mercy and justice for company.

7. You will draw water joyfully from the wellsprings of salvation.
   Give thanks to the LORD, give praise to his holy name.

8. Make the LORD's deeds known among the nations;
   proclaim the greatness of his name.

9. Sing a psalm to the LORD, for he has done glorious deeds;
   make known his works to all of the earth.

10. People of Zion, sing for joy,
    for great in your midst is the Holy One of Israel.

Laughter Fills Our Mouths

Second Sunday of Advent, Song for the Word
Fifth Sunday of Lent, Song for the Word

Psalm 126

1. When the LORD delivered Zion from bondage,
   it seemed like a dream.
   Then was our mouth filled with laughter,
   on our lips there were songs.

2. The heathens themselves said: "What marvels
   the LORD worked for them!"
   What marvels the LORD worked for us!
   Indeed we were glad.

3. Deliver us, O LORD, from our bondage
   as streams in dry land.
   Those who are sowing in tears
   will sing when they reap.

4. They go out, they go out, full of tears,
   carrying seed for the sowing;
   they come back, they come back, full of song,
   carrying their sheaves.

Performance Notes *Both Antiphon and Verse Tone are repeated each time they are sung.*

Every Valley Shall Be Filled

Second Sunday of Advent, Song for the Table

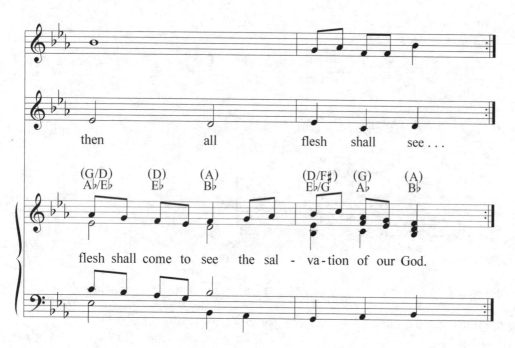

Verses *Isaiah 40:1-11*
Superimposed tone

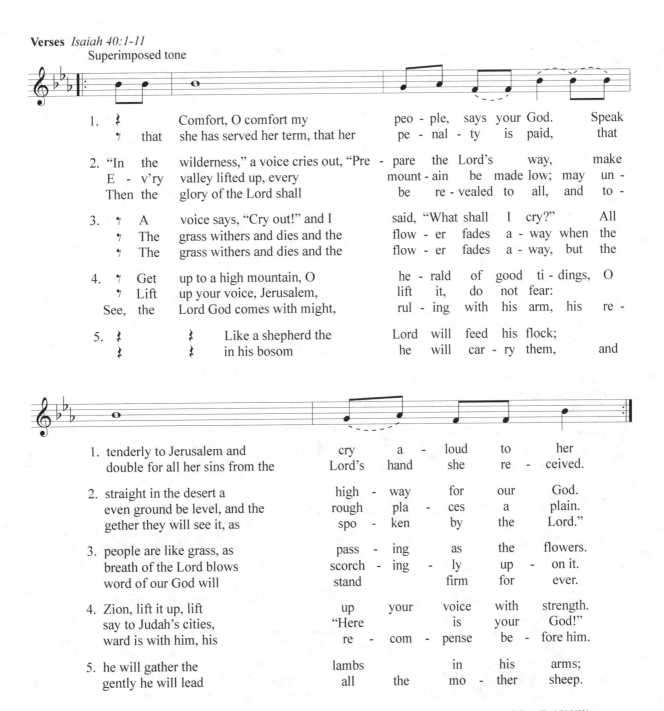

1. Comfort, O comfort my peo - ple, says your God. Speak
   that she has served her term, that her pe - nal - ty is paid, that

2. "In the wilderness," a voice cries out, "Pre - pare the Lord's way, make
   E - v'ry valley lifted up, every mount - ain be made low; may un -
   Then the glory of the Lord shall be re - vealed to all, and to -

3. A voice says, "Cry out!" and I said, "What shall I cry?" All
   The grass withers and dies and the flow - er fades a - way when the
   The grass withers and dies and the flow - er fades a - way, but the

4. Get up to a high mountain, O he - rald of good ti - dings, O
   Lift up your voice, Jerusalem, lift it, do not fear:
   See, the Lord God comes with might, rul - ing with his arm, his re -

5. Like a shepherd the Lord will feed his flock;
   in his bosom he will car - ry them, and

1. tenderly to Jerusalem and cry a - loud to her
   double for all her sins from the Lord's hand she re - ceived.

2. straight in the desert a high - way for our God.
   even ground be level, and the rough pla - ces a plain.
   gether they will see it, as spo - ken by the Lord."

3. people are like grass, as pass - ing as the flowers.
   breath of the Lord blows scorch - ing - ly up - on it.
   word of our God will stand firm for ever.

4. Zion, lift it up, lift up your voice with strength.
   say to Judah's cities, "Here is your God!"
   ward is with him, his re - com - pense be - fore him.

5. he will gather the lambs in his arms;
   gently he will lead all the mo - ther sheep.

Rejoice in the Lord, Again Rejoice!

Third Sunday of Advent, Song for the Week

Tone for Three-line Verses

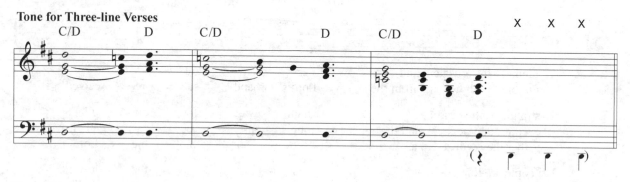

Psalm 96

1. O sing a new song to the LORD,
   sing to the LORD, all the earth.
   O sing to the LORD, bless his name.

2. Proclaim God's help day by day,
   tell among the nations his glory
   and his wonders among all the peoples.

3. The LORD is great and worthy of praise,
   to be feared above all gods;
   the gods of the heathens are naught.

4. It was the LORD who made the heavens,
   his are majesty and honor and power
   and splendor in the holy place.

5. Give the LORD, you families of peoples,
   give the LORD glory and power,
   give the LORD the glory of his name.

6. Bring an offering and enter God's courts,
   worship the LORD in the temple.
   O earth, stand in fear of the LORD.

7. Proclaim to the nations: "God is king."
   The world was made firm in its place;
   God will judge the people in fairness.

Tone for Four-line Verses

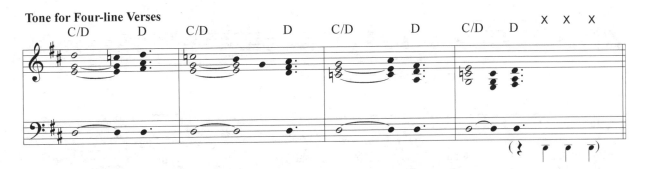

8. Let the heavens rejoice and earth <u>be</u> glad,
   let the sea and all within it <u>thunder</u> praise,
   let the land and all it bears <u>re</u>joice,
   all the trees of the wood shout <u>for</u> joy,

9. at the presence of the L<small>ORD</small> <u>who</u> comes,
   who comes to <u>rule</u> the earth,
   comes with justice to rule <u>the</u> world,
   and to judge the peoples <u>with</u> truth.

Performance Notes
Both Antiphon and Verses are preferably sung unaccompanied. The Antiphon is sung twice every time.

X = *fingersnaps/handclaps/other percussion on the 2nd and 3rd beats of the measure within the Antiphon,
and three strong beats at the end of each verse to lead back into the Antiphon.*

Great in Our Midst Is the Holy One

Third Sunday of Advent, Song for the Word

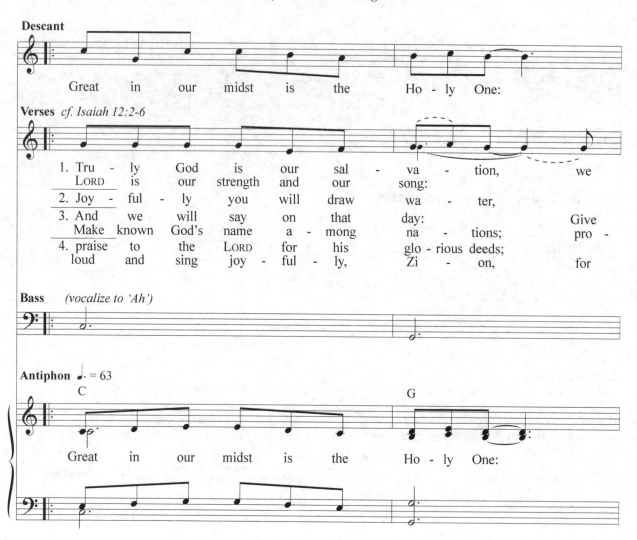

Descant

Great in our midst is the Ho - ly One:

Verses *cf. Isaiah 12:2-6*

1. Tru - ly God is our sal - va - tion, we
   LORD is our strength and our song:
2. Joy - ful - ly you will draw wa - ter,
3. And we will say on that day: Give
   Make known God's name a - mong na - tions; pro -
4. praise to the LORD for his glo - rious deeds;
   loud and sing joy - ful - ly, Zi - on, for

Bass *(vocalize to 'Ah')*

Antiphon ♩. = 63

C   G

Great in our midst is the Ho - ly One:

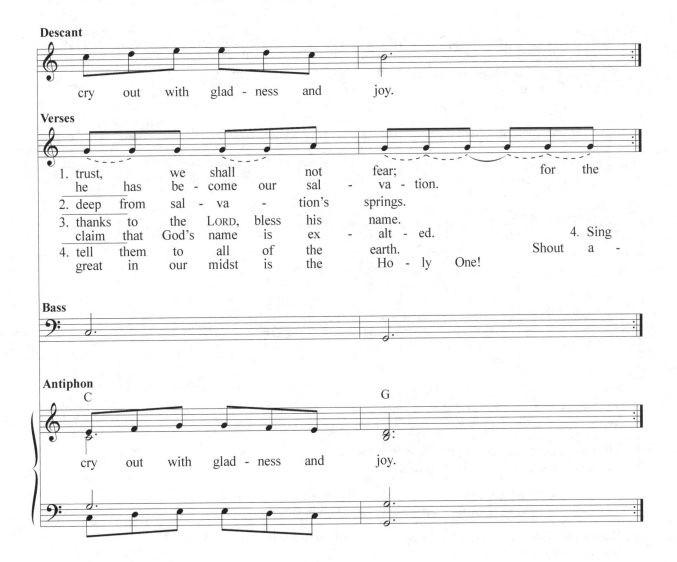

Descant

cry out with glad - ness and joy.

Verses

1. trust, we shall not fear; for the
   he has be - come our sal - va - tion.
2. deep from sal - va - tion's springs.
3. thanks to the LORD, bless his name.
   claim that God's name is ex - alt - ed. 4. Sing
4. tell them to all of the earth. Shout a -
   great in our midst is the Ho - ly One!

Bass

Antiphon

C   G

cry out with glad - ness and joy.

Performance Notes

The Psalm Tone can be superimposed on the Antiphon as shown, or it may be sung separately (but still in rhythm) using a simple chordal accompaniment.

Be Strong, Our God Has Come to Save Us

Third Sunday of Advent, Song for the Table

Isaiah 35:1-10

1. The wilderness and the dry land shall be glad, the desert shall re<u>joice</u> and blossom;
   like the crocus it shall blossom abundantly, and re<u>joice</u> with joy and singing.

2. The glory of Lebanon shall be given to it, the majesty of Car<u>mel</u> and Sharon.
   They shall see the glory of the LORD, the ma<u>jes</u>ty of our God.

3. Strengthen the weak hands, and make firm the <u>feeble</u> knees.
   Say to those who are of a fearful heart, "Be <u>strong</u>, do not fear!"

4. "Here is your God. He will come with vengeance, with ter<u>rible</u> recompense.
   He <u>will</u> come and save you."

5. Then the eyes of the blind shall be opened, and the ears of the deaf <u>be</u> unstopped:
   then the lame shall leap like a deer, and the tongue of the <u>speech</u>less sing for joy.

6. For waters shall break forth in the wilderness, and streams <u>in</u> the desert;
   the burning sand shall become a pool, and the thirsty <u>ground</u> springs of water;
[Repeat B]
   the haunt of jackals shall become a swamp, the grass shall be<u>come</u> reeds and rushes.

7. A highway shall be there, and it shall be called the <u>Holy</u> Way;
   the unclean shall not travel upon it, but it shall <u>be</u> for God's people;
[Repeat B]
   no traveler, not even <u>fools</u>, shall go astray.

8. No lion shall be there, nor shall any ravenous beast <u>come</u> up on it;
   they shall not be found there, but the re<u>deemed</u> shall walk there.

9. And the ransomed of the LORD shall return, and come to <u>Zion</u> with singing;
   everlasting joy shall be upon their heads; they shall obtain joy and gladness,
   and sorrow and <u>sighing</u> shall flee away.

Open, You Skies: Rain Down the Just One

Fourth Sunday of Advent, Song for the Week

Antiphon ♩. = 63

O-pen, you skies: rain down the Just One. O-pen, O earth, let sal-va-tion spring forth.

Verse Tone

Psalm 72

1. O God, give your judgement to the king,
   to a king's son your justice,
   that he may judge your people in justice
   and your poor in right judgement.

2. May the mountains bring forth peace for the people
   and the hills, justice.
   May he defend the poor of the people
   and save the children of the needy.

3. He shall endure like the sun and the moon
   from age to age.
   He shall descend like rain on the meadow,
   like raindrops on the earth.

4. In his days justice shall flourish
   and peace till the moon fails.
   He shall rule from sea to sea,
   from the Great River to earth's bounds.

5. Before him his enemies shall fall,
   his foes lick the dust.
   The kings of Tarshish and the seacoasts
   shall pay him tribute.

6. The kings of Sheba and Seba
   shall bring him gifts.
   Before him all rulers shall fall prostrate,
   all nations shall serve him.

7. For he shall save the poor when they cry,
   and the needy who are helpless.
   He will have pity on the weak
   and save the lives of the poor.

8. From oppression he will rescue their lives,
   to him their blood is dear.
   They shall pray for him without ceasing
   and bless him all the day.

9. May corn be abundant in the land
   to the peaks of the mountains.
   May its fruit rustle like Lebanon;
   may people flourish in the cities
      like grass on the earth.

10. May his name be blessed for ever
    and endure like the sun.
    Every tribe shall be blessed in him,
    all nations bless his name.

11. Blessed be the LORD, the God of Israel,
    who alone works wonders,
    ever blessed God's glorious name.
    Let his glory fill the earth. Amen! Amen!

God of Hosts, Bring Us Back

Fourth Sunday of Advent, Song for the Word

Psalm 80:2ac, 3bc, 5, 7, 15, 18-19

1. O shepherd of Israel, hear us,
   shine forth from your cherubim throne.
   O LORD, rouse up your might,
   O LORD, come to our help.

2. LORD God of hosts, how long
   will you frown on the plea of your people?
   You have made us the taunt of our neighbors,
   our enemies laugh us to scorn.

3. God of hosts, turn again, we implore,
   look down from heaven and see.
   Visit this vine and protect it,
   the vine your right hand has planted.

4. May your hand be on the one you have chosen,
   the one you have given your strength.
   And we shall never forsake you again;
   give us life that we may call on your name.

Performance Notes

For accompaniment with organ, the low E's with stems down should be played on the pedals, and the canonic counter-melody in the bass stave can be solo'd on a separate manual.

With piano or keyboard, either transpose the low E's up an octave or omit the counter-melody completely.

My Soul Rejoices in God

Fourth Sunday of Advent, Song for the Table
Immaculate Conception (December 8), Song for the Table

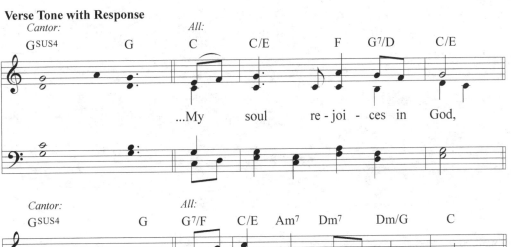

Luke 1:46-55

1. My soul glorifies the Lord,   *My soul rejoices . . .*
   my spirit rejoices in God, my Savior.   *All my being . . .*

2. He looks on his servant in her lowliness;   *(simile)*
   henceforth all generations will call me blessed.

3. The Almighty works marvels for me.
   Holy his name!

4. His mercy is from age to age
   on those who fear him.

5. He puts forth his arm in strength
   and scatters the proud-hearted.

6. He casts the mighty from their thrones
   and raises the lowly.

7. He fills the starving with good things,
   sends the rich away empty.

8. He protects Israel his servant,
   remembering his mercy,

9. the mercy promised to our fathers,
   for Abraham and his children for ever.

A Light Will Shine on Us This Day

Christmas, Song for the Week

Antiphon ♩ = 69

A light will shine on us this day: the Lord is born for us.

Verse Tone with Response

...the Lord is born for us.

Isaiah 9:2-3, 6-7

1. The people who walked in darkness have seen a <u>great</u> light;   *the Lord is born . . .*

2. those who lived in a land of deep shadow, on them light <u>has</u> shone.   *the Lord is born . . .*

3. You have multiplied the nation, you have increased <u>its</u> joy;   *(simile)*

4. they rejoice before you as with joy at the harvest, as people exult when dividing <u>plun</u>der.

5. For a child has been born for us, a son <u>giv'n</u> to us;

6. authority rests upon his <u>shoul</u>ders;

7. and he is named Wonderful Counsellor, Mighty God, Everlasting Father, <u>Prince</u> of Peace.

8. His authority shall grow con<u>tin</u>ually,

9. and there shall be endless peace for the throne of David and his <u>king</u>dom.

10. He will establish and uphold it with justice and with righteousness
    from this time onward and for <u>ever</u>more.

11. The zeal of the LORD of hosts will <u>do</u> this.

Christmas, Song for the Word: Option I

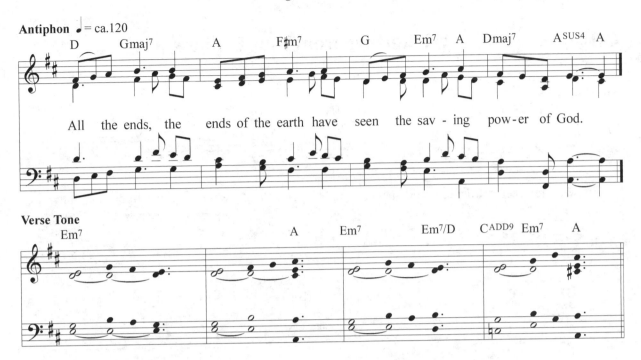

Antiphon ♩ = ca.120

All the ends, the ends of the earth have seen the sav - ing pow-er of God.

Verse Tone

Psalm 98 *[The Lectionary selections for the day are indicated by an asterisk.]*

1. * Sing a new song <u>to</u> the LORD
   * who <u>has</u> worked wonders;
   * whose right hand and <u>holy</u> arm
   * have <u>brought</u> salvation.

2. * The LORD has made <u>known</u> salvation;
   * has shown justice <u>to</u> the nations;
   * has remembered <u>truth</u> and love
   * for the <u>house</u> of Israel.

3. * All the ends of the <u>earth</u> have seen
   * the salvation <u>of</u> our God.
   * Shout to the LORD, <u>all</u> the earth,
   * ring <u>out</u> your joy.

4. * Sing psalms to the LORD <u>with</u> the harp,
   * with the <u>sound</u> of music.
   * With trumpets and the sound <u>of</u> the horn
   * acclaim the <u>King</u>, the LORD.

5. Let the sea and all with<u>in</u> it thunder;
   the world and <u>all</u> its peoples.
   Let the rivers <u>clap</u> their hands
   and the hills ring <u>out</u> their joy

6. at the presence of the <u>LORD</u>, who comes,
   who comes to <u>rule</u> the earth.
   God will rule the <u>world</u> with justice
   and the peo<u>ples</u> with fairness.

Performance Notes
The Antiphon may be sung twice through each time.

C-16

We Receive from Your Fullness

Christmas, Song for the Table

We re-ceive from your full-ness light up-on light; we re-ceive from your full-ness truth up-on truth; we re-ceive from your full-ness grace up-on grace; we re-ceive from your full-ness, O Lord.

Verse Tone

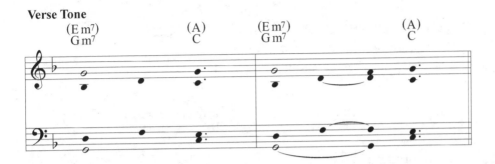

1 John 1:5-7; Isaiah 35:1-4

1. This is the message we have heard from him and proclaim to you,
   that God is light and in him there is no darkness <u>at</u> all.

2. If we say that we have fellowship with him while we are walking in darkness,
   we lie and do not do what <u>is</u> true;

3. but if we walk in the light as he himself is the light,
   we have fellowship with one another, and the blood of Jesus cleanses us from <u>all</u> sin.

4. The wilderness and the dry land shall be glad, the desert shall rejoice and blossom;
   like the crocus it shall blossom abundantly, and rejoice with joy <u>and</u> singing.

5. The glory of Lebanon shall be given to it, the majesty of Carmel and Sharon.
   They shall see the glory of the LORD, the majesty of <u>our</u> God.

6. Strengthen the weak hands, and make firm the feeble knees.
   Say to those who are of a fearful heart, "Be strong, do <u>not</u> fear!

7. Here is your God. He will come with vengeance, with terrible recompense.
   He will come <u>and</u> save you."

C-18

Happy Are They Who Dwell in Your House

Holy Family, Song for the Word
Anniversary of the Dedication of a Church, Song for the Word: Option I

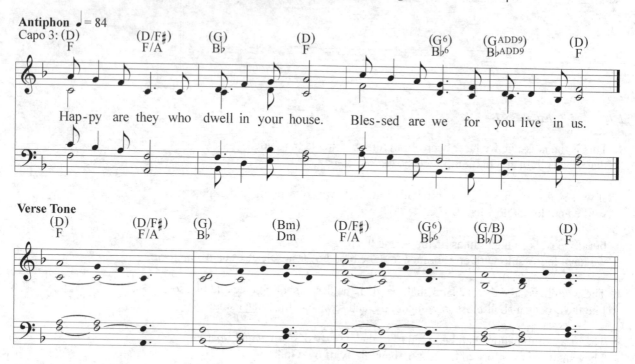

Psalm 84:3-12   *[The * indicates Lectionary selections for the Feast of the Holy Family; the + indicates those for the Dedication of a Church.]*

1. +* My soul is longing and yearning,
   +* is yearning for the courts of the LORD.
   +* My heart and my soul ring out their joy
   +* to God, the living God.

2. + The sparrow herself finds a home
   + and the swallow a home for her brood;
   + she lays her young by your altars,
   + LORD of hosts, my king and my God.

3. +* They are happy, who dwell in your house,
   +* for ever singing your praise.
     * They are happy, whose strength is in you,
     * in whose hearts are the roads to Zion.

4.   As they go through the Bitter Valley
   they make it a place of springs.
   They walk with ever-growing strength,
   they will see the God of gods in Zion.

5.   * O LORD God of hosts, hear my prayer,
     * give ear, O God of Jacob.
   +* Turn your eyes, O God, our shield,
   +* look on the face of your anointed.

6. + One day within your courts
   + is better than a thousand elsewhere.
   + The threshold of the house of God
   + I prefer to the dwellings of the wicked.

7.   For the LORD God is a rampart, a shield.
   The LORD will give us favor and glory.
   The LORD will not refuse any good
   to those who walk without blame.

A Light Will Shine on Us This Day

C-20

Solemnity of Mary, Mother of God, Song for the Week

Isaiah 9:2-3, 6-7

1. The people who walked in darkness have seen a <u>great</u> light;   *the Lord is born . . .*

2. those who lived in a land of deep shadow, on them light <u>has</u> shone.   *the Lord is born . . .*

3. You have multiplied the nation, you have increased <u>its</u> joy;   *(simile)*

4. they rejoice before you as with joy at the harvest, as people exult when dividing <u>plun</u>der.

5. For a child has been born for us, a son <u>giv'n</u> to us;

6. authority rests upon his <u>shoul</u>ders;

7. and he is named Wonderful Counsellor, Mighty God, Everlasting Father, <u>Prince</u> of Peace.

8. His authority shall grow con<u>tin</u>ually,

9. and there shall be endless peace for the throne of David and his <u>king</u>dom.

10. He will establish and uphold it with justice and with righteousness
    from this time onward and for <u>ev</u>ermore.

11. The zeal of the Lᴏʀᴅ of hosts will <u>do</u> this.

May God Bless Us in Mercy

Solemnity of Mary, Mother of God, Song for the Word

Psalm 67 [*The Lectionary selections for the day are indicated by an asterisk.*]

1. * O God, be gracious <u>and</u> bless us
   * and let your face shed its light up<u>on</u> us.
   * So will your ways be known up<u>on</u> earth
   * and all nations learn your <u>saving</u> help.

2. * Let the nations be glad and <u>ex</u>ult
   * for you rule the world <u>with</u> justice.
   * With fairness you <u>rule</u> the peoples,
   * you guide the <u>nations</u> on earth.

3. The earth has yielded <u>its</u> fruit
   for God, our God, <u>has</u> blessed us.
   May God still <u>give</u> us blessing
   till the ends of the earth <u>stand</u> in awe.

4. * Let the peoples praise you, <u>O</u> God;
   * let all the <u>peoples</u> praise you.
   * Let the peoples praise <u>you</u>, O God,
   * let all the <u>peoples</u> praise you.

Psalm text: The Grail (England), © 1963, 1986, 1993, 2000, The Grail, GIA Publications, Inc., agent. All rights reserved. Used with permission.
Music and antiphon text: © 2005, The Collegeville Composers Group. All rights reserved. Published and administered by the Liturgical Press, Collegeville, MN 56321.

Jesus Christ, the Same Today, Yesterday and Evermore
C-22

Solemnity of Mary, Mother of God, Song for the Table
Fifteenth Sunday in Ordinary Time, Song for the Week: Option II
Christ the King, Song for the Table

Colossians 1:11-20

1. May you be made strong with all the strength that comes from his <u>glorious</u> <u>power</u>,
   and may you be prepared to endure <u>everything</u> with patience,
   while joyfully giving <u>thanks</u> to the <u>Father</u>,
   who has enabled you to share in the in<u>her</u>itance of the saints in the <u>light</u>.

2. He has rescued us from the <u>power</u> of <u>darkness</u>
   and transferred us into the kingdom of his be<u>lov</u>ed Son,
   in whom we <u>have</u> redemption,
   the for<u>give</u>ness of <u>sins</u>.

3. He is the image of the invisible God, the <u>first</u>born of all cre<u>a</u>tion:
   for in him all things in heaven and on earth <u>were</u> created,
   things visible and invisible, whether thrones or do<u>min</u>ions or rulers or <u>powers</u>—
   all things have been created <u>through</u> him and <u>for</u> him.

4. He himself is before all things, and in <u>him</u> all things hold to<u>geth</u>er.
   He is the head of the bo<u>dy</u>, the Church;
   he is the beginning, the <u>first</u>born from the <u>dead</u>,
   so that he might come to have <u>first</u> place in <u>everything</u>.

5. For in him all the <u>full</u>ness of God was pleased to <u>dwell</u>,
   and through him God was pleased to reconcile to him<u>self</u> all things,
   whether on <u>earth</u> or in <u>heaven</u>,
   by making peace through the <u>blood</u> of his <u>cross</u>.

C-23

Arise, Jerusalem, Look to the East

Epiphany, Song for the Week

Antiphon ♩ = 92

A-rise, Je-ru-sa-lem, look to the East. Your child-ren come to you: o - pen your gates.

Verse Tone

Baruch 5:1-2, 5-7, 9; Isaiah 12:3-6

1. Jerusalem, take off your robe of mourning and misery,
   put on forever the beauty of glory!

2. Wrapped in the robe of your justice and righteousness,
   put on your head the miter of majesty!

3. Jerusalem, arise, and look east from the highest heights!
   Your children are gathered at the word of your holy one.

4. Even though you went, led away by your enemies,
   God brings them back, borne aloft as if royalty.

5. God has ordered valleys and hills made into level ground
   so you can march safely in the light of God's glory.

6. God himself in joy will be the leader of Israel
   in glory, with mercy and justice for company.

7. You will draw water joyfully from the wellsprings of salvation.
   Give thanks to the LORD, give praise to his holy name.

8. Make the LORD's deeds known among the nations;
   proclaim the greatness of his name.

9. Sing a psalm to the LORD, for he has done glorious deeds;
   make known his works to all of the earth.

10. People of Zion, sing for joy,
    for great in your midst is the Holy One of Israel.

Music and text: © 2005, The Collegeville Composers Group. All rights reserved. Published and administered by the Liturgical Press, Collegeville, MN 56321.

Epiphany, Song for the Word

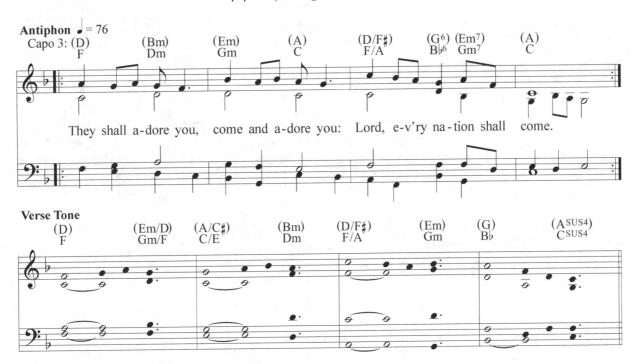

Psalm 72   *[The Lectionary selections for the day are indicated by an asterisk.]*

1. * O God, give your judgement to the king,
   * to a king's son your justice,
   * that he may judge your people in justice
   * and your poor in right judgement.

2. May the mountains bring forth peace for the people
   and the hills justice.
   May he defend the poor of the people
   and save the children of the needy.

3. He shall endure like the sun and the moon
   from age to age.
   He shall descend like rain on the meadow,
   like raindrops on the earth.

4. * In his days justice shall flourish
   * and peace till the moon fails.
   * He shall rule from sea to sea,
   * from the Great River to earth's bounds.

5. Before him his enemies shall fall,
   his foes lick the dust.
   * The kings of Tarshish and the seacoasts
   * shall pay him tribute.

6. * The kings of Sheba and Seba
   * shall bring him gifts.
   * Before him all rulers shall fall prostrate,
   * all nations shall serve him.

7. * For he shall save the poor when they cry,
   * and the needy who are helpless.
   * He will have pity on the weak
   * and save the lives of the poor.

8. From oppression he will rescue their lives,
   to him their blood is dear.
   They shall pray for him without ceasing
   and bless him all the day.

9. May corn be abundant in the land
   to the peaks of the mountains.
   May its fruit rustle like Lebanon;
   may people flourish in the cities
      like grass on the earth.

10. May his name be blessed for ever
    and endure like the sun.
    Every tribe shall be blessed in him,
    all nations bless his name.

11. Blessed be the LORD, the God of Israel,
    who alone works wonders,
    ever blessed God's glorious name.
    Let his glory fill the earth. Amen! Amen!

Our City Has No Need of Sun or Moon

Epiphany, Song for the Table

Revelation 21:24-27ac; 22:3b-5

1. The nations will walk <u>by</u> its light,
   and the kings of the earth
      will bring their <u>glo</u>ry into it.

2. Its gates will never be <u>shut</u> by day,
   and there will <u>be</u> no night there.

3. People will bring into <u>it</u> the glory
   and the honor <u>of</u> the nations.

4. Nothing un<u>clean</u> will enter it,
   but only those who are written
      in the Lamb's <u>book</u> of life.

5. The throne of God
      and of the Lamb <u>will</u> be in it,
   and his ser<u>vants</u> will worship him.

6. They will <u>see</u> his face,
   and his name will be <u>on</u> their foreheads.

7. And there will be <u>no</u> more night;
   they need no light of <u>lamp</u> or sun,

8. for the LORD God will <u>be</u> their light,
   and they will reign for <u>ev</u>er and ever.

Here Is My Servant, Here Is My Son

Baptism of the Lord, Song for the Week
Second Sunday of Lent, Song for the Table
The Transfiguration of the Lord (August 6), Song for the Day

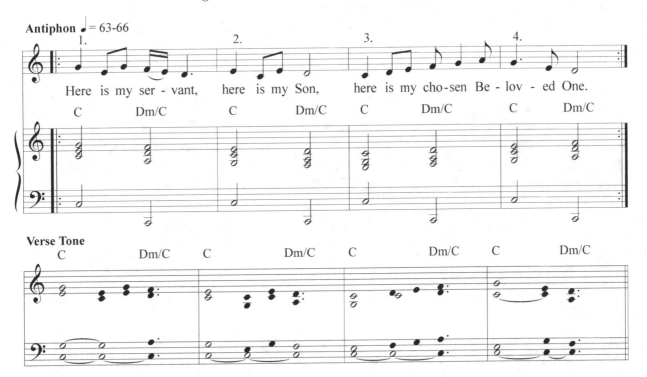

Isaiah 40:1-11

1. Comfort, O comfort my people, <u>says</u> your God.
   Speak tenderly to Jerusalem and <u>cry</u> to her
   that she has served her term, that her penal<u>ty</u> is paid,
   that she has received from the LORD's hand double for
      all <u>her</u> sins.

2. A voice cries out: "In the wilderness prepare the way
      <u>of</u> the LORD,
   make straight in the desert a highway <u>for</u> our God.
   Every valley shall be <u>lifted</u> up,
   and every mountain and hill be <u>made</u> low;

3. the uneven ground shall become level, and the rough
      <u>places</u> a plain.
   Then the glory of the LORD shall <u>be</u> revealed,
   and all people shall see <u>it</u> together,
   for the mouth of the LORD <u>has</u> spoken."

4. A voice <u>says</u>, "Cry out!"
   And I said, "What <u>shall</u> I cry?"
   All peo<u>ple</u> are grass,
   their constancy is like the flower of <u>the</u> field.

5. The grass withers, the flower fades, when the
      breath of the LORD <u>blows</u> upon it;
   surely the peo<u>ple</u> are grass.
   The grass withers, the <u>flower</u> fades;
   but the word of our God will stand <u>forever</u>.

6. Get you up to a high mountain, O Zion, herald
      <u>of</u> good tidings,
   lift up your voice with strength, O Jerusalem,
      herald <u>of</u> good tidings,
   lift it up, <u>do</u> not fear;
   say to the cities of Judah, "Here is <u>your</u> God!"

7. See, the LORD God <u>comes</u> with might,
   and his arm <u>rules</u> for him;
   his <u>reward</u> is with him,
   and his recompense <u>before</u> him.

8. He will feed his flock <u>like</u> a shepherd;
   he will gather the lambs <u>in</u> his arms,
   and carry them <u>in</u> his bosom,
   and gently lead the <u>mother</u> sheep.

Performance Notes
The Antiphon may be sung as a round.

Bless the Lord, My Soul

Baptism of the Lord, Song for the Word

End at the fermata if the descant is not used.

Verse Tone

Psalm 104:1b-4, 24-25, 27-28, 29b-30

1. LORD God, how great <u>you</u> are,
   clothed in majes<u>ty</u> and glory,
   wrapped in light as in <u>a</u> robe!
   You stretch out the heavens like <u>a</u> tent.

2. Above the rains you build <u>your</u> dwelling.
   You make the clouds your chariot,
      you walk on the wings <u>of</u> the wind;
   you make the winds <u>your</u> messengers
   and flashing fire <u>your</u> servants.

3. How many are your works, <u>O</u> LORD!
   In wisdom you have <u>made</u> them all.
   The earth is full of <u>your</u> riches.

   There is the sea, vast <u>and</u> wide,
   [repeat C-D]
      with its moving swarms <u>past</u> counting,
   living things, great <u>and</u> small.

4. All of these look <u>to</u> you
   to give them their food <u>in</u> due season.
   You give it, they gather <u>it</u> up;
   you open your hand, they have <u>their</u> fill.

5. You take back your spirit, <u>they</u> die,
   returning to the dust from <u>which</u> they came.
   You send forth your spirit, they are <u>created</u>;
   and you renew the face of <u>the</u> earth.

Performance Notes

Percussion or handclaps may be added, as indicated by the X's, both during the Antiphon and at the end of the psalm verses to lead back into the Antiphon.

God's Love Is Revealed to Us

Baptism of the Lord, Song for the Table
Christmas, Song for the Word: Option II
Holy Family, Song for the Table

Antiphon *(1 John 4:9)* ♩ = 88

God's love is re-vealed to us, that we might have life through him.

God's love is re-vealed.

Verse Tone

Psalm 98; Ephesians 1:3-4   [The Lectionary selections for Christmas are indicated by an asterisk.]

1. * Sing a new <u>song</u> to the L<small>ORD</small>
   * who <u>has</u> worked <u>won</u>ders;
   * whose right hand and ho<u>ly</u> arm
   * have <u>brought</u> salvation.

2. * The L<small>ORD</small> has made <u>known</u> sal<u>va</u>tion;
   * has shown <u>jus</u>tice to the <u>na</u>tions;
   * has remembered truth <u>and</u> love
   * for the <u>house</u> of Israel.

3. * All the ends of the <u>earth</u> have <u>seen</u>
   * the salvation <u>of</u> our <u>God</u>.
   * Shout to the L<small>ORD</small>, all <u>the</u> earth,
   * ring <u>out</u> your joy.

4. * Sing psalms to the L<small>ORD</small> with the <u>harp</u>,
   * with the <u>sound</u> of <u>mu</u>sic.
   * With trumpets and the sound of <u>the</u> horn
   * acclaim the <u>King</u>, the L<small>ORD</small>.

5. Let the sea and all with<u>in</u> it, <u>thun</u>der;
   the world and <u>all</u> its <u>peo</u>ples.
   Let the rivers clap <u>their</u> hands
   and the hills ring <u>out</u> their joy

6. at the presence of the L<small>ORD</small>, who <u>comes</u>,
   who comes to <u>rule</u> the <u>earth</u>.
   God will rule the world <u>with</u> justice
   and the <u>peo</u>ples with fairness.

Verses 7 and 8 are sung on the Baptism of the Lord:

7. Blessed be the <u>God</u> and <u>Fa</u>ther
   of our L<small>ORD</small> Jesus <u>Christ</u>,
   who has blessed us <u>in</u> Christ
   with every spiritual blessing in the <u>heav</u>'nly places.

8. He <u>chose</u> us in <u>Christ</u>
   before the foun<u>da</u>tion of the <u>world</u>
   to be holy <u>and</u> blameless
   before <u>him</u> in love.

Optional Coda to the Final Antiphon

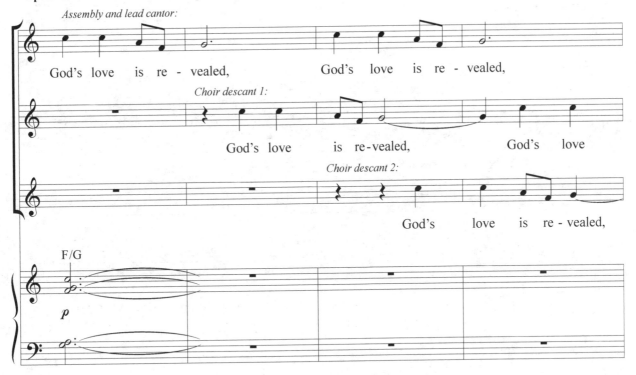

Performance Notes

Verses 7 and 8 are sung on the Baptism of the Lord only; omit these verses on Christmas.

Each two-measure phrase of the Antiphon is sung first by a cantor and then repeated by all.

Instead of repeating the last two measures of the final Antiphon, use the optional three-part coda above at a distance of two quarter-notes to create the effect of gently pealing bells, as shown. The top line is the Assembly, led by a cantor, the lower two lines being taken by other members of the choir.

The sustained accompaniment chord can easily be omitted if not required.

The canon may be repeated at any time as desired, gradually fading out.

Those Who Love Me, I Will Deliver

First Sunday of Lent, Song for the Week

Verse Tone

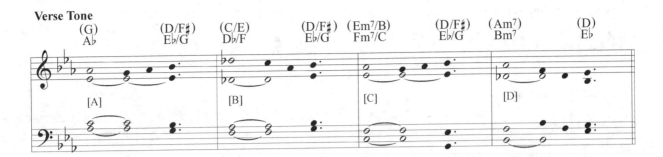

Psalm 91; Isaiah 58:8, 9c-10, 11c-12, 14

1. Those who dwell in the shelter of <u>the</u> Most High
   and abide in the shade of <u>the</u> Almighty
   say to the LORD: "My re<u>fuge</u>, my stronghold,
   the God in <u>whom</u> I trust."

2. It is God who will free you <u>from</u> the snare
   of the fowler who seeks <u>to</u> destroy you;
   God will conceal you <u>with</u> his pinions,
   and under his wings you <u>will</u> find refuge.

3. You will not fear the terror <u>of</u> the night
   nor the arrow that <u>flies</u> by day,
   nor the plague that prowls <u>in</u> the darkness
   nor the scourge that lays <u>waste</u> at noon.

4. A thousand may fall <u>at</u> your side,
   ten thousand fall <u>at</u> your right,
   you, it will ne<u>ver</u> approach;
   God's faithfulness is buck<u>ler</u> and shield.

5. Your eyes have on<u>ly</u> to look
   to see how the wicked <u>are</u> repaid,
   you who have said: "<u>LORD</u>, my refuge!"
   and have made the Most <u>High</u> your dwelling.

6. Upon you no e<u>vil</u> shall fall,
   no plague approach <u>where</u> you dwell.
   For you God has comman<u>ded</u> the angels
   to keep you in <u>all</u> your ways.

7. They shall bear you up<u>on</u> their hands
   lest you strike your foot a<u>gainst</u> a stone.
   On the lion and the viper <u>you</u> will tread
   and trample the young lion <u>and</u> the dragon.

8. You set your love on me so <u>I</u> will save you,
   protect you for you <u>know</u> my name.

When you call I shall answer: "<u>I</u> am with you,"
I will save you in distress and <u>give</u> you glory.

9. *[omit A-B]*
   With length of days I <u>will</u> content you;
   I shall let you see my <u>saving</u> power.

10. Your light shall break forth <u>like</u> the dawn,
    and your healing shall <u>spring</u> up quickly;
    your vindicator shall <u>go</u> before you,
    the glory of the LORD shall <u>be</u> your rearguard.

11. If you remove the yoke <u>from</u> among you,
    the pointing of the finger, the <u>speaking</u> of evil,
    if you offer your food <u>to</u> the hungry
    and satisfy the needs of <u>the</u> afflicted,

12. then your light shall rise <u>in</u> the darkness
    and your gloom be <u>like</u> the noonday.
    You shall be like a <u>watered</u> garden,
    like a spring of water, whose waters <u>never</u> fail.

13. Your ancient ruins shall <u>be</u> rebuilt;
    you shall raise up the foundations
       of many <u>generations</u>:
    you shall be called the repairer <u>of</u> the breach,
    the restorer of <u>streets</u> to live in.

14. Then you shall take delight <u>in</u> the LORD,
    and I will make you ride
       upon the heights <u>of</u> the earth;
    I will feed you with the heritage
       of your an<u>cestor</u> Jacob,
    for the mouth of the LORD has spoken.

I Am with You

First Sunday of Lent, Song for the Word

Verses *Psalm 91:1-2, 10-15*
Superimposed tone

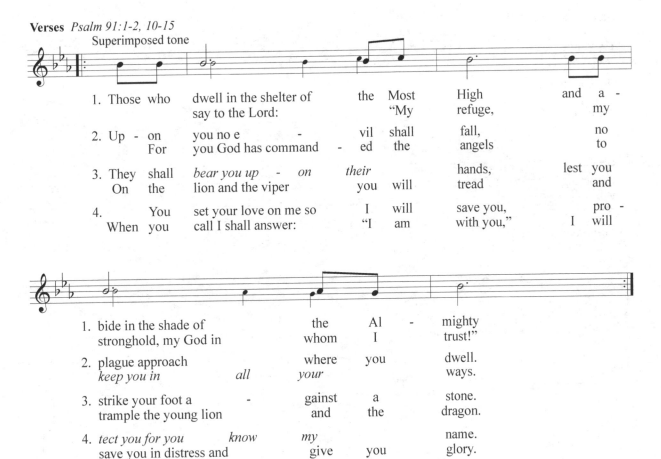

1. Those who dwell in the shelter of the Most High and a -
   say to the Lord: "My refuge, my
2. Up - on you no e - vil shall fall, no
   For you God has command - ed the angels to
3. They shall *bear you up - on their* hands, lest you
   On the lion and the viper you will tread and
4. You set your love on me so I will save you, pro -
   When you call I shall answer: "I am with you," I will

1. bide in the shade of the Al - mighty
   stronghold, my God in whom I trust!"
2. plague approach where you dwell.
   keep you in all your ways.
3. strike your foot a - gainst a stone.
   trample the young lion and the dragon.
4. *tect you for you know my* name.
   save you in distress and give you glory.

Performance Notes

The Psalm is chanted rhythmically. If desired, it may be sung superimposed on the Antiphon, or separately without the Antiphon being sung beneath (though still with accompaniment if accompaniment is being used).
Syllables in italic type indicate places where the dotted half + two eighth-notes pattern is replaced by the half note and two quarter notes (cue-size notes).

C-31   Not on Bread Alone Are We Nourished

First Sunday of Lent, Song for the Table

* *The word God lasts for four beats only, unless Descant 1 is being sung,*
when it is prolonged for an additional measure.

Drone

Verse Tone

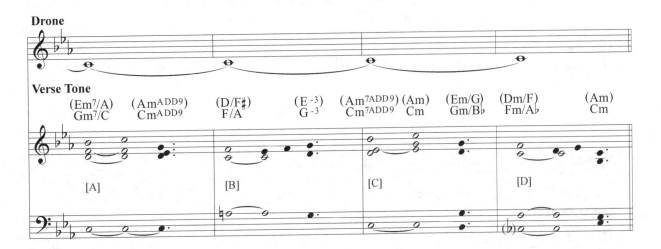

Psalm 19

1. The heavens proclaim the <u>glory</u> of <u>God</u>,
   and the firmament shows forth the work <u>of</u> God's hands.
   Day unto <u>day</u> takes up the <u>story</u>
   and night unto night makes <u>known</u> the message.

2. No speech, no word, no <u>voice</u> is <u>heard</u>
   yet their span extends through <u>all</u> the earth,
   [omit C]
   their words to the utmost bounds <u>of</u> the world.

3. There God has placed a <u>tent</u> for the <u>sun</u>;
   it comes forth like a bridegroom coming <u>from</u> his tent,
   [omit C]
   rejoices like a champion to <u>run</u> its course.

4. At the end of the sky is the <u>rising</u> of the <u>sun</u>;
   to the furthest end of the sky <u>is</u> its course.
   [omit C]
   There is nothing concealed from its <u>burn</u>ing heat.

5. The law of the Lord is <u>perfect</u>,
   it re<u>vives</u> the soul.
   The rule of the Lord is to be <u>trusted</u>,
   it gives wisdom <u>to</u> the simple.

6. The precepts of the Lord are <u>right</u>,
   they <u>glad</u>den the heart.
   The command of the Lord is <u>clear</u>,
   it gives light <u>to</u> the eyes.

7. The fear of the Lord is <u>holy</u>,
   abi<u>ding</u> for ever.
   The decrees of the Lord are <u>truth</u>
   and all <u>of</u> them just.

8. They are more to be de<u>sired</u> than <u>gold</u>,
   than the pur<u>est</u> of gold
   and sweeter are <u>they</u> than <u>honey</u>,
   than honey <u>from</u> the comb.

9. So in them your <u>servant</u> finds in<u>struction</u>;
   great reward is <u>in</u> their keeping.
   But can we dis<u>cern</u> all our <u>errors</u>?
   From hidden <u>faults</u> acquit us.

10. From presumption re<u>strain</u> your <u>servant</u>
    and let <u>it</u> not rule me.
    Then shall <u>I</u> be <u>blameless</u>,
    clean <u>from</u> grave sin.

11. May the spoken <u>words</u> of my <u>mouth</u>,
    the thoughts <u>of</u> my heart,
    win favor in your <u>sight</u>, O Lord,
    my rescu<u>er</u>, my rock!

Performance Notes
The Antiphon melody is derived from the hymn tune PICARDY.

C-32

Seek the Lord! Long for the Lord!

Second Sunday of Lent, Song for the Week
Twenty-sixth Sunday in Ordinary Time, Song for the Week
Thirtieth Sunday in Ordinary Time, Song for the Week

Verse Tone with Response

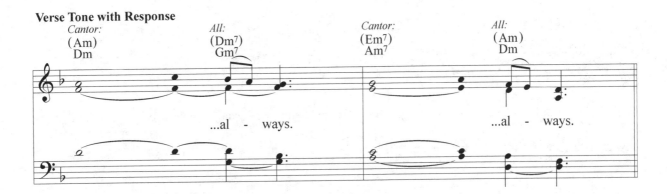

Psalm 105:1-5

1. Give thanks and acclaim God's <u>name</u> *al-ways*,
   make known God's deeds among the peo<u>ples</u> *al-ways*.

2. O sing to the LORD, sing <u>praise</u> *al-ways*;
   tell all his wonderful <u>works</u> *al-ways*!

3. Be proud of God's holy <u>name</u> *al-ways*,
   let the hearts that seek the LORD re<u>joice</u> *al-ways*.

4. Consider the LORD, who is <u>strong</u> *al-ways*;
   constantly seek his <u>face</u> *al-ways*.

5. Remember the wonders of the LORD *al-ways*,
   the miracles and judgements pro<u>nounced</u> *al-ways*.

The Lord Is My Light

Second Sunday of Lent, Song for the Word

Antiphon ♩ = 72

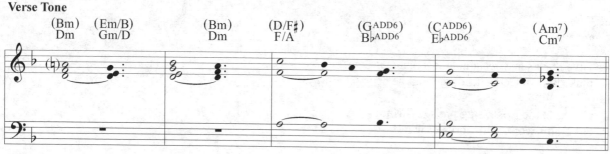

Verse Tone

Psalm 27:1, 3-5, 7-14   *[The Lectionary selections for the day are indicated by an asterisk.]*

1. * The LORD is my light and my <u>help</u>;
   * whom shall I <u>fear</u>?
   * The LORD is the stronghold <u>of</u> my life;
   * before whom <u>shall</u> I shrink?

2. Though an army encamp a<u>gainst</u> me
   my heart would not <u>fear</u>.
   Though war break <u>out</u> against me
   even then <u>would</u> I trust.

3. There is one thing I ask of the LORD, for this I <u>long</u>,
   to live in the house of the LORD all the days of my <u>life</u>,
   to savor the sweetness <u>of</u> the LORD,
   to be<u>hold</u> his temple.

4. For God makes me safe in his <u>tent</u>
   in the day of <u>evil</u>.
   God hides me in the shelter <u>of</u> his tent,
   on a rock I <u>am</u> secure.

5. * O LORD, hear my voice when I <u>call</u>;
   * have mercy and <u>answer</u>.
   * Of you my <u>heart</u> has spoken:
   * "<u>Seek</u> God's face."

6. * It is your face, O LORD, that I <u>seek</u>;
   * hide not your <u>face</u>.
   * Dismiss not your ser<u>vant</u> in anger;
   * you have <u>been</u> my help.

7. Do not abandon or for<u>sake</u> me,
   O God my <u>help</u>!
   Though father and <u>mother</u> forsake me,
   the LORD <u>will</u> receive me.

8. Instruct me, LORD, in your <u>way</u>;
   on an even path <u>lead</u> me.
   When they lie in ambush, protect me
   from my e<u>nemies'</u> greed.
   False witnesses rise against me,
   breath<u>ing</u> out fury.

9. * I am sure I shall see the LORD's <u>goodness</u>
   * in the land of the <u>living</u>.
   * In the LORD, hold firm <u>and</u> take heart.
   * Hope <u>in</u> the LORD!

Turn Our Hearts from Stone to Flesh

C-35

Third Sunday of Lent, Song for the Week

Ezekiel 36:24-28; Jeremiah 31:33; Ezekiel 37:12-14

1. I will take you from the nations,
   and gather you from all the countries,
   and bring you into your own land.

2. I will sprinkle clean water upon you
   and you shall be clean from all your uncleannesses,
   and from all your idols I will cleanse you.

3. A new heart I will give you,
   and a new spirit I will put within you;
   and I will remove from your body the heart of stone
   and give you a heart of flesh.

4. I will put my spirit within you,
   and make you follow my statutes
   and be careful to observe my ordinances.

5. Then you shall live in the land
   that I gave to your ancestors;
   and you shall be my people,
   and I will be your God.

6. I will put my law within you,
   and I will write it on your hearts;
   and I will be your God,
   and you shall be my people.

7. I am going to open your graves,
   and bring you up from your graves, O my people;
   and I will bring you back
   to the land of Israel.

8. And you shall know that I am the LORD,
   when I open your graves,
   and bring you up from your graves,
   O my people.

9. I will put my spirit within you,
   and you shall live
   and I will place you on your own soil;
   then you shall know that I, the LORD,
      have spoken and will act.

Performance Notes
Percussion or handclaps may be added, as indicated by X's, both during the Antiphon and at the end of the psalm verses to lead back into the Antiphon.
The Antiphon should be repeated every time it is sung.
The entire piece may be transposed down a whole step.

Merciful and Tender

Third Sunday of Lent, Song for the Word

Psalm 103 [The Lectionary selections for the day are indicated by an asterisk.]

1. * My soul, give thanks to the LORD,
   * all my being, bless God's holy name.
   * My soul, give thanks to the LORD
   * and never forget all God's blessings.

2. * It is God who forgives all your guilt,
   * who heals every one of your ills,
   * who redeems your life from the grave,
   * who crowns you with love and compassion,
   [repeat C-D]
   who fills your life with good things,
   renewing your youth like an eagle's.

3. The LORD does deeds of justice,
   gives judgement for all who are oppressed.
   The LORD's ways were made known to Moses;
   the LORD's deeds to Israel's children.

4. * The LORD is compassion and love,
   * slow to anger and rich in mercy.
   The LORD will not always chide,
   will not be angry forever.
   [repeat C-D]
   * God does not treat us according to our sins
   * nor repay us according to our faults.

5. For as the heavens are high above the earth
   so strong is God's love for the God-fearing;
   * as far as the east is from the west
   * so far does he remove our sins.

6. * As parents have compassion on their children,
   * the LORD has pity on those who are God-fearing
   for he knows of what we are made,
   and remembers that we are dust.

7. As for us, our days are like grass;
   we flower like the flower of the field;
   the wind blows and we are gone
   and our place never sees us again.

8. *A* But the love of the LORD is everlasting
   B upon those who fear the LORD.
   A God's justice reaches out to children's children
   B when they keep his covenant in truth,
   D when they keep his will in their mind.

9. *A* The LORD has set his throne in heaven
   B and his kingdom rules over all.
   A Give thanks to the LORD, all you angels,
   B mighty in power, fulfilling God's word,
   D who heed the voice of that word.

10. *A* Give thanks to the LORD, all you hosts,
    B you servants who do God's will.
    A Give thanks to the LORD, all his works,
    B in every place where God rules.
    D My soul, give thanks to the LORD!

Listen! Listen! Open Your Hearts!

Third Sunday of Lent, Song for the Word: RCIA Option
Twenty-seventh Sunday in Ordinary Time, Song for the Word

Lis-ten! Lis - ten! O-pen your hearts! Lis-ten! Lis - ten! O-pen your hearts!

Psalm 95:1-9 [*The Lectionary selections for the day are indicated by an asterisk.*]

1. * Come, ring out our joy to the L<small>ORD</small>;
   * hail the rock <u>who</u> saves us.

2. * Let us come before God, giving <u>thanks</u>;
   * with songs let us hail <u>the</u> L<small>ORD</small>.

3. A mighty God is the L<small>ORD</small>,
   a great king above <u>all</u> gods.

4. In God's hands are the depths of the <u>earth</u>;
   the heights of the mountains <u>as</u> well.

5. The sea belongs to God, who <u>made</u> it
   and the dry land shaped by <u>his</u> hands.

6. * Come in; let us bow and bend <u>low</u>;
   * let us kneel before the God <u>who</u> made us.

7. * This is our God, and we the people
   *   who belong to his <u>pasture</u>,
   * the flock that is led by <u>his</u> hand.

8. * O that today you would listen to God's <u>voice</u>!
   * "Harden not your hearts as at <u>Meribah</u>,
   [repeat the tone]
      * as on that day at Massah in the <u>desert</u>
      * when your ancestors put me to the test;
      *   when they tried me, though they saw <u>my</u> work."

Those Who Love Me, I Will Deliver

Third Sunday of Lent, Song for the Table
Fourth Sunday in Ordinary Time, Song for the Week

Verse Tone

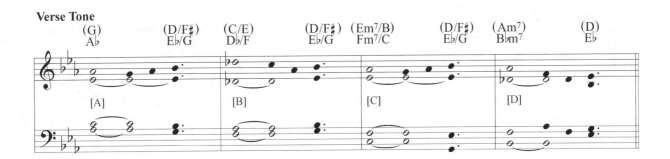

Psalm 91

1. Those who dwell in the shelter of the Most High
   and abide in the shade of the Almighty
   say to the LORD: "My refuge, my stronghold,
   the God in whom I trust."

2. It is God who will free you from the snare
   of the fowler who seeks to destroy you;
   God will conceal you with his pinions,
   and under his wings you will find refuge.

3. You will not fear the terror of the night
   nor the arrow that flies by day,
   nor the plague that prowls in the darkness
   nor the scourge that lays waste at noon.

4. A thousand may fall at your side,
   ten thousand fall at your right,
   you, it will never approach;
   God's faithfulness is buckler and shield.

5. Your eyes have only to look
   to see how the wicked are repaid,
   you who have said: "LORD, my refuge!"
   and have made the Most High your dwelling.

6. Upon you no evil shall fall,
   no plague approach where you dwell.
   For you God has commanded the angels
   to keep you in all your ways.

7. They shall bear you upon their hands
   lest you strike your foot against a stone.
   On the lion and the viper you will tread
   and trample the young lion and the dragon.

8. You set your love on me so I will save you,
   protect you for you know my name.
   When you call I shall answer: "I am with you,"
   I will save you in distress and give you glory.

9. *[omit A-B]*
   With length of days I will content you;
   I shall let you see my saving power.

Give Us Living Water

Third Sunday of Lent, Song for the Table: RCIA Option

Verses *John 4:13-14, 34; Psalm 34:2-15*

Superimposed tone

1. Everyone who	drinks of this	wa -	ter
2. Those who	drink of the	water that I will	give them
3. water that I will	give will be -	come in	them a spring of
4. food is to	do the	will of him who	sent me
5. bless the	LORD at	all	times,
6. LORD my	soul shall	make its	boast; the
7. Glori -	fy the	LORD with	me. To -
8. sought the	LORD	and was	heard; from
9. Look towards	God and be	ra -	diant;
10. When the	poor cry	out the LORD	hears them and
11. The	angel of the	LORD is en -	camped a -
12. Taste and	see that the	LORD is	good.
13. vere the	LORD,	you his	saints.
14. Strong	lions suffer	want and go	hungry but
15. Come,	children, and	hear	me that
16. Who are	those who	long for	life and
17. Keep your	tongue from	e -	vil and your
18. Turn a -	side from	evil and do	good;

1. will be	thirsty a -	gain.		
2. will	never be	thirst -	y.	*3. The*
3. water gushing	up to e -	ternal	life.	*4. My*
4. and to com -	plete his	work.		*5. I will*
5. God's	praise always	on my	lips;	*6. In the*
6. humble shall	hear and be	glad.		
7. gether	let us	praise God's	name.	*8. I*
8. all my	terrors set	free.		
9. let your	faces	not be a -	bashed.	
10. rescues	them from	all their dis -	tress.	
11. round	those who	fear God, to	rescue them.	
12. They are	happy who seek	refuge in	God.	*13. Re -*
13. They lack	nothing, who re -	vere the	LORD.	
14. those who	seek the	LORD lack no	blessing.	
15. I may	teach you the	fear of the	LORD.	
16. many	days to en -	joy their pros -	perity?	
17. lips from	speaking de -	ceit.		
18. seek and	strive after	peace.		

C-40   Rejoice, Rejoice, All You Who Love Jerusalem!

Fourth Sunday of Lent, Song for the Week

Antiphon ♩ = 100

Re - joice, re - joice, all you who love Je - ru - sa - lem! Re -

joice, be glad, for you will be con - soled.

Verse Tone

Psalm 122

1. I rejoiced when I heard them say:
   "Let us go to God's house."
   And now our feet are standing
   within your gates, O Jerusalem.

2. Jerusalem is built as a city
   strongly compact.
   It is there that the tribes go up,
   the tribes of the LORD.

3. For Israel's law it is,
   there to praise the LORD's name.
   There were set the thrones of judgement
   of the house of David.

4. For the peace of Jerusalem pray:
   "Peace be to your homes!
   May peace reign in your walls,
   in your palaces, peace!"

5. For love of my fam'ly and friends
   I say: "Peace upon you."
   For love of the house of the LORD
   I will ask for your good.

The Goodness of the Lord

Fourth Sunday of Lent, Song for the Word

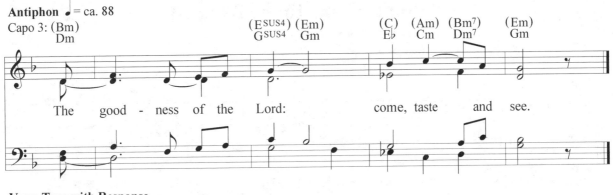

Verse Tone with Response

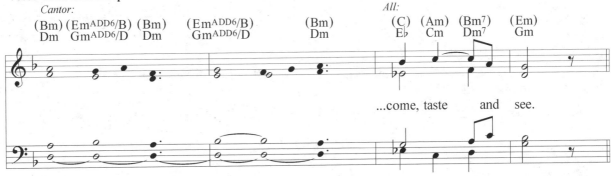

Psalm 34:2-15

1. I will bless the LORD <u>at</u> all times,
   God's praise always <u>on</u> my lips;   *come, taste . . .*

2. In the LORD my soul shall <u>make</u> its boast;
   the humble shall hear <u>and</u> be glad.   *come, taste . . .*

3. Glorify the <u>LORD</u> with me.
   Together let us <u>praise</u> God's name.   *(simile)*

4. I sought the LORD <u>and</u> was heard;
   from all my te<u>rrors</u> set free.

5. Look towards God <u>and</u> be radiant;
   let your faces not <u>be</u> abashed.

6. When the poor cry out <u>the</u> LORD hears them
   and rescues them from all <u>their</u> distress.

7. The angel of the LORD <u>is</u> encamped
   around those who fear <u>God</u>, to rescue them.

8. Taste and see that the <u>LORD</u> is good.
   They are happy who seek re<u>fuge</u> in God.

9. Revere the LORD, <u>you</u> his saints.
   They lack nothing, who re<u>vere</u> the LORD.

10. Strong lions suffer want <u>and</u> go hungry
    but those who seek the LORD <u>lack</u> no blessing.

11. Come, child<u>ren</u>, and hear me
    that I may teach you the fear <u>of</u> the LORD.

12. Who are those who <u>long</u> for life
    and many days to enjoy <u>their</u> prosperity?

13. Keep your <u>tongue</u> from evil
    and your lips from speak<u>ing</u> deceit.

14. Turn aside from evil <u>and</u> do good;
    seek and strive <u>after</u> peace.

C-42 ➜ Fourth Sunday of Lent, Song for the Word, RCIA Option, *same as C-82*

C-43

Come, Come to the Banquet

Fourth Sunday of Lent, Song for the Table
Twenty-fourth Sunday in Ordinary Time, Song for the Table

Verses for the Fourth Sunday of Lent *Psalm 78:13-16, 23-29, 35, 52-53*

1. God divided the sea and <u>led</u> them through
    and made the waters stand up <u>like</u> a wall;
    leading them by day <u>with</u> a cloud,
    by night, with a light <u>of</u> fire.

2. God split the rocks <u>in</u> the desert;
    gave them plentiful drink as <u>from</u> the deep;
    made streams flow out <u>from</u> the rock,
    and made waters run down <u>like</u> rivers.

Verse Tone

Verses for the Fourth Sunday of Lent *continued*

3. God commanded the <u>clouds</u> above
and opened the <u>gates</u> of heaven;
rained down manna <u>for</u> their food,
and gave them bread <u>from</u> heaven.

4. Mere mortals ate the <u>bread</u> of angels.
The LORD sent them meat <u>in</u> abundance;
made the east wind <u>blow</u> from heaven
and roused the south wind <u>with</u> might.

5. God rained food on <u>them</u> like dust,
winged fowl like the sands <u>of</u> the sea;

let it fall in the midst <u>of</u> their camp
and all around <u>their</u> tents.

6. So they ate and <u>had</u> their fill;
for God gave them <u>all</u> they craved.
They remembered that God <u>was</u> their rock,
God, the Most High, their <u>redeemer</u>.

7. God brought forth the peo<u>ple</u> like sheep;
guided them like a flock <u>in</u> the desert;
led them safely with no<u>thing</u> to fear,
while the sea engulfed <u>their</u> foes.

Verses for the Twenty-fourth Sunday in Ordinary Time *Psalm 32*

1. Happy those whose offense <u>is</u> forgiven,
whose sin <u>is</u> remitted.
O happy those to whom the LORD im<u>putes</u> no guilt,
in whose spirit is <u>no</u> guile.

2. I kept it secret and my <u>frame</u> was wasted.
I groaned <u>all</u> day long,
for night and day your hand was hea<u>vy</u> upon me.
Indeed my strength was dried up as by the sum<u>mer's</u> heat.

3. But now I have acknow<u>ledged</u> my sins;
my guilt I <u>did</u> not hide.
I said: "I will confess my offense <u>to</u> the LORD."
And you, LORD, have forgiven the guilt of <u>my</u> sin.

4. So let faithful <u>people</u> pray to you
in the <u>time</u> of need.
The floods of water <u>may</u> reach high
but they shall stand <u>secure</u>.

5. You are my hiding <u>place</u>, O LORD;
you save me <u>from</u> distress.
[Omit C]
You surround me with cries of <u>deliverance</u>.

6. I will instruct <u>you</u> and teach you
the way <u>you</u> should go;
I will <u>give</u> you counsel
with my eye u<u>pon</u> you.

7. Be not like <u>horse</u> and mule,
unintelligent, needing bri<u>dle</u> and bit,
[Omit C]
else they will not <u>approach</u> you.

8. *[Omit A-B]*
Many sorrows <u>have</u> the wicked,
but those who trust in the LORD are
surrounded with lo<u>ving</u> mercy.

9. Rejoice, rejoice <u>in</u> the LORD,
e<u>xult</u>, you just!
O come, ring <u>out</u> your joy,
all you upright <u>of</u> heart.

Performance Notes
Verses from Psalm 78 are for the Fourth Sunday of Lent.
Verses from Psalm 32 are for the Twenty-fourth Sunday in Ordinary Time.

You Are Light in the Lord

Fourth Sunday of Lent, Song for the Table: RCIA Option

Verse Tone

Isaiah 58:8-12; 60:1-5, 19-22

1. Your light shall break <u>forth</u> like the <u>dawn</u>,
   and your healing shall spring <u>up</u> quickly;
   your vindicator shall <u>go</u> before you,
   the glory of the Lord shall be <u>your</u> rear guard.

2. Then you shall <u>call</u> and the Lord will <u>answer</u>;
   you shall cry for help, and he will say, Here <u>I</u> am.
   If you remove the yoke <u>from</u> among you,
   the pointing of the finger, the speaking <u>of</u> evil,
   [repeat entire tone]
   if you offer your <u>food</u> to the <u>hungry</u>
   and satisfy the needs of the <u>afflicted</u>,
   then your light shall rise <u>in</u> the darkness
   and your gloom be like <u>the</u> noonday.

3. The Lord will <u>guide</u> you con<u>tin</u>ually,
   and satisfy your needs in parched places,
   and make your <u>bones</u> strong;
   and you shall be like a <u>watered</u> garden,
   like a spring of water, whose waters will ne<u>ver</u> fail.

4. Your ancient <u>ruins</u> shall be re<u>built</u>;
   you shall raise up the foundations
   of many ge<u>ner</u>ations;
   you shall be called the repairer <u>of</u> the breach,
   the restorer of streets <u>to</u> live in.

5. Arise, shine; for your <u>light</u> has <u>come</u>,
   the glory of the Lord has risen u<u>pon</u> you.
   For darkness shall c<u>over</u> the earth,
   and thick darkness <u>the</u> peoples.

6. The Lord will <u>rise</u> up<u>on</u> you,
   and his glory will appear <u>over</u> you.
   Nations shall come <u>to</u> your light,
   and kings to the brightness of <u>your</u> dawn.

7. Lift up your <u>eyes</u> and look a<u>round</u>;
   they all gather together, <u>they</u> come to you;
   your sons shall come from <u>far</u> away,
   and your daughters shall be carried
   on their nur<u>ses</u>' arms.

8. Then you shall <u>see</u> and be <u>radiant</u>;
   [omit B-C]
   your heart shall thrill and re<u>joice</u>.

9. The sun shall no longer be your <u>light</u> by <u>day</u>,
   nor for brightness shall the moon
   give light to you <u>by</u> night;
   but the Lord will be your ever<u>last</u>ing light,
   and your God will be <u>your</u> glory.

10. Your sun shall no <u>more</u> go <u>down</u>,
    or your moon withdraw <u>itself</u>;
    for the Lord will be your everlasting light,
    and your days of mourning shall <u>be</u> ended.

11. Your people shall <u>all</u> be <u>righteous</u>;
    they shall possess the land <u>forever</u>.
    They are the shoot that I planted,
    the work <u>of</u> my hands,
    so that I might <u>be</u> glorified.

12. The least of them shall be<u>come</u> a <u>clan</u>,
    and the smallest one a <u>mighty</u> nation:
    I <u>am</u> the Lord;
    in its time I will accomplish <u>it</u> quickly.

My God, My Strength, Defend My Cause

Fifth Sunday of Lent, Song for the Week

Verse Tone with Response

...my God,   my strength,   de - fend my cause.

...save me from the hands   of the   wick - ed.

Psalm 43

1. Defend me, O God, and plead my cause against a <u>god</u>less nation.   *my God, my strength . . .*
   From a deceitful and cunning people rescue <u>me</u>, O God.   *save me from the hands . . .*

2. Since you, O God, are my stronghold, why have <u>you</u> rejected me?   *(simile)*
   Why do I go mourning, oppressed <u>by</u> the foe?

3. O send forth your light and your truth; let these <u>be</u> my guide.
   Let them bring me to your holy mountain, to the place <u>where</u> you dwell.

4. And I will come to your altar, O God, the God <u>of</u> my joy.
   My redeemer, I will thank you on the harp, O <u>God</u>, my God.

5. Why are you cast down, my soul, why <u>groan</u> within me?
   Hope in God; I will praise yet again my savior <u>and</u> my God.

Fifth Sunday of Lent, Song for the Word, *same as C-5* ← **C-46**

There Is Mercy in the Lord

Fifth Sunday of Lent, Song for the Word: RCIA Option

Verse Tone

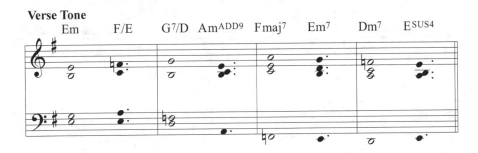

Psalm 130:1-6b, 7b-8

1. Out of the depths I cry to you, O LORD,
   LORD, hear my voice!
   O let your ears be attentive
   to the voice of my pleading.

2. If you, O LORD, should mark our guilt,
   LORD, who would survive?
   But with you is found forgiveness:
   for this we revere you.

3. My soul is waiting for the LORD,
   I count on God's word.
   My soul is longing for the LORD
   more than those who watch for daybreak.

4. Because with the LORD there is mercy
   and fullness of redemption,
   Israel indeed God will redeem
   from all its iniquity.

Performance Notes

The Antiphon may be sung in a two or four-part round as indicated. After the final stanza, the round may continue as long as desired.
The Optional Bass part is only used once the four-part round is firmly established.

C-48

You Are My Hiding-Place, O Lord

Fifth Sunday of Lent, Song for the Table

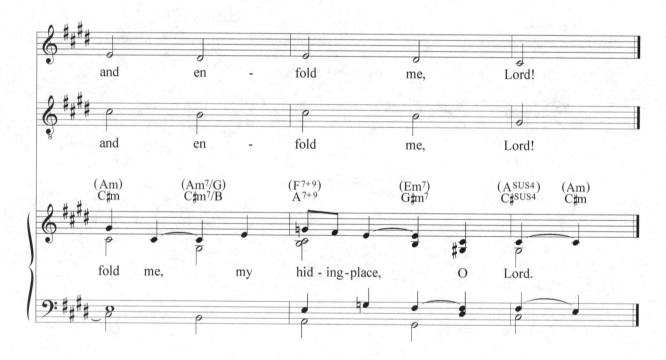

Verse Tone

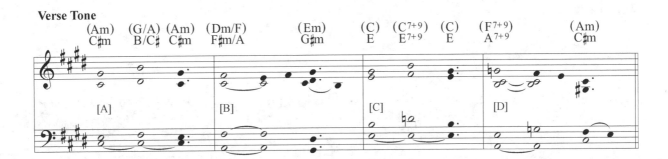

Psalm 32:1-3, 4c-5b, 5e-7, 10-11

1. Happy those whose of<u>fense</u> is for<u>given</u>,
   whose sin <u>is</u> remitted.
   O happy those to whom the Lord imputes no <u>guilt</u>,
   in whose spirit <u>is</u> no guile.

2. I kept it secret and my <u>frame</u> was <u>wasted</u>.
   I groaned <u>all</u> day long.
   Indeed my <u>strength</u> was dried <u>up</u>
   as by the <u>summer</u>'s heat.

3. But now I have ac<u>knowledged</u> my <u>sins</u>;
   my guilt I <u>did</u> not hide.
   And you, Lord, have for<u>given</u>
   the guilt <u>of</u> my sin.

4. So let faithful people <u>pray</u> to <u>you</u>
   in the <u>time</u> of need.
   The floods of <u>water</u> may reach <u>high</u>
   but they shall <u>stand</u> secure.

5. You are my <u>hiding</u> place, O Lord;
   you save me <u>from</u> distress.
   [omit C]
   You surround me with cries <u>of</u> deliverance.

6. Many <u>sorrows</u> have the <u>wicked</u>,
   but those who trust <u>in</u> the Lord
   [omit C]
   are surrounded with <u>loving</u> mercy.

7. Rejoice, re<u>joice</u> in the Lord,
   ex<u>ult</u>, you just!
   O come, <u>ring</u> out your <u>joy</u>,
   all you up<u>right</u> of heart.

I Am the Resurrection

Fifth Sunday of Lent, Song for the Table: RCIA Option

John 12:23-26, 31-32, 35-36 (option I)

1. The hour has come for the
   Son of Man to be glorified.
   Very truly, I tell you, unless a grain of wheat
   falls to the ground and dies,
   it remains just a single grain;
   but if it dies, it bears much fruit.

2. Those who love their life lose it,
   and those who hate their life in this world
   will keep it for eternal life.

3. Whoever serves me must follow me,
   and where I am, there will my servant be also.
   Whoever serves me, the Father will honor.

4. Now is the judgement of this world;
   now the ruler of this world will be driven out.
   And I, when I am lifted up from the earth,
   will draw all people to myself.

5. The light is with you for a little longer.
   Walk while you have the light,
   so that the darkness may not overtake you.

6. If you walk in the darkness,
   you do not know where you are going.
   While you have the light, believe in the light,
   so that you may become children of light.

Verse Tone

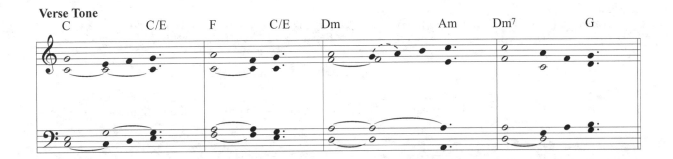

Psalm 34 (option II)

1. I will bless the LORD at all times,
   God's praise always on <u>my</u> lips;
   in the LORD my soul <u>shall</u> make its boast.
   The humble shall hear <u>and</u> be glad.

2. Glorify the LORD with me.
   Together let us praise <u>God's</u> name.
   I sought the LORD and was heard;
   from all my ter<u>rors</u> set free.

3. Look towards God <u>and</u> be radiant;
   let your faces not be a<u>bashed</u>.
   When the poor cry <u>out</u> the LORD hears them
   and rescues them from all <u>their</u> distress.

4. The angel of the LORD <u>is</u> encamped
   around those who fear God, <u>to</u> rescue them.
   Taste and see that the <u>LORD</u> is good.
   They are happy who seek re<u>fuge</u> in God.

5. Revere the LORD, you saints.
   They lack nothing, who revere <u>the</u> LORD.
   Strong lions suffer <u>want</u> and go hungry
   but those who seek the LORD <u>lack</u> no blessing.

6. Come, chil<u>dren</u> and hear me
   that I may teach you the fear of <u>the</u> LORD.
   Who are those who <u>long</u> for life
   and many days, to enjoy <u>their</u> prosperity?

7. Then keep your <u>tongue</u> from evil
   and your lips from speaking <u>deceit</u>.
   Turn aside from e<u>vil</u> and do good;
   seek and strive <u>after</u> peace.

8. The eyes of the LORD are to<u>ward</u> the just
   and his ears toward their <u>appeal</u>.
   The face of the LORD <u>rebuffs</u> the wicked
   to destroy their remembrance <u>from</u> the earth.

9. They call <u>and</u> the LORD hears
   and rescues them in all their <u>distress</u>.
   The LORD is close to the <u>bro</u>-ken-hearted;
   those whose spirit is crushed <u>God</u> will save.

10. Many are the trials <u>of</u> the upright
    but the LORD will come <u>to</u> rescue them,
    keeping guard over <u>all</u> their bones,
    not one of their bones <u>shall</u> be broken.

11. Evil brings death <u>to</u> the wicked;
    those who hate the good <u>are</u> doomed.
    The LORD ransoms the <u>souls</u> of the faithful.
    None who trust in God shall <u>be</u> condemned.

Performance Notes
Words with a double underline are sung over the slurred G–A.

Hosanna, Hosanna, Hosanna in the Highest

Palm Sunday of the Lord's Passion, Opening Song

* Final note of tone: sing either G or C

1. The children of Jerusalem
   welcomed Christ the King.
   They carried olive branches
      and loudly praised the Lord.

2. The children of Jerusalem
   welcomed Christ the King.
   They spread their cloaks before him
      and loudly praised the Lord.

3. Hosanna to the Son of David!
   Blessed is he who comes
   in the name of the Lord!

4. The children of Jerusalem
   welcomed Christ the King.
   They proclaimed the resurrection of life.

5. Waving olive branches,
   they loudly praised the Lord:
   Hosanna in the highest.

6. When the people heard that Jesus
   was entering Jerusalem,
   they went to meet him.

7. Waving olive branches,
   they loudly praised the Lord:
   Hosanna in the highest.

Palm Sunday of the Lord's Passion, Song for the Word

Antiphon ♩ = 54

My God, my God, why have you a - ban-doned me, my God?

Verse Tone

Psalm 22:8-9, 17-18a, 19-20, 23-24

1. All who see me deride me.
   They curl their lips, they toss their heads.
   "He trusted in the LORD, let him save him,
   and release him if this is his friend."

2. Many dogs have surrounded me,
   a band of the wicked beset me.
   They tear holes in my hands and my feet.
   I can count every one of my bones.

3. They divide my clothing among them.
   They cast lots for my robe.
   O LORD, do not leave me alone,
   my strength, make haste to help me.

4. I will tell of your name to my people
   and praise you where they are assembled.
   "You who fear the LORD, give praise;
   all children of Jacob, give glory.
        Revere God, children of Israel."

If I Must Drink This Cup

Palm Sunday of the Lord's Passion, Song for the Table

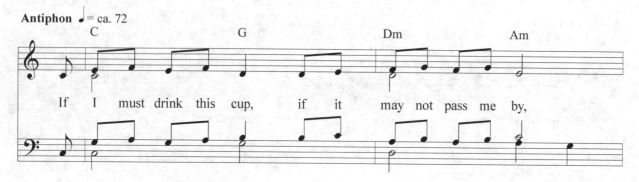

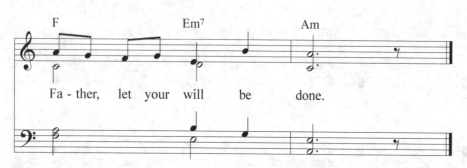

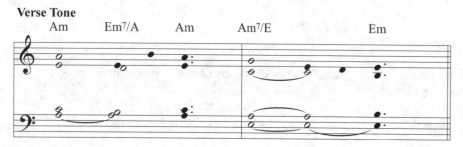

Psalm 116

1. I love the LORD, for the LORD has heard
   the cry of <u>my</u> appeal.

2. The LORD was atten<u>tive</u> to me
   in the day <u>when</u> I called.

3. They surrounded me, the <u>snares</u> of death,
   with the anguish <u>of</u> the tomb;

4. they caught me, sorrow <u>and</u> distress.
   I called <u>on</u> the LORD's name.

5. O LORD, my <u>God</u>, deliver me!
   O LORD, my <u>God</u>, deliver me!

6. How gracious is the LORD and just;
   our God <u>has</u> compassion.

7. The LORD protects the <u>simple</u> hearts;
   I was helpless <u>so</u> God saved me.

8. Turn back, my soul, <u>to</u> your rest
   for the LORD <u>has</u> been good.

9. The LORD has kept my <u>soul</u> from death,
   my eyes from tears, my <u>feet</u> from stumbling.

10. I will walk in the presence <u>of</u> the LORD
    in the land <u>of</u> the living.

Our Glory and Pride Is the Cross of Jesus Christ

Holy Thursday, Entrance Song

Psalm 67

1. O God, be gracious <u>and</u> bless us
   and let your face shed <u>its</u> light upon us.
   So will your ways be known up<u>on</u> earth
   and all nations learn your sav<u>ing</u> help.
   Let the peoples . . .

2. Let the nations be glad and <u>ex</u>ult
   for you rule the world <u>with</u> justice.

With fairness you rule <u>the</u> peoples,
you guide the nations <u>on</u> earth.
   (simile)

3. The earth has yielded <u>its</u> fruit
   for God, our God, <u>has</u> blessed us.
   May God still give <u>us</u> blessing
   till the ends of the earth stand <u>in</u> awe.

Our Cup of Blessing

Holy Thursday, Song for the Word

Psalm 116:12-19

1. How can I repay the LORD
   for his goodness to me?
   The cup of salvation I will raise;
   I will call on the name of the LORD.

2. My vows to the LORD I will fulfill
   before all the people.
   O precious in the eyes of the LORD
   is the death of the faithful.

3. Your servant, LORD, your servant am I;
   you have loosened my bonds.
   A thanksgiving sacrifice I make;
   I will call on the name of the LORD.

4. My vows to the LORD I will fulfill
   before all the people,
   in the courts of the house of the LORD,
   in your midst, O Jerusalem.

A New Commandment I Give to You

Holy Thursday, Song for the Washing of Feet
Fifth Sunday of Easter, Song for the Table

Verses for Holy Thursday *cf. Matthew 20:21, 24; John 13:5, 8, 15, 14, 35, 34; 1 Corinthians 13:13*

A
1. Christ heard the Twelve dis-put-ing a-bout the high-est seat; he
2. I set you an ex-am-ple of what you ought to do, since
3. I give a new com-mand-ment to those I choose and send: that

Verses for the Fifth Sunday of Easter *cf. Revelation 21:2-4, 6; John 13:34; 1 Corinthians 13:13*

B
1. I saw the ho-ly ci-ty, the new Je-ru-sa-lem
2. And God will wipe their tears, and death will be no more,
3. I give a new com-mand-ment to those I choose and send: that

Antiphon ♩ = 72

Capo 5: (Am) (Dm⁷)   (G)   (Em⁷)   (Am)
Dm Gm⁷   C   Am⁷   Dm

A new com-mand-ment I give to you, that you

A
1. took a bowl of wa-ter, and knelt to wash their feet. He
2. I, your Lord and Mas-ter, have wash'd your feet for you. By
3. you should love each o-ther as I have, to the end. So

B
1. com-ing down from hea-ven as love-ly as a bride. I
2. cry-ing, pain and mourn-ing, these things have passed a-way.
3. you should love each o-ther as I have, to the end. So

(Dm)   (G)   (C)   (G/B) (Am^ADD9)
Gm   C   F   C/E Dm^ADD9

love one an-o-ther as I have loved you. A

Performance Notes

*In verse 2 for the Fifth Sunday of Easter, if you are used to pronouncing "Omega" with the stress on the first and not
the second syllable – you should sing "Omega and Alpha."*

This Is My Body

Holy Thursday, Song for the Table
The Most Holy Body and Blood of Christ, Song for the Table

Verses *Psalm 23*
Superimposed tone

1. Lord, you are my shep - herd; there is
2. Fresh and green are the pas - tures where you
3. rest - ful wa - ters you lead me, to re -
4. guide me a - long the right path; you are
5. walk in the val - ley of dark - ness no
6. there with your crook and your staff; you give
7. pared a ban - quet for me in the
8. head you a - noint - ed with oil; my
9. good - ness and kind - ness shall fol - low me all the
10. Lord's own house shall I dwell for

Descant 1

This is my bo - dy, gi - ven for you;

Descant 2

This is my bo - dy, gi - ven for you;

Antiphon ♩. = 58

This is my bo - dy, gi - ven for you;

C   Dm/F

Performance Notes

The first four measures of the Descants and Antiphon are vocalized (perhaps to 'oo') or hummed when a verse is superimposed.

Father, into Your Hands

Good Friday, Song for the Word

Psalm 31:2, 6, 12-13, 15-17, 25

1. In you, O Lord, I take refuge.
   Let me never be put to shame.
   In your justice, set me free.
   Into your hands I commend my spirit.
   It is you who will redeem me, Lord.

2. In the face of all my foes
   I am a reproach,
   an object of scorn to my neighbors
   and of fear to my friends.

3. Those who see me in the street
   run far away from me.
   I am like the dead, forgotten by all,
   like a thing thrown away.

4. But as for me, I trust in you, Lord;
   I say: "You are my God.
   My life is in your hands, deliver me
   from the hands of those who hate me.

5. Let your face shine on your servant.
   Save me in your love."
   Be strong, let your heart take courage,
   all who hope in the Lord.

Send Out Your Spirit

Easter Vigil, Song for the Word: Reading I-a Response

Psalm 104:1-2a, 5-6, 10, 12, 13-14, 24, 35c

1. Bless the LORD, <u>my</u> soul!
   LORD God, how <u>great</u> you are,
   clothed in majesty <u>and</u> glory,
   wrapped in light as in <u>a</u> robe!

2. You founded the earth on <u>its</u> base,
   to stand firm from <u>age</u> to age.
   You wrapped it with the ocean like <u>a</u> cloak:
   the waters stood higher than <u>the</u> mountains.

3. You make springs gush forth in <u>the</u> valleys;
   they flow in be<u>tween</u> the hills.
   On their banks dwell the birds <u>of</u> heaven;
   from the branches they sing <u>their</u> song.

4. From your dwelling you water <u>the</u> hills;
   earth drinks its fill <u>of</u> your gift.
   You make the grass grow for <u>the</u> cattle
   and the plants to serve <u>our</u> needs.

5. How many are your works, <u>O</u> LORD!
   In wisdom you have <u>made</u> them all.
   The earth is full of <u>your</u> riches.
   Bless the LORD, <u>my</u> soul.

Performance Notes

Percussion or handclaps may be added, as indicated by X's, both during the Antiphon and at the end of the psalm verses to lead back into the Antiphon.
The Antiphon should be repeated every time it is sung.
The entire piece may be transposed down a whole step.

The Earth Is Full of the Goodness of God

Easter Vigil, Song for the Word: Reading I-b Response

Verse Tone with Response *Psalm 33:4-7, 12-13, 20, 22*

1. The word of the LORD is faithful
   The LORD loves just - ice and right
2. By God's word the heav'ns were made,
   God collects the waves of the ocean;
3. They are happy whose God is the LORD,
   From the heavens the LORD looks forth
4. Our soul is waiting for the LORD.
   May your love be upon us, O LORD,

Bles-sed be God, Bles-sed be God!

1. and all his works done in truth.
   and fills the earth with love.
2. by the breath of his mouth all the stars.
   and stores up the depths of the sea.
3. the people who are chosen as his own.
   and sees all the peoples of the earth.
4. The LORD is our help and our shield.
   as we place all our hope in you.

Bles-sed be God's name!

My Portion and My Cup

Easter Vigil, Song for the Word: Reading II Response

Psalm 16:5, 8-11

1. O LORD, it is you who are my portion <u>and</u> cup,
   it is you yourself who <u>are</u> my prize.

2. I keep you, LORD, ever in <u>my</u> sight;
   since you are at my right hand, I <u>shall</u> stand firm.

3. And so my heart re<u>joic</u>es, † my soul <u>is</u> glad;
   even my body shall <u>rest</u> in safety.

4. For you will not leave my soul among <u>the</u> dead,
   nor let your beloved <u>know</u> decay.

5. You will show me the path of <u>life</u>, † the fullness of joy in <u>your</u> presence,
   at your right hand happ<u>iness</u> for ever.

Sing to the Lord

Easter Vigil, Song for the Word: Reading III Response

Exodus 15:1-6, 17-18

1. I will sing to the LORD, glorious his triumph!
   Horse and rider he has thrown in<u>to</u> the sea!
   The LORD is my strength, my song, <u>my</u> salvation.
   [repeat C]
       This is my God and <u>I</u> extol him,
       my father's God and I <u>give</u> him praise.

2. The LORD is a warrior! The LORD <u>is</u> his name.
   The chariots of Pharaoh he hurled in<u>to</u> the sea,
   the flower of his army is drowned <u>in</u> the sea.
   The deeps hide them; they sank <u>like</u> a stone.

3. Your right hand, LORD, glorious <u>in</u> its power,
   your right hand, LORD, has shat<u>tered</u> the enemy.
   [omit C]
       In the greatness of your glory you <u>crushed</u> the foe.

4. You will lead your people and plant them <u>on</u> your mountain,
       the place, O LORD, where you have <u>made</u> your home,
       the sanctuary, LORD, which your <u>hands</u> have made.
       The LORD will reign for <u>ever</u> and ever.

I Will Praise You, Lord

Easter Vigil, Song for the Word: Reading IV Response
Tenth Sunday in Ordinary Time, Song for the Word

Descant I

I will praise you, Lord.

Descant II

Praise you, Lord, O praise you, Lord.

Antiphon ♩ = 108

Em   Am⁷   D   Gmaj⁷   Am⁷ Bm⁷ Em

I will praise you, Lord, you have res-cued me; I will praise you, Lord.

Verse Tone

Em   Am/C Am   Em

Psalm 30:2, 4-6, 11-12a, 13b

1. I will praise you, LORD, <u>you</u> have rescued me
   and have not let my enemies rejoice <u>o</u>ver me.
   O LORD, you have raised my soul <u>from</u> the dead,
   restored me to life from those who sink in<u>to</u> the grave.

2. Sing psalms to the LORD, <u>all</u> you faithful,
   give thanks to his <u>ho</u>ly name.
   God's anger lasts a moment, God's fa<u>vor</u> through life.
   At night there are tears, but joy <u>comes</u> with dawn.

3. The LORD listened <u>and</u> had pity.
   The LORD came <u>to</u> my help.
   For me you have changed my mourning <u>into</u> dancing.
   O LORD my God, I will thank <u>you</u> for ever.

Joyfully You Will Draw Water

Easter Vigil, Song for the Word: Reading V Response
Easter Vigil, Song for the Word: Reading VII-b Response

Descant

Joy - ful - ly you will draw wa - ter

Verses *cf. Isaiah 12:2-6*

1. Tru - ly God is our sal - va - tion, we
   LORD is our strength and our song:
2. And we will say on that day: Give
   Make known God's name a - mong na - tions; pro -
3. praise to the LORD for his glo - rious deeds;
   loud and sing joy - ful - ly, Zi - on, for

Bass *(vocalize to 'Ah')*

Antiphon ♩. = 63

C   G

Joy - ful - ly you will draw wa - ter

deep from sal - va - tion's springs.

1. trust, we shall not fear; for the
   he has be - come our sal - va - tion.
2. thanks to the LORD, bless his name.
   claim that God's name is ex - alt - ed. 3. Sing
3. tell them to all of the earth. Shout a -
   great in our midst is the Ho - ly One!

C   G

deep from sal - va - tion's springs.

Performance Notes *The psalm-tone can be superimposed on the Antiphon as shown, or it may be sung separately (but still in rhythm) using a simple chordal accompaniment.*

Your Word Is Life, Lord

Easter Vigil, Song for the Word: Reading VI Response
Third Sunday in Ordinary Time, Song for the Word
Fifteenth Sunday in Ordinary Time, Song for the Word

Verses for the Easter Vigil and the Fifteenth Sunday in Ordinary Time   *Psalm 19:8-11*

1. The law of the LORD is perfect,
   it revives the soul.
   The rule of the LORD is to be trusted,
   it gives wisdom to the simple.

2. The precepts of the LORD are right,
   they gladden the heart.
   The command of the LORD is clear,
   it gives light to the eyes.

3. The fear of the LORD is holy,
   abiding for ever.
   The decrees of the LORD are truth
   and all of them just.

4. They are more to be desired than gold,
   than the purest of gold
   and sweeter are they than honey,
   than honey from the comb.

Verses for the Third Sunday in Ordinary Time   *Psalm 19:8-10, 15*

1. The law of the LORD is perfect,
   it revives the soul.
   The rule of the LORD is to be trusted,
   it gives wisdom to the simple.

2. The precepts of the LORD are right,
   they gladden the heart.
   The command of the LORD is clear,
   it gives light to the eyes.

3. The fear of the LORD is holy,
   abiding for ever.
   The decrees of the LORD are truth
   and all of them just.

4. May the spoken words of my mouth,
   the thoughts of my heart,
   win favor in your sight, O LORD,
   my rescuer, my rock!

Like a Deer That Longs for Running Streams

Easter Vigil, Song for the Word: Reading VII-a Response

Psalm 42:3, 5; 43:3-4

1. My soul is thirsting for God, the God <u>of</u> my life;   *like a deer . . .*
   when can I enter and see the <u>face</u> of God?   *so my soul . . .*

2. These things will I remember as I pour out my soul:
   how I would lead the rejoicing crowd into the <u>house</u> of God,   *(simile)*
   amid cries of gladness and thanksgiving, the throng <u>wild</u> with joy.

3. O send forth your light and your truth; let these <u>be</u> my guide.
   Let them bring me to your holy mountain, to the place <u>where</u> you dwell.

4. And I will come to your altar, O God, the God <u>of</u> my joy.
   My redeemer, I will thank you on the harp, O <u>God</u>, my God.

C-66 ➔ Easter Vigil, Song for the Word: Reading VII-b Response, *same as C-63*

C-67

Lord, Cleanse My Heart

Easter Vigil, Song for the Word: Reading VII-c Response

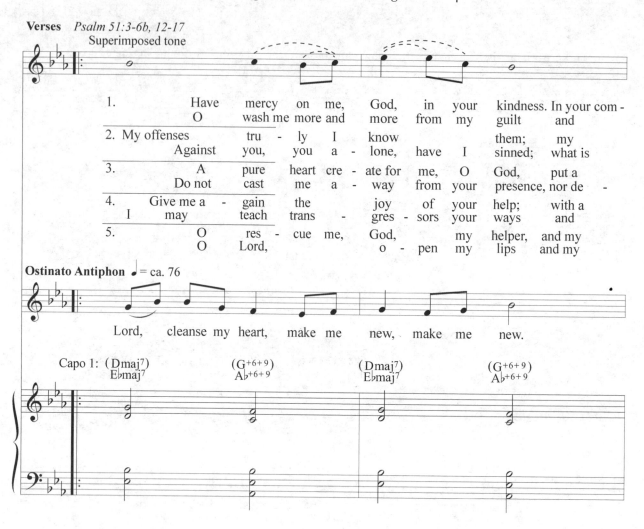

Verses *Psalm 51:3-6b, 12-17*

Superimposed tone

1. Have mercy on me, God, in your kindness. In your com-
   O wash me more and more from my guilt and
2. My offenses tru - ly I know them; my
   Against you, you a - lone, have I sinned; what is
3. A pure heart cre - ate for me, O God, put a
   Do not cast me a - way from your presence, nor de -
4. Give me a - gain the joy of your help; with a
   I may teach trans - gres - sors your ways and
5. O res - cue me, God, my helper, and my
   O Lord, o - pen my lips and my

Ostinato Antiphon ♩ = ca. 76

Lord, cleanse my heart, make me new, make me new.

Capo 1: (Dmaj⁷)   (G⁺⁶⁺⁹)   (Dmaj⁷)   (G⁺⁶⁺⁹)
        E♭maj⁷   A♭⁺⁶⁺⁹   E♭maj⁷   A♭⁺⁶⁺⁹

Verses Superimposed tone

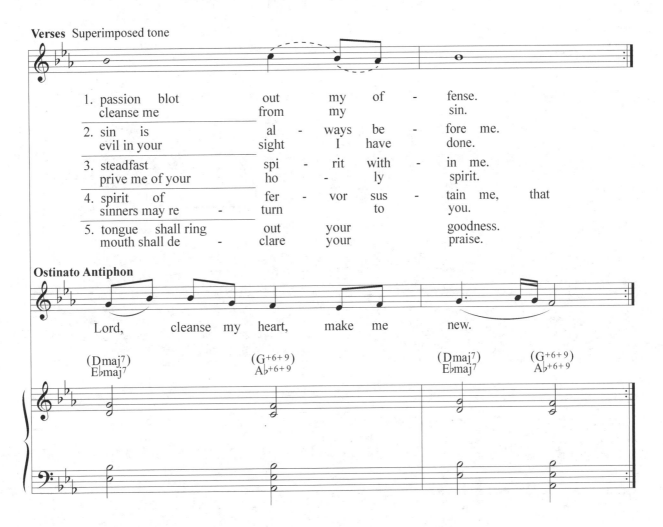

1. passion blot out my of - fense.
   cleanse me from my sin.
2. sin is al - ways be - fore me.
   evil in your sight I have done.
3. steadfast spi - rit with - in me.
   prive me of your ho - ly spirit.
4. spirit of fer - vor sus - tain me, that
   sinners may re - turn to you.
5. tongue shall ring out your goodness.
   mouth shall de - clare your praise.

Ostinato Antiphon

Lord, cleanse my heart, make me new.

(Dmaj7)   (G+6+9)   (Dmaj7)   (G+6+9)
Ebmaj7   Ab+6+9   Ebmaj7   Ab+6+9

C-68

Alleluia, Alleluia, Alleluia!

Easter Vigil, Song for the Word: Epistle Response

Clothed in Christ, One in Christ

Easter Vigil, Baptismal Acclamation

Performance Notes

This acclamation may be used immediately after each baptism, or at the clothing with a white garment, or at both these points in the rite.

Christ, Our Pasch

Easter Vigil, Song for the Table
Easter Sunday, Song for the Table

♩ = 84   *Adaptations from Psalm 66*

1. Christ, our pasch, is sa - cri - ficed, al - le - lu - ia. Un - lea - vened
2. Make a joy - ful noise to God, al - le - lu - ia. O sing the
3. Won - drous are your deeds, O Lord, al - le - lu - ia, and all the
4. Come and see what God has done, al - le - lu - ia. How awe - some

1. bread will be our feast, al - le - lu - ia. Bread of truth and sin -
2. glo - ry of God's name, al - le - lu - ia. Praise the Lord for his
3. earth will wor - ship you, al - le - lu - ia. They will sing prais - es
4. are God's deeds for us, al - le - lu - ia. We re - joice in God's

1. ce - ri - ty, al - le - lu - ia, al - le - lu - ia, al - le - lu - ia!
2. ma - jes - ty, al - le - lu - ia, al - le - lu - ia, al - le - lu - ia!
3. to your name, al - le - lu - ia, al - le - lu - ia, al - le - lu - ia!
4. might - y pow'r, al - le - lu - ia, al - le - lu - ia, al - le - lu - ia!

Christt the Lord Is Risen Again

Easter Sunday, Song for the Week

♩ = 84 *Adaptations from Psalm 95*

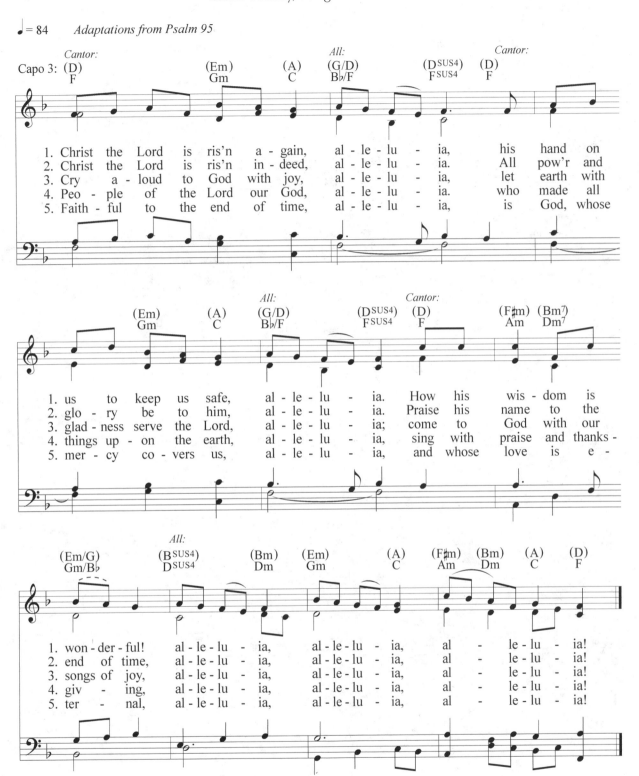

1. Christ the Lord is ris'n a - gain, al - le - lu - ia, his hand on
2. Christ the Lord is ris'n in - deed, al - le - lu - ia. All pow'r and
3. Cry a - loud to God with joy, al - le - lu - ia, let earth with
4. Peo - ple of the Lord our God, al - le - lu - ia. who made all
5. Faith - ful to the end of time, al - le - lu - ia, is God, whose

1. us to keep us safe, al - le - lu - ia. How his wis - dom is
2. glo - ry be to him, al - le - lu - ia. Praise his name to the
3. glad - ness serve the Lord, al - le - lu - ia; come to God with our
4. things up - on the earth, al - le - lu - ia, sing with praise and thanks -
5. mer - cy co - vers us, al - le - lu - ia, and whose love is e -

1. won - der - ful! al - le - lu - ia, al - le - lu - ia, al - le - lu - ia!
2. end of time, al - le - lu - ia, al - le - lu - ia, al - le - lu - ia!
3. songs of joy, al - le - lu - ia, al - le - lu - ia, al - le - lu - ia!
4. giv - ing, al - le - lu - ia, al - le - lu - ia, al - le - lu - ia!
5. ter - nal, al - le - lu - ia, al - le - lu - ia, al - le - lu - ia!

This Is the Day

Easter Sunday, Song for the Word

Verses *Psalm 118:1-2, 16-17, 22-23*

Superimposed tone

1. Give thanks to the LORD who is good, for God's
2. The LORD's right hand has triumphed; God's
3. The stone which the build - ers re - jected has be -

Descant

This is the day, this is the day,

Antiphon ♩ = 132

Capo 3: (C) (Dm/C)
E♭ Fm/E♭

This is the day, this is the day,

1. love endures for e - ver. Let the
2. right hand raised me up.
3. come the cor - ner - stone.

this is the day, let us re - joice,

(C) (Dm/C)
E♭ Fm/E♭

this is the day the Lord has made;

Music and antiphon text: © 2005, The Collegeville Composers Group. All rights reserved. Published and administered by the Liturgical Press, Collegeville, MN 56321.

C-73 → Easter Sunday, Song for the Table, *same as C-70*

C-74

Like Newborn Children

Second Sunday of Easter, Song for the Week

Isaiah 66:10-14

1. Rejoice with Jerusalem,
   and be glad for her, all you who love her;
   rejoice with her in joy,
   all you who mourn over her—

2. that you may nurse and be satisfied
   from her consoling breast;
   that you may drink deeply
   with delight from her glorious bosom.

3. For thus says the LORD:
   I will extend prosperity to her like a river,
   and the wealth of the nations
   like an overflowing stream;

4. and you shall nurse and be carried on her arm,
   and dandled on her knees.
   As a mother comforts her child,
   so I will comfort you.

5. You shall be comforted in Jerusalem.
   You shall see, and your heart shall rejoice;
   your bodies shall flourish
   like the grass.

6. And it shall be known
   that the hand of the LORD is with his servants,
   and his indignation
   is against his enemies.

Alleluia, Alleluia, Alleluia!

Second Sunday of Easter, Song for the Word

Antiphon ♩. = ca. 60

Al - le - lu - ia, al - le - lu - ia, al - le - lu - ia!

Verses *Psalm 118:2-4, 13-15, 22-23*

1. Chil - dren of Is - rael and Aa - ron, say, "God's
2. Though thrust down and fall - ing, God came to my aid. My
3. The stone which the build - ers re - ject - ed and scorn'd is

1. love has no end, God's love has no end." All those who
2. sa - vior gives cou - rage and strength to my soul. Loud shouts of
3. now the key, the cor - ner - stone. This is the

1. fear the LORD, now let them say: "God's love has no end."
2. vic - to - ry joy - ful - ly fill the tents of the just.
3. work of the LORD our God, great in our eyes.

Put Your Hand Here, Thomas

Second Sunday of Easter, Song for the Table

Psalm 30

1. I will praise you, LORD, you have rescued me
[omit B-C]
   and have not let my enemies rejoice over me.

2. O LORD, I cried to you for help
   and you, my God, have healed me.
   O LORD, you have raised my soul from the dead,
   restored me to life from those who sink into the
   grave.

3. Sing psalms to the LORD, you faithful ones,
   give thanks to his holy name.
   God's anger lasts a moment, God's favor through
   life.
   At night there are tears, but joy comes with dawn.

4. I said to myself in my good fortune:
   "Nothing will ever disturb me."
   Your favor had set me on a mountain fastness,
   then you hid your face and I was put to confusion.

5. To you, LORD, I cried,
   to my God I made appeal:
   "What profit would my death be,
      my going to the grave?
   Can dust give you praise or proclaim your truth?"

6. The LORD listened and had pity.
   The LORD came to my help.
   For me you have changed my mourning into dancing,
   you removed my sackcloth and clothed me with joy.
[Repeat C-D]
   So my soul sings psalms to you unceasingly.
   O LORD my God, I will thank you for ever.

C-77

Let All the Earth Cry Out Your Praises
Third Sunday of Easter, Song for the Week

Let All the Earth Adore and Praise You
Second Sunday in Ordinary Time, Song for the Week
Fourteenth Sunday in Ordinary Time, Song for the Word

Antiphon ♩ = 138

Let all the earth cry out your prais - es,
*Let all the earth a - dore and praise you,

al - le - lu - ia, al - le - lu - ia!
sing to your name, O God Most High!

Antiphon (same melody, alternate setting)

Let all the earth cry out your prais - es,
*Let all the earth a - dore and praise you,

al - le - lu - ia, al - le - lu - ia!
sing to your name, O God Most High!

The alternate text (italic) is used on the Second and Fourteenth Sundays in Ordinary Time.

Verse Tone with Response

...al - le - lu - ia, al - le - lu - ia!
...sing to your name, O God Most High!

Psalm 66:1-12, 16-20 [Lectionary selections for the Fourteenth Sunday in Ordinary Time are indicated by an asterisk.]

1. * Cry out with <u>joy</u> to
   * God, <u>all</u> the earth;
   alleluia, alleluia! (or *Sing to your name . . .*)

2. * O sing to the glory of his <u>name</u>,
   * rendering <u>glorious</u> praise.
   alleluia, alleluia! (or *Sing to your name . . .*)

3. * Say to <u>God</u>: "How tre-
   * men<u>dous</u> your deeds!   *(simile)*

4. Because of the greatness of your <u>strength</u>
   your enemies <u>cringe</u> before you.

5. * Before you all the earth shall <u>bow</u>,
   * shall sing to you, sing <u>to</u> your name!"

6. * Come and see the works of <u>God</u>,
   * tremendous deeds <u>for</u> the people.

7. * God turned the sea into <u>dry</u> land,
   * they passed through the ri<u>ver</u> dry-shod.

8. * Let our <u>joy</u> then
   * be <u>in</u> the LORD.

9. * The LORD rules for <u>ever</u>,
   * for <u>ever</u> in power.

10. The LORD's eyes keep watch over <u>nations</u>;
    let rebels not lift <u>them</u>selves up.

11. O peoples, bless our <u>God</u>, let the
    voice of God's <u>praise</u> resound.

12. Praise God who gave life to our <u>souls</u>
    and kept our <u>feet</u> from stumbling.

13. For you, our God, have <u>tested</u> us,
    you have tried us as sil<u>ver</u> is tried;

14. you led us, God, into the <u>snare</u>;
    you laid a heavy burden <u>on</u> our backs.

15. You let foes ride over our <u>heads</u>;
    we went through fire <u>and</u> through water

16. but then you <u>brought</u> us,
    you brought <u>us</u> relief.

17. * Come and hear, all who fear <u>God</u>,
    * I will tell what God did <u>for</u> my soul;

18. to God I cried a<u>loud</u>,
    with high praise ready <u>on</u> my tongue.

19. If there had been evil in my <u>heart</u>,
    the LORD would <u>not</u> have listened.

20. But truly God has <u>listened</u>;
    has heeded the voice <u>of</u> my prayer.

21. * Blessed be <u>God</u> who has
    * not re<u>jected</u> me.

22. * Blessed be <u>God</u> who has not with-
    * held his <u>love</u> from me.

Performance Notes
Since the psalm verses are fairly short and brisk, it is recommended that the Antiphon only be sung after every two or three verses.

I Will Praise You, Lord

Third Sunday of Easter, Song for the Word

Psalm 30:2, 4-6, 11-12a, 13b

1. I will praise you, LORD, <u>you</u> have rescued me
   and have not let my enemies rejoice <u>over</u> me.
   O LORD, you have raised my soul <u>from</u> the dead,
   restored me to life from those who sink in<u>to</u> the grave.

2. Sing psalms to the LORD, <u>all</u> you faithful,
   give thanks to his <u>holy</u> name.
   God's anger lasts a moment, God's fa<u>vor</u> through life.
   At night there are tears, but joy <u>comes</u> with dawn.

3. The LORD listened <u>and</u> had pity.
   The LORD came <u>to</u> my help.
   For me you have changed my mourning <u>into</u> dancing.
   O LORD my God, I will thank <u>you</u> for ever.

If You Love Me, Feed My Lambs

Third Sunday of Easter, Song for the Table

Psalm 78:13-16, 23-29, 35, 52-53

1. God divided the sea and led <u>them</u> through
   and made the waters stand up like <u>a</u> wall;
   leading them by day with <u>a</u> cloud,
   by night, with a light <u>of</u> fire.

2. God split the rocks in <u>the</u> desert;
   gave them plentiful drink as from <u>the</u> deep;
   made streams flow out from <u>the</u> rock,
   and made waters run down <u>like</u> rivers.

3. God commanded the clouds <u>above</u>
   and opened the gates <u>of</u> heaven;
   rained down manna for <u>their</u> food,
   and gave them bread <u>from</u> heaven.

4. Mere mortals ate the bread <u>of</u> angels.
   The LORD sent them meat in <u>abundance</u>;

made the east wind blow <u>from</u> heaven
and roused the south wind <u>with</u> might.

5. God rained food on them <u>like</u> dust,
   winged fowl like the sands of <u>the</u> sea;
   let it fall in the midst of <u>their</u> camp
   and all around <u>their</u> tents.

6. So they ate and had <u>their</u> fill;
   for God gave them all <u>they</u> craved.
   They remembered that God was <u>their</u> rock,
   God, the Most High, their <u>redeemer</u>.

7. God brought forth the people <u>like</u> sheep;
   guided them like a flock in <u>the</u> desert;
   led them safely with nothing <u>to</u> fear,
   while the sea engulfed <u>their</u> foes.

Performance Note *The Antiphon may be sung SATB.*

C-80   The Earth Is Full of the Goodness of God
Fourth Sunday of Easter, Song for the Week

Antiphon ♩. = ca. 76

The earth is full of the good-ness of God, al-le-lu-ia, al-le-lu-ia; the hea-vens were made by the word of the Lord, al-le-lu-ia!

Verse Tone with Response

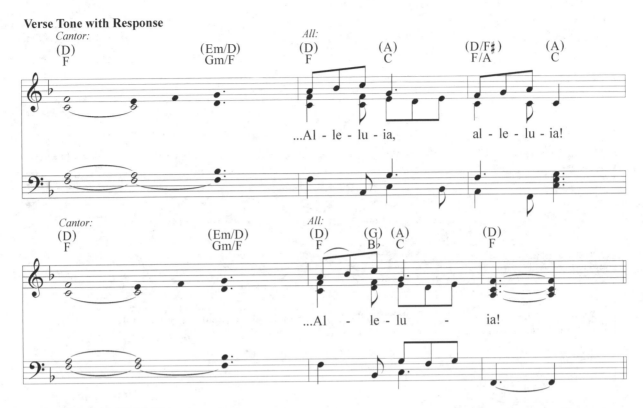

Psalm 33:1-9, 12-13, 20-22

1. Ring out your joy to the LORD, <u>O</u> you just;
   Alleluia, alleluia;
   for praise is fitting for <u>loy</u>al hearts.
   Alleluia!

2. Give thanks to the LORD up<u>on</u> the harp, *(simile)*
   with a ten-stringed lute <u>play</u> your songs.

3. Sing to the LORD a song <u>that</u> is new,
   play loudly with <u>all</u> your skill.

Antiphon

4. The word of the <u>LORD</u> is faithful
   and all his works <u>done</u> in truth.

5. The LORD loves jus<u>tice</u> and right
   and fills the <u>earth</u> with love.

Antiphon

6. By God's word the <u>heav'ns</u> were made,
   by the breath of his mouth <u>all</u> the stars.

7. God collects the waves <u>of</u> the ocean;
   and stores up the depths <u>of</u> the sea.

Antiphon

8. Let all the earth <u>fear</u> the LORD,
   all who live in the world <u>stand</u> in awe.

9. For God spoke; it <u>came</u> to be.
   God commanded; it sprang <u>into</u> being.

Antiphon

10. They are happy whose God <u>is</u> the LORD,
    the people who are chosen <u>as</u> his own.

11. From the heavens the <u>LORD</u> looks forth
    and sees all the peoples <u>of</u> the earth.

Antiphon

12. Our soul is waiting <u>for</u> the LORD.
    The LORD is our help <u>and</u> our shield.

13. Our hearts find joy <u>in</u> the LORD.
    We trust in God's <u>holy</u> name.

14. May your love be upon <u>us</u>, O LORD,
    as we place all our <u>hope</u> in you.

Antiphon

People of God, Flock of the Lord

Fourth Sunday of Easter, Song for the Word

Verses Superimposed tone

(Verse 4)

Descant 1 (Soprano)

Al - le-lu - ia, al-le-lu - ia, al-le-lu - ia, O sing to the

Al-le-lu - ia, al-le-lu - ia, al-le-lu - ia, al - le-lu -

Descant 2 (Alto)

Peo - ple, sing, sing to God, al - le - lu -

Al - le - lu - ia, al - le - lu -

Descant 3 (Bass)

Peo-ple of God, flock of the Lord, al-le-lu-ia, sing, O sing!

Al - le-lu - ia, al - le-lu - ia, al-le-lu-ia, al - le-lu - ia.

Antiphon ♩ = ca. 46

Capo 4: (Am) (Dm) (G) (C) (F) (Dm/F) (E)

C#m F#m B E A F#m/A G#

Peo-ple of God, flock of the Lord, al-le-lu-ia, sing to the Lord.

Al - le-lu - ia, al - le-lu - ia, al-le-lu-ia, al - le-lu - ia.

Verses Superimposed tone

Descant 1 (Soprano)

Lord. Al-le-lu - ia, al-le-lu - ia, O peo-ple, sing to the Lord.
ia. Al-le-lu - ia, al-le-lu - ia, al - le - lu - ia.

Descant 2 (Alto)

ia. Peo-ple, sing, sing to God, al - le - lu - ia.
ia. Al - le - lu - ia, al - le lu - ia.

Descant 3 (Bass)

Peo-ple of God, flock of the Lord, al-le-lu-ia, sing to the Lord.
Al - le-lu - ia, al - le-lu - ia, al-le-lu-ia, al - le-lu - ia.

Antiphon

(Am) (Dm) (G) (C) (F) (Dm/F) (E) (Am)
C♯m F♯m B E A F♯m/A G♯ C♯m

Peo-ple of God, flock of the Lord, al-le-lu-ia, sing to the Lord.
Al - le-lu - ia, al - le-lu - ia, al-le-lu-ia, al - le-lu - ia.

Psalm 100 [*The Lectionary selections for the day are indicated by an asterisk.*]

1. * Cry out with joy to the LORD, all the earth.
   * Serve the LORD with gladness.
   * Come before God,
   * singing for joy.

2. * Know that the LORD is God,
   * our Maker, to whom we belong.
   * We are God's people,
   * sheep of the flock.

3. * Enter the gates with thanksgiving,
   God's courts with songs of praise.
   Give thanks to God
   and bless his name.

4. * Indeed how good is the LORD,
   * whose merciful love is eternal,
   * whose faithfulness
   * lasts forever.

Performance Notes
The text in italics could be used for an additional final refrain instead of the main text.

C-82

My Shepherd Is the Lord

Fourth Sunday of Easter, Song for the Table
Fourth Sunday of Lent, Song for the Word: RCIA Option

Antiphon ♩ = 76

My shep-herd is the Lord, there is no-thing I shall need. Beside the rest-ful wa-ters my God re-fresh-es me.

Verse Tone with Response

Cantor: *All:*   *Cantor:*   *All:*

...there is no-thing I shall need.   ...my God re-fresh-es me.

Psalm 23

1. Fresh and green are <u>the</u> pastures *there is . . .*
   where you give me <u>repose.</u> *my God . . .*
   Near restful waters <u>you</u> lead me *there is . . .*
   to revive my droop<u>ing</u> spirit. *my God . . .*

2. You guide me along the <u>right</u> path; *(simile)*
   you are true to <u>your</u> name.
   If I should walk in the valley <u>of</u> darkness
   no evil would <u>I</u> fear.
   You are there with your crook and <u>your</u> staff;
   with these you give <u>me</u> comfort.

3. You have prepared a banquet <u>for</u> me
   in the sight of <u>my</u> foes.
   My head you have anointed <u>with</u> oil;
   my cup is o<u>ver</u>flowing.

4. Surely goodness and kindness <u>shall</u> follow me
   all the days of <u>my</u> life.
   In the LORD's own house shall <u>I</u> dwell
   for ever <u>and</u> ever.

Sing to God a New Song

Fifth Sunday of Easter, Song for the Week
Immaculate Conception (December 8), Song for the Word

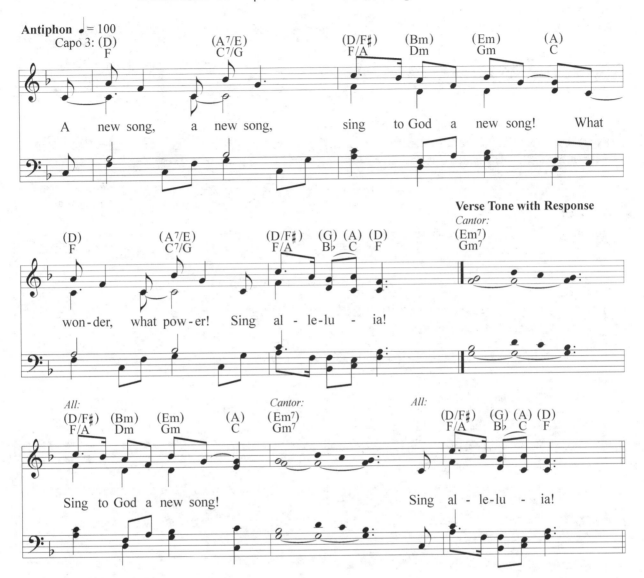

Psalm 98   *[The Lectionary selections for the Immaculate Conception are indicated by an asterisk.]*

1. * Sing a new song to the Lord who
   *   has worked wonders;   *Sing to God . . .*
   * whose right hand and holy arm have
   *   brought salvation.   *Sing alleluia!*

2. * The Lord has made known salvation;
   *   has shown justice to the nations;   *(simile)*
   * has remembered truth and love
   *   for the house of Israel.

3. * All the ends of the earth have seen
   *   the salvation of our God.
   * Shout to the Lord, all the earth,
   *   ring out your joy.

4. Sing psalms to the Lord with the harp,
      with the sound of music.
   With trumpets and the sound of the horn
      acclaim the King, the Lord.

5. Let the sea and all within it thunder;
      the world, and all its peoples.
   Let the rivers clap their hands
      and the hills ring out their joy

6. at the presence of the Lord who comes,
      who comes to rule the earth.
   God will rule the world with justice
      and the peoples with fairness.

C-84

I Will Praise Your Name For Ever

Fifth Sunday of Easter, Song for the Word

Psalm 145:8-13

1. You are kind and full <u>of</u> compassion,
   slow to anger, abound<u>ing</u> in love. *Alleluia . . .*

2. How good you are, L<small>ORD</small>, to all,
   compassionate to <u>all</u> your creatures. *Alleluia . . .*

3. All your creatures shall thank <u>you</u>, O L<small>ORD</small>,
   and your friends shall re<u>peat</u> their blessing. *(simile)*

4. They shall speak of the glory <u>of</u> your reign
   and declare your <u>might</u>, O God.

5. Let them make known to all your <u>mighty</u> deeds
   and the glorious splendor <u>of</u> your reign.

6. Yours is an ever<u>lasting</u> kingdom;
   your rule lasts from <u>age</u> to age.

C-85 → Fifth Sunday of Easter, Song for the Table, *see C-55*

C-86   Shout to the Ends of the Earth

Sixth Sunday of Easter, Song for the Week

Psalm 66:1-12, 16-20

1. Cry out with joy to God, all the <u>earth</u>.   *alleluia!*
   O sing to the glory of his name, rendering <u>glor</u>ious praise.   *alleluia!*

2. Say to God: "How tremendous your <u>deeds</u>!   *(simile)*
   Because of the greatness of your strength your enemies <u>cringe</u> before you.

3. Before you all the earth shall <u>bow</u>,
   shall sing to you, sing <u>to</u> your name!"

Verse Tone with Response

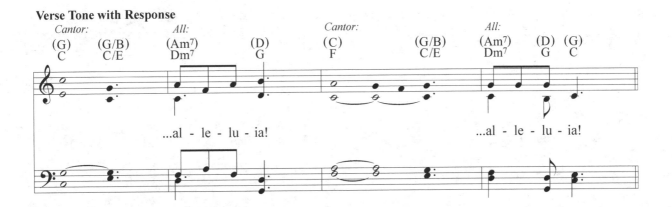

4. Come and see the works of <u>God</u>,
   tremendous deeds <u>for</u> the people.

5. God turned the sea into <u>dry</u> land,
   they passed through the ri<u>ver</u> dry-shod.

6. Let our joy then be in the Lord,
   who rules for e<u>ver</u> in power.

7. The Lord's eyes keep watch over <u>nations</u>;
   let rebels not lift <u>them</u>selves up.

8. O peoples, bless our <u>God</u>,
   let the voice of God's <u>praise</u> resound.

9. Praise God who gave life to our <u>souls</u>
   and kept our <u>feet</u> from stumbling.

10. For you, our God, have <u>tested</u> us,
    you have tried us as sil<u>ver</u> is tried;

11. you led us, God, into the <u>snare</u>;
    you laid a heavy burden <u>on</u> our backs.

12. You let foes ride over our <u>heads</u>;
    we went through fire <u>and</u> through water

13. but then you <u>brought</u> us,
    you brought <u>us</u> relief.

14. Come and hear, all who fear <u>God</u>,
    I will tell what God did <u>for</u> my soul;

15. to God I cried a<u>loud</u>,
    with high praise ready <u>on</u> my tongue.

16. If there had been evil in my <u>heart</u>,
    the Lord would <u>not</u> have listened.

17. But truly God has <u>listened</u>;
    has heeded the voice <u>of</u> my prayer.

18. Blessed be <u>God</u>
    who has not re<u>jected</u> me.

19. Blessed be <u>God</u>
    who has not withheld his <u>love</u> from me.

God, Let All the Peoples Praise You

C-87

Sixth Sunday of Easter, Song for the Word

Descant *Use the lower set of words for the descant if this setting is used during Lent.*

Al - le - lu - ia, al - le - lu - ia.
Let all peo - ples praise you, O God.

Antiphon ♩ = 88

C Cmaj7 AmADD9 F Em/G Dm7 Am

Alleluia (lower set of words) may be used during Eastertide.

God, let all the peo-ples praise you, all the na-tions of the earth.
or: al - le - lu - ia.

Verse Tone

C G/C F/C C Am Em/G F Dm7 Em7 F

Psalm 67 *[The Lectionary selections for the day are indicated by an asterisk.]*

1. * O God, be gracious <u>and</u> bless us
   * and let your face shed its light up<u>on</u> us.
   * So will your ways be known up<u>on</u> earth
   * and all nations learn your <u>sav</u>ing help.

2. * Let the nations be glad and e<u>xult</u>
   * for you rule the world <u>with</u> justice.
   * With fairness you <u>rule</u> the peoples,
   * you guide the <u>nations</u> on earth.

3. The earth has yielded <u>its</u> fruit
   for God, our God, has <u>blessed</u> us.
   May God still <u>give</u> us blessing
   till the ends of the earth <u>stand</u> in awe.

4. * Let the peoples praise you, <u>O</u> God;
   * let all the <u>peo</u>ples praise you.
   * Let the peoples praise <u>you</u>, O God,
   * let all the <u>peo</u>ples praise you.

Live On in My Love

C-88

Sixth Sunday of Easter, Song for the Table

Verses *John 15:9-16*

1. As the Fa - ther loved me, so I have loved you:
2. If you keep my com - mands, you will live in my love,
3. May my joy be in you, may your joy be com - plete:
4. Love one an - o - ther as I have loved you:
5. No great - er love than to lay down your life:
6. You are my friends if you keep to my word:
7. No long - er slaves, but I call you friends:
8. Not you who chose me, but I who chose you:
9. Go forth and bear fruit, and your fruit must en - dure:

Alto Descant

(Text as above)

G   D   A   Em   Bm

♩. = ca.36

(Verses) *All:*

live on in my love.   **Antiphon** Live on in my love, live on in my love.

Alto Descant

Live on in my love.   Live on in my love, live on in my love.

Tenor Descant

Live on in my love.   Live on in my love, live on in my love.

Bass Descant

Live on in my love, live on in my love.

D/F♯ G   A   D Em/G   Bm   Em⁷ Em⁷/G   Bm

Why Stare into the Sky?

The Ascension of the Lord, Song for the Day/Week

Psalm 68:2-6, 19-22, 33-36

1. Let God arise, let the foes be scattered.
   Let those who hate God take to flight.

2. As smoke is blown away so will they be blown away;
   like wax that melts before the fire,
   so the wicked shall perish at the presence of God.

3. But the just shall rejoice at the presence of God,
   they shall exult and dance for joy.
   O sing to the LORD, make music to God's name;
   make a highway for the One who rides upon the clouds.

4. Rejoice in the LORD, exult before God.
   Father of the orphan, defender of the widow,
   such is God in the holy place.

5. You have gone up on high; you have taken captives,
   receiving people in tribute, O God,
   even those who rebel, into your dwelling, O LORD.
   May the LORD be blessed day after day.

6. God our savior bears our burdens;
   this God of ours is a God who saves.
   The LORD our God holds the keys of death.
   And God will smite the heads of foes,
   the crowns of those who persist in their sins.

7. Kingdoms of the earth, sing to God,
       praise the LORD
   who rides on the heavens, the ancient
       heavens.
   God's mighty voice thunders and roars.

8. Come, acknowledge the power of God,
   whose glory is on Israel;
   whose might is in the skies.

9. God is to be feared in the holy place.
   This is the LORD, Israel's God,
   who gives strength and power to the people.

God Goes Up with Shouts of Joy

The Ascension of the Lord, Song for the Word

Psalm 47   [The Lectionary selections for the day are indicated by an asterisk.]

1. * All peoples, <u>clap</u> your hands,
   * cry to God with <u>shouts</u> of joy!   *alleluia!*
   * For the LORD, the Most High, <u>we</u> must fear,
   * great king over <u>all</u> the earth.   *alleluia!*

2. God subdues <u>peoples</u> under us
   and nations <u>under</u> our feet.   *(simile)*
   Our inheritance, our glory <u>is</u> from God,
   given to Jacob <u>out</u> of love.

3. * God goes up with <u>shouts</u> of joy;
   * the LORD goes up with <u>trum</u>pet blast.
   * Sing praise for <u>God</u>, sing praise,
   * sing praise to our <u>king</u>, sing praise.

4. * God is king of <u>all</u> the earth,
   * sing praise with <u>all</u> your skill.
   * God is king <u>over</u> the nations;
   * God reigns <u>enthroned</u> in holiness.

5. The leaders of the people <u>are</u> assembled
   with the people of A<u>braham's</u> God.
   The rulers of the earth be<u>long</u> to God,
   to God who reigns <u>over</u> all.

I Will See You Again

The Ascension of the Lord, Song for the Table

Verse Tone

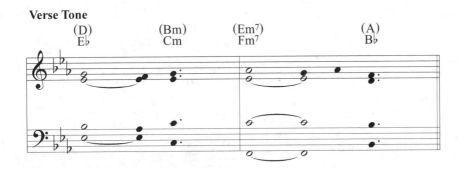

cf. John 14:18; 16:22; Revelation 1:17-18; John 14:26; 16:7; 16:13; 15:26-27; Acts 1:8

1. I will not leave you orphans;
   I will come back to you and your hearts will rejoice.

2. I am the beginning and the end of all things;
   I have met death, but I am alive.

3. The Holy Spirit whom the Father will send
   will teach you, and remind you of all I have said.

4. It is best for me to leave you,
   because if I do not go the Spirit will not come to you.

5. When the Spirit of truth comes to you,
   you will be led to the fullness of truth.

6. When the Advocate comes whom I will send you from the Father,
   the Spirit of truth who comes from my Father,
   he will testify on my behalf.

7. You also are to testify
   because you have been with me from the beginning.

8. When the Holy Spirit comes to you,
   you will be my witnesses to all the world.

"Come," Says My Heart

Seventh Sunday of Easter, Song for the Week

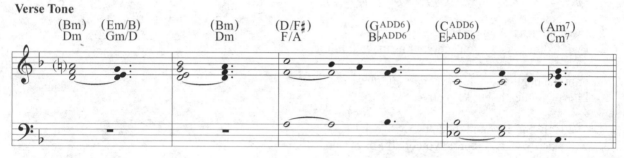

Psalm 27:1, 3-5, 7-14

1. The LORD is my light and my help;
   whom shall I fear?
   The LORD is the stronghold of my life;
   before whom shall I shrink?

2. Though an army encamp against me
   my heart would not fear.
   Though war break out against me
   even then would I trust.

3. There is one thing I ask of the LORD, for this I long,
   to live in the house of the LORD all the days of my life,
   to savor the sweetness of the LORD,
   to behold his temple.

4. For God makes me safe in his tent
   in the day of evil.
   God hides me in the shelter of his tent,
   on a rock I am secure.

5. O LORD, hear my voice when I call;
   have mercy and answer.
   Of you my heart has spoken:
   "Seek God's face."

6. It is your face, O LORD, that I seek;
   hide not your face.
   Dismiss not your servant in anger;
   you have been my help.

7. Do not abandon or forsake me,
   O God my help!
   Though father and mother forsake me,
   the LORD will receive me.

8. Instruct me, LORD, in your way;
   on an even path lead me.
   When they lie in ambush, protect me
   from my enemies' greed.
   False witnesses rise against me,
   breathing out fury.

9. I am sure I shall see the LORD's goodness
   in the land of the living.
   In the LORD, hold firm and take heart.
   Hope in the LORD!

The Lord Is King

C-93

Seventh Sunday of Easter, Song for the Word
The Transfiguration of the Lord (August 6), Song for the Word

Descant

Easter: The Lord is king: al - le - lu - ia!
Transfiguration: The Lord is king of all the earth.

Antiphon ♩. = 63

The Lord is king, most high a - bove all the earth.

Verse Tone

[A] [B] [C] [D]

Verses for the Seventh Sunday of Easter   *Psalm 97:1-2, 6, 7c, 9*

1. The LORD is king, let earth rejoice,
   let all the coastlands be glad.
   Surrounded by cloud and darkness;
   justice and right, God's throne.

2. The skies proclaim God's justice;
   all peoples see God's glory.
   [Omit C]
   All you spirits, worship the LORD.

3. For you indeed are the LORD
   most high above all the earth,
   [Omit C]
   exalted far above all spirits.

Verses for the Transfiguration of the Lord   *Psalm 97:1-6, 9*

1. The LORD is king, let earth rejoice,
   let all the coastlands be glad.
   Surrounded by cloud and darkness;
   justice and right, God's throne.

2. A fire prepares the way;
   it burns up foes on every side.
   God's lightnings light up the world,
   the earth trembles at the sight.

3. The mountains melt like wax
   before the LORD of all the earth.
   The skies proclaim God's justice;
   all peoples see God's glory.

4. For you indeed are the LORD
   most high above all the earth,
   [Omit C]
   exalted far above all spirits.

Keep Us in Your Name
Seventh Sunday of Easter, Song for the Table

Jeremiah 31:10-14

1. Hear the | word of the LORD, O nations,
   and de- | clare it in the coastlands far <u>a</u>way;
   say, | "He who scattered Israel <u>will</u> gather him,
   and will | keep him as a shepherd <u>a</u> flock."

2. For the | LORD has <u>ran</u>somed Jacob,
   and has re- | deemed him from hands <u>too</u> strong for him.
   They shall come and | sing aloud on the height <u>of</u> Zion,
   and they shall be | radiant over the goodness of <u>the</u> LORD,

3. over the | grain, the wine, <u>and</u> the oil,
   and over the | young of the flock and <u>the</u> herd:
   their life shall be- | come like a <u>wa</u>tered garden,
   and they shall | never languish <u>a</u>gain.

4. Then shall the young | women rejoice <u>in</u> the dance,
   and the | young men and the old shall <u>be</u> merry.
   I will | turn their mourning in<u>to</u> joy,
   I will comfort | them and give them gladness <u>for</u> sorrow.

5. I will | give the priests their <u>fill</u> of fatness,
   and my people shall be | satisfied with my bounty, says <u>the</u> LORD.

C-95

The Love of God

Pentecost Sunday, Song for the Week
The Most Holy Trinity, Song for the Table

Performance Notes

The verses of Psalm 103 are used on Pentecost Sunday.
The verses from the Canticle of Ephesians are used on Trinity Sunday.

Verse Tone

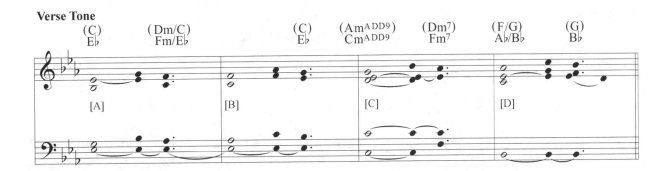

[A] [B] [C] [D]

Verses for Pentecost Sunday *Psalm 103*

1. My soul, give thanks to the LORD,
   all my being, bless God's holy name.
   My soul, give thanks to the LORD
   and never forget all God's blessings.

2. It is God who forgives all your guilt,
   who heals every one of your ills,
   who redeems your life from the grave,
   who crowns you with love and compassion,
   [repeat C-D]
      who fills your life with good things,
      renewing your youth like an eagle's.

3. The LORD does deeds of justice,
   gives judgement for all who are oppressed.
   The LORD's ways were made known to Moses;
   the LORD's deeds to Israel's children.

4. The LORD is compassion and love,
   slow to anger and rich in mercy.
   The LORD will not always chide,
   will not be angry for ever.
   [repeat C-D]
      God does not treat us according to our sins
      nor repay us according to our faults.

5. For as the heavens are high above the earth,
   so strong is God's love for the God-fearing;
   as far as the east is from the west,
   so far does God remove our sins.

6. As parents have compassion on their children,
   the LORD has pity on those who are God-fearing
   for God knows of what we are made,
   and remembers that we are dust.

7. As for us, our days are like grass;
   we flower like the flower of the field;
   the wind blows and we are gone
   and our place never sees us again.

8. But the love of the LORD is everlasting
   upon those who fear the LORD.
   God's justice reaches out to children's children
   when they keep his covenant in truth,
   [repeat D]
      when they keep his will in their mind.

9. The LORD has set his throne in heaven
   and his kingdom rules over all.
   Give thanks to the LORD, all you angels,
   mighty in power, fulfilling God's word,
   [repeat D]
      who heed the voice of that word.

10. Give thanks to the LORD, all you hosts,
    you servants who do God's will.
    Give thanks to the LORD, all God's works,
    in every place where God rules.
    [repeat D]
       My soul, give thanks to the LORD!

Verse Tone

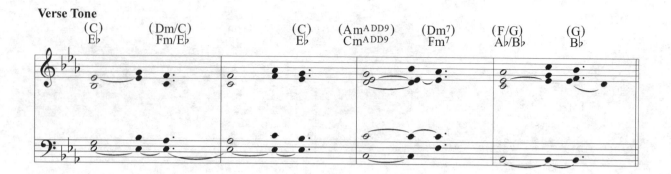

Verses for Trinity Sunday *Ephesians 1:3-14*

1. Blessed be the God and Father of our Lord Jesus Christ,
   who has blessed us in Christ with every spiritual blessing in the heavenly places,
   just as he chose us in Christ before the foundation of the world
   to be holy and blameless before him in love.

2. He destined us for adoption as his children through Jesus Christ,
   according to the good pleasure of his will,
   to the praise of his glorious grace
   that he freely bestowed on us in the Beloved.

3. In him we have redemption through his blood,
   the forgiveness of our trespasses,
   according to the riches of his grace
   that he lavished on us.

4. With all wisdom and insight he has made known to us the mystery of his will,
   according to his good pleasure that he set forth in Christ,
   as a plan for the fullness of time,
   to gather up all things in him, things in heaven and things on earth.

5. In Christ we have also obtained an inheritance,
   having been destined according to the purpose of him who accomplishes all things
      according to his counsel and will,
   so that we, who were the first to set our hope on Christ,
   might live for the praise of his glory.

6. In him you also, when you had heard the word of truth, the gospel of your salvation,
      and had believed in him,
   were marked with the seal of the promised Holy Spirit;
   this is the pledge of our inheritance toward redemption as God's own people,
   to the praise of his glory.

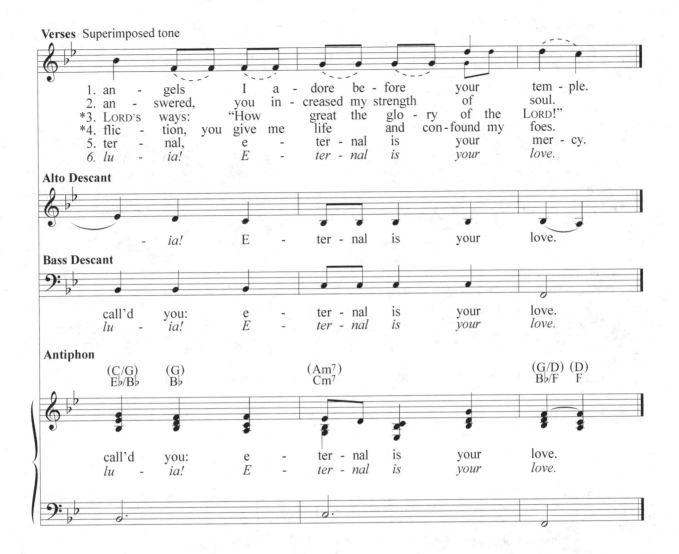

Verses Superimposed tone

1. an - gels I a - dore be - fore your tem - ple.
2. an - swered, you in - creased my strength of soul.
*3. LORD's ways: "How great the glo - ry of the LORD!"
*4. flic - tion, you give me life and con-found my foes.
5. ter - nal, e - ter - nal is your mer - cy.
6. *lu - ia! E - ter - nal is your love.*

Alto Descant

- ia! E - ter - nal is your love.

Bass Descant

call'd you: e - ter - nal is your love.
lu - ia! E - ter - nal is your love.

Antiphon

(C/G)   (G)   (Am⁷)   (G/D) (D)
E♭/B♭   B♭   Cm⁷   B♭/F F

call'd you: e - ter - nal is your love.
lu - ia! E - ter - nal is your love.

Performance Notes
At the end of the piece, the Antiphon may be repeated using the Alleluias in italics instead of the usual text.
On the 5th Sunday in Ordinary Time, Year C, omit verse 4;
on the 17th Sunday in Ordinary Time, Year C, omit verse 3.

Cast Out into the Deep

Fifth Sunday in Ordinary Time, Song for the Table

(Play G♯ only if Antiphon is sung without the bass descant)

Verse Tone

Psalm 107:23-26, 28-31

1. Some sailed to the sea in ships
   to trade on the mighty waters.
   They saw the deeds of the LORD,
   the wonders he does in the deep.

2. For God spoke and summoned the gale,
   tossing the waves of the sea
   up to heaven and back into the deep;
   their souls melted away in distress.

3. Then they cried to the LORD in their need
   and he rescued them from their distress.
   God stilled the storm to a whisper;
   all the waves of the sea were hushed.

4. They rejoiced because of the calm
   and God led them to the haven they desired.
   Let them confess the love of the LORD,
   the wonders God does for the people.

Performance Notes
In the Antiphon, the alternation between measures of 4/4 and 3/4 is intentional.

Lead Me, Guide Me

Sixth Sunday in Ordinary Time, Song for the Week

Psalm 31:2-6, 10, 15-17, 25

1. In you, O LORD, I take refuge.
   Let me never be put to shame.

2. In your justice, set me free,
   *hear me and speedily rescue me.

3. Be a rock of refuge for me,
   *a mighty stronghold to save me,

4. for you are my rock, my stronghold.
   *For your name's sake lead me and guide me.

5. Release me from the snares they have hidden
   for you are my refuge, LORD.

6. Into your hands I commend my spirit.
   It is you who will redeem me, LORD.

7. Have mercy on me, O LORD,
   for I am in distress.

8. Tears have wasted my eyes,
   my throat and my heart.

9. As for me, I trust in you, LORD.
   I say: "You are my God.

10. My life is in your hands, deliver me
    *from the hands of those who hate me.

11. Let your face shine on your servant.
    Save me in your love."

12. Be strong, let your heart take courage,
    all who hope in the LORD.

Performance Notes

Use the small cue-size notes (second measure of the verse tone) on the verse lines marked with an asterisk.

Planted Like a Tree

Sixth Sunday in Ordinary Time, Song for the Word

Psalm 1:1-4, 6

Happy indeed <u>are</u> those
who follow not the counsel <u>of</u> the wicked,
nor linger in the way <u>of</u> sinners
nor sit in the company <u>of</u> scorners,
but whose delight is the law of <u>the</u> L<small>ORD</small>
and who ponder God's law <u>day</u> and night.

They are like a tree that <u>is</u> planted
beside the flow<u>ing</u> waters,

that yields its fruit in <u>due</u> season
and whose leaves shall <u>never</u> fade;
and all that they do <u>shall</u> prosper.

Not so are the wicked, <u>not</u> so!
for they like winnow<u>èd</u> chaff
shall be driven away <u>by</u> the wind.
For the L<small>ORD</small> guards the way of <u>the</u> just
but the way of the wicked leads <u>to</u> doom.

Performance Notes

The Drone is preferably hummed (to an 'n' sound rather than an 'm' sound), but may also be sustained on the organ at the written pitch or an octave lower, or played by guitars strumming an E chord, without the 3rd, on the first beat of every measure only. When the assembly sings the Antiphon without a superimposed verse, choir voices may add drones an octave lower than printed.

The Antiphon should be sung through several times before starting the verses, and several times more after the verses are finished.

During the verses, the melody line of the Antiphon may be vocalized to 'oo' instead of singing the text. Although the verses are of unequal length, the total number of lines equals 16, which means the 4-line chant is sung through a total of four times, the verses sung without pausing between stanzas.

Blest Are You Who Weep

Sixth Sunday in Ordinary Time, Song for the Table

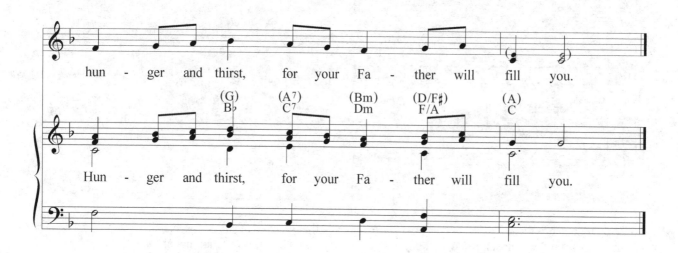

Verse Tone

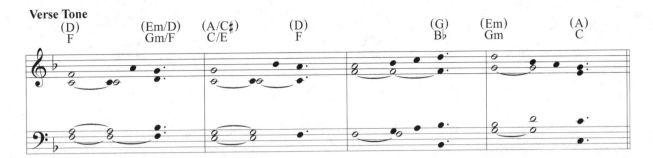

Matthew 5:3-10; Psalm 103:3-4, 8, 10-12, 17-18

1. Blessed are the poor in spirit,
   for theirs is the kingdom of heaven.
   Blessed are those who mourn,
   for they will be comforted.

2. Blessed are the meek,
   for they will inherit the earth.
   Blessed are those who hunger
      and thirst for righteousness,
   for they will be filled.

3. Blessed are the merciful,
   for they will receive mercy.
   Blessed are the pure in heart,
   for they will see God.

4. Blessed are the peacemakers,
   for they will be called children of God.
   Blessed are those who are persecuted
      for righteousness' sake,
   for theirs is the kingdom of heaven.

5. It is God who forgives all your guilt,
   who heals every one of your ills,
   who redeems your life from the grave,
   who crowns you with love and compassion.

6. The LORD is compassion and love,
   slow to anger and rich in mercy.
   God does not treat us according to our sins
   nor repay us according to our faults.

7. As the heavens are high above the earth
   so strong is God's love for the God-fearing;
   as far as the east is from the west
   so far does he remove our sins.

8. The love of the LORD is everlasting
   upon those who fear the LORD.
   God's justice reaches out to children's children
   when they keep his covenant in truth,
      when they keep his will in their mind.

C-113

Your Mercy Is My Hope

Seventh Sunday in Ordinary Time, Song for the Week
Twentieth Sunday in Ordinary Time, Song for the Week

Antiphon ♩ = ca. 76

Your mer-cy is my hope, your pro-mise is my song: my

heart re-joi-ces in your pow'r to save.

Verse Tone

*Flex †
when required*

Psalm 13

1. How long, O LORD, will you <u>for</u>get me?
   How long will you <u>hide</u> your face?

2. How long must I bear grief in my † <u>soul</u>,
   this sorrow in my heart day <u>and</u> night?
   How long shall my ene<u>my</u> prevail?

3. Look at me, answer me, LORD <u>my</u> God!
   Give light to my eyes lest I fall <u>asleep</u> in death,
   [verse continues above, repeating the tone]

   lest my enemy say: "I have <u>pre</u>vailed";
   lest my foes rejoice to <u>see</u> my fall.

4. As for † <u>me</u>, I trust in your merci<u>ful</u> love.
   Let my heart rejoice in your <u>saving</u> help.

5. Let me sing to you, LORD, for your goodness <u>to</u> me,
   sing psalms to your name, O <u>LORD</u>, Most High.

Merciful and Tender

Seventh Sunday in Ordinary Time, Song for the Word

Antiphon ♩ = 76-80

Mer - ci - ful and ten - der, faith - ful is the Lord.

Verse Tone

[A]   [B]   [C]   [D]

Psalm 103 [The Lectionary selections for the day are indicated by an asterisk.]

1. * My soul, give thanks to the Lord,
   * all my being, bless God's holy name.
   * My soul, give thanks to the Lord
   * and never forget all God's blessings.

2. * It is God who forgives all your guilt,
   * who heals every one of your ills,
   * who redeems your life from the grave,
   * who crowns you with love and compassion,
   [repeat C-D]
   who fills your life with good things,
   renewing your youth like an eagle's.

3. The Lord does deeds of justice,
   gives judgement for all who are oppressed.
   The Lord's ways were made known to Moses;
   the Lord's deeds to Israel's children.

4. * The Lord is compassion and love,
   * slow to anger and rich in mercy.
   The Lord will not always chide,
   will not be angry forever.
   [repeat C-D]
   * God does not treat us according to our sins
   * nor repay us according to our faults.

5. For as the heavens are high above the earth
   so strong is God's love for the God-fearing;
   * as far as the east is from the west
   * so far does he remove our sins.

6. * As parents have compassion on their children,
   * the Lord has pity on those who are God-fearing
   for he knows of what we are made,
   and remembers that we are dust.

7. As for us, our days are like grass;
   we flower like the flower of the field;
   the wind blows and we are gone
   and our place never sees us again.

8. *A* But the love of the Lord is everlasting
   B upon those who fear the Lord.
   A God's justice reaches out to children's children
   B when they keep his covenant in truth,
   D when they keep his will in their mind.

9. *A* The Lord has set his throne in heaven
   B and his kingdom rules over all.
   A Give thanks to the Lord, all you angels,
   B mighty in power, fulfilling God's word,
   D who heed the voice of that word.

10. *A* Give thanks to the Lord, all you hosts,
    B you servants who do God's will.
    A Give thanks to the Lord, all his works,
    B in every place where God rules.
    D My soul, give thanks to the Lord!

Forgive, and You Will Be Forgiven

Seventh Sunday in Ordinary Time, Song for the Table

C-115

Verse Tone

Psalm 119:33-48

1. Teach me the demands of <u>your</u> statutes
   and I will keep them to <u>the</u> end.
   Train me to ob<u>serve</u> your law,
   to keep it <u>with</u> my heart.

2. Guide me in the path of your <u>com</u>mands;
   for there is my <u>de</u>light.
   Bend my heart <u>to</u> your will
   and not to <u>love</u> of gain.

3. Keep my eyes from what <u>is</u> false;
   by your word, give <u>me</u> life.
   Keep the promise <u>you</u> have made
   to the ser<u>vant</u> who fears you.

4. Keep me from the scorn <u>I</u> dread,
   for your decrees <u>are</u> good.
   See, I long <u>for</u> your precepts;
   then in your justice, <u>give</u> me life.

5. Lord, let your love come <u>up</u>on me,
   the saving help of <u>your</u> promise.
   And I shall answer <u>those</u> who taunt me
   for I trust <u>in</u> your word.

6. Do not take the word of truth from <u>my</u> mouth
   for I trust in your <u>de</u>crees.
   I shall keep <u>your</u> law always
   for <u>ev</u>er and ever.

7. I shall walk in the path <u>of</u> freedom
   for I seek <u>your</u> precepts.
   I will speak of your will be<u>fore</u> the powerful
   and not <u>be</u> abashed.

8. Your commands have been my <u>de</u>light;
   these I <u>have</u> loved.
   I will worship your com<u>mands</u> and love them
   and pon<u>der</u> your statutes.

The Strong Lord Sets Me Free

Eighth Sunday in Ordinary Time, Song for the Week

Antiphon ♩ = 80

The strong Lord sets me free, in his love de-lights in me.

Verse Tone

[A]   [B]   [C]   [D]

Psalm 18

1. I love you, LORD, my strength,
   my rock, my for<u>tress</u>, my savior.
   God, you are the rock where <u>I</u> take refuge;
   my shield, my mighty <u>help</u>, my stronghold.
   [repeat A and D]
     LORD, you are worthy <u>of</u> all praise,
     when I call I am saved <u>from</u> my foes.

2. The waves of death <u>rose</u> about me;
   the torrents of destruc<u>tion</u> assailed me;
   the snares of the <u>grave</u> entangled me;
   the traps of <u>death</u> confronted me.

3. In my anguish I called <u>to</u> you, LORD;
   I cried to you, <u>God</u>, for help.
   From your temple you <u>heard</u> my voice;
   my cry came <u>to</u> your ears.

4. Then the earth reeled and rocked;
     the mountains were shaken <u>to</u> their base,
   they reeled at your ter<u>rible</u> anger.
   Smoke came forth from your nostrils
     and scorching fire <u>from</u> your mouth,
   coals were set ablaze <u>by</u> its heat.

5. You lowered the heavens <u>and</u> came down,
   a black cloud <u>under</u> your feet.
   You came enthroned <u>on</u> the cherubim,
   you flew on the wings <u>of</u> the wind.

6. You made the dark<u>ness</u> your covering,
   the dark waters of the <u>clouds</u>, your tent.
   A brightness shone <u>out</u> before you
   with hailstones and flash<u>es</u> of fire.

7. LORD, you thundered <u>in</u> the heavens,
   Most High, you let your <u>voice</u> be heard.
   You shot your arrows, scat<u>tered</u> the foe,
   flashed your lightnings and put <u>them</u> to flight.

8. The bed of the ocean <u>was</u> revealed;
   the foundations of the world <u>were</u> laid bare
   at the thunder of your <u>threat</u>, O LORD,
   at the blast of the breath <u>of</u> your anger.

9. From on high you reached <u>down</u> and seized me;
   you drew me out of the <u>mighty</u> waters.
   You snatched me from my p<u>owerful</u> foe,
   from my enemies whose strength I <u>could</u> not match.

10. They assailed me in the day of <u>my</u> misfortune,
    but you, LORD, were <u>my</u> support.
    You brought me forth <u>into</u> freedom,
    you saved me be<u>cause</u> you loved me.

11. You rewarded me because <u>I</u> was just,
    repaid me, for my <u>hands</u> were clean,
    for I have kept your <u>way</u>, O LORD,
    and have not fallen a<u>way</u> from you.

Verse Tone

12. Your judgements are <u>all</u> before me;
    I have never neglected <u>your</u> commands.
    I have always been up<u>right</u> before you;
    I have kept my<u>self</u> from guilt.

13. You repaid me because <u>I</u> was just
    and my hands were clean <u>in</u> your eyes.
    You are loving with <u>those</u> who love you,
    you show yourself perfect <u>with</u> the perfect.

14. With the sincere you show your<u>self</u> sincere,
    but the cunning you out<u>do</u> in cunning.
    For you save a <u>humble</u> people
    but humble the eyes <u>that</u> are proud.

15. You, O Lord, <u>are</u> my lamp,
    my God who ligh<u>tens</u> my darkness.
    With you I can break through <u>any</u> barrier,
    with my God I can scale <u>any</u> wall.

16. Your ways, O <u>God</u>, are perfect;
    your word, O Lord, is pu<u>rest</u> gold.
    You indeed <u>are</u> the shield
    of all who make <u>you</u> their refuge.

17. For who is <u>God</u> but you, Lord?
    Who is a rock but <u>you</u>, my God?
    You who gird <u>me</u> with strength
    and make the path <u>safe</u> before me.

18. My feet you made swift <u>as</u> the deer's,
    you have made me stand firm <u>on</u> the heights.
    You have trained my <u>hands</u> for battle
    and my arms to bend the <u>heavy</u> bow.

19. You gave me your <u>saving</u> shield;
    you upheld me, trained <u>me</u> with care.
    You gave me freedom <u>for</u> my steps;
    my feet have <u>never</u> slipped.

20. I pursued and over<u>took</u> my foes,
    never turning back till <u>they</u> were slain.
    I smote them so they <u>could</u> not rise;
    they fell be<u>neath</u> my feet.

21. You girded me with <u>strength</u> for battle,
    you made my enemies <u>fall</u> beneath me,
    you made my <u>foes</u> take flight;
    those who hated me <u>I</u> destroyed.

22. They cried, but there was no <u>one</u> to save them;
    they cried to you, Lord, <u>but</u> in vain.
    I crushed them fine as dust be<u>fore</u> the wind;
    trod them down like dirt <u>in</u> the streets.

23. You saved me from the feuds <u>of</u> the people
    and put me at the head <u>of</u> the nations.
    People unknown <u>to</u> me served me;
    when they heard of me <u>they</u> obeyed me.

24. Foreign nations came <u>to</u> me cringing,
    foreign nations faded away.
    [omit C]
    They came trembling out <u>of</u> their strongholds.

25. Long life to you, Lord, my rock!
    Praise to you, <u>God</u>, who saves me,
    the God who gives <u>me</u> redress
    and subdues <u>people</u> under me.

26. *A* You saved me from my <u>furious</u> foes.
    B You set me above <u>my</u> assailants.
    A You saved me from <u>violent</u> hands,
    B so I will praise you, Lord, <u>among</u> the nations;
    D I will sing a psalm <u>to</u> your name.

27. You have given great victories <u>to</u> your king
    and shown your love for <u>your</u> anointed,
    [omit C]
    for David and his <u>line</u> for ever.

It Is Good to Give You Thanks, O Lord

Eighth Sunday in Ordinary Time, Song for the Word

Psalm 92:2-3, 13-16

1. It is good to give thanks to the LORD,
   to make music to your name, O Most High,
   to proclaim your love in the morning
   and your truth in the watches of the night.

2. The just will flourish like the palm tree
   and grow like a Lebanon cedar.
   Planted in the house of the LORD,
   they will flourish in the courts of our God.

3. They will still bear fruit when they are old,
   still full of sap, still green,
   to proclaim that the LORD is just:
   my rock, in whom there is no wrong.

From the Fullness of Our Hearts

Eighth Sunday in Ordinary Time, Song for the Table

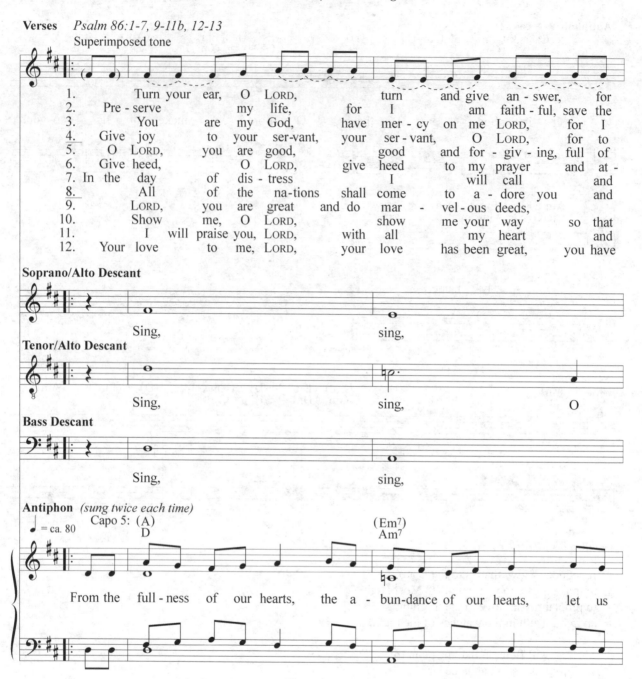

Verses *Psalm 86:1-7, 9-11b, 12-13*
Superimposed tone

1. Turn your ear, O LORD, turn and give an-swer, for
2. Pre - serve my life, for I am faith - ful, save the
3. You are my God, have mer - cy on me LORD, for I
4. Give joy to your ser-vant, your ser - vant, O LORD, for to
5. O LORD, you are good, good and for - giv - ing, full of
6. Give heed, O LORD, give heed to my prayer and at -
7. In the day of dis - tress I will call and
8. All of the na-tions shall come to a - dore you and
9. LORD, you are great and do mar - vel - ous deeds,
10. Show me, O LORD, show me your way so that
11. I will praise you, LORD, with all my heart and
12. Your love to me, LORD, your love has been great, you have

Soprano/Alto Descant

Sing, sing,

Tenor/Alto Descant

Sing, sing, O

Bass Descant

Sing, sing,

Antiphon *(sung twice each time)*

Capo 5: (A)
♩ = ca. 80   D   (Em⁷)
                               Am⁷

From the full - ness of our hearts, the a - bun-dance of our hearts, let us

Alleluia, Send Out Your Spirit

Pentecost Sunday, Song for the Word

Psalm 104:1, 24ac, 29b-31, 34

1. Bless the LORD, <u>my</u> soul!
   LORD God, how <u>great</u> you are!
   How many are your works, <u>O</u> LORD!
   The earth is full of <u>your</u> riches.

2. You take back your spirit, <u>they</u> die,
   returning to the dust from <u>which</u> they came.
   You send forth your spirit, they are <u>created</u>;
   and you renew the face of <u>the</u> earth.

3. May the glory of the LORD last <u>for</u> ever!
   May the LORD rejoice <u>in</u> creation!
   May my thoughts be pleasing <u>to</u> God.
   I find my joy in <u>the</u> LORD.

Performance Notes

Percussion or handclaps may be added, as indicated by X's, both during the Antiphon and at the end of the psalm verses to lead back into the Antiphon.
The Antiphon should be repeated every time it is sung.
The entire piece may be transposed down a whole step.

Come to Me and Drink
Pentecost Sunday, Song for the Table

Psalm 63:2-9; 42:2-3, 8-9

1. O God, you are my God, for <u>you</u> I long;
   for you my <u>soul</u> is thirsting.
   My body <u>pines</u> for you
   like a dry, weary land with<u>out</u> water.

2. So I gaze on you <u>in</u> the sanctuary
   to see your strength <u>and</u> your glory.
   For your love is bet<u>ter</u> than life,
   my lips will <u>speak</u> your praise.

3. So I will bless you <u>all</u> my life,
   in your name I will lift <u>up</u> my hands.
   My soul shall be filled as <u>with</u> a banquet,
   my mouth shall praise <u>you</u> with joy.

4. On my bed <u>I</u> remember you.
   On you I muse <u>through</u> the night

for you have <u>been</u> my help;
in the shadow of your wings <u>I</u> rejoice.

5. My soul <u>clings</u> to you;
   [omit B-C]
   your right hand <u>holds</u> me fast.

6. Like the deer that yearns for <u>running</u> streams,
   so my soul is yearning for <u>you</u>, my God.
   My soul is thirsting for God, the God <u>of</u> my life;
   when can I enter and see the <u>face</u> of God?

7. Deep is calling on deep, in the <u>roar</u> of waters;
   your torrents and all your waves swept <u>over</u> me.
   By day the LORD will send forth <u>loving</u> kindness;
   by night I will sing to the LORD,
       praise the God <u>of</u> my life.

Proclaim the Wonders God Has Done

C-99

Second Sunday in Ordinary Time, Song for the Word

Psalm 96:1-3, 7-8a, 9-10a, 10c

1. O sing a new song to the LORD,
   sing to the LORD, all the earth.
   O sing to the LORD, bless his name.

2. Proclaim God's help day by day,
   tell among the nations his glory
   and his wonders among all the peoples.

3. Give the LORD, you families of peoples,
   give the LORD glory and power,
   give the LORD the glory of his name.

4. Worship the Lord in the temple.
   O earth, stand in fear of the LORD.
   Proclaim to the nations: "God is king."
   God will judge the peoples in fairness.

Performance Notes

Percussion or handclaps may be added, as indicated by the X's, both during the Antiphon and at the end of the psalm verses to lead back into the Antiphon.

As a Bridegroom Rejoices

Second Sunday in Ordinary Time, Song for the Table
The Immaculate Conception of the Blessed Virgin Mary (December 8), Song for the Day

Descant 2

...and your God will re - joice, will re - joice o - ver you.

Verse Tone with Response

Cantor:
C   Cmaj7/E   Dm7   G   *All:*   F/A   Cmaj7/E   Dm7 GSUS4   C

...and your God will re - joice, will re - joice o - ver you.

Isaiah 61:10–62:5

1. *[For this verse only, omit the tone repeat.]*
   I will greatly rejoice in the LORD,
   my whole being shall exult in my God.
       and your God will rejoice . . .

2. He has clothed me with the garments of salvation,
   he has covered me with the robe of righteousness,
       and your God will rejoice . . .
   as a bridegroom decks himself with a garland,
   and as a bride adorns herself with her jewels.
       and your God will rejoice . . .

3. For as the earth brings forth its shoots,
   and as a garden causes what is sown in it
       to spring up,   *(simile)*
   so the LORD God will cause righteousness
       and praise
   to spring up before all the nations.

4. For Zion's sake I will not keep silent,
   and for Jerusalem's sake I will not rest,
   until her vindication shines out like the dawn,
   and her salvation like a burning torch.

5. The nations shall see your vindication,
   and all the kings your glory;
   and you shall be called by a new name
   that the mouth of the LORD shall give.

6. You shall be a crown of beauty
       in the hand of the LORD
   and a royal diadem in the hand of your God.
   You shall no more be termed Forsaken,
   and your land shall no more be termed Desolate;

7. but you shall be called My Delight Is in Her,
   and your land Married;
   for the LORD delights in you,
   and your land shall be married.

8. For as a young man marries a young woman,
   so shall your builder marry you,
   and as the bridegroom rejoices over the bride,
   so shall your God rejoice over you.

C-101   This Day Is Holy to the Lord Our God
Third Sunday in Ordinary Time, Song for the Week

Alto Descant

Ho - ly,   this day is ho - ly.   Ho -   ly,

Tenor Descant

This day is ho - ly: re - joice,   re -

Bass Descant

This   day is ho - ly: re - joice,   re -

Antiphon ♩. = 42

Capo 2: (D)   (Bm)   (Em)   (A)   (D)   (Bm)
         E   C#m   F#m   B   E   C#m

This day is ho - ly to the Lord   our God; the joy of the Lord will

Performance Notes

The Antiphon is sung twice through each time. It also works by itself as a two-part round, the second part entering at "(the) joy of the Lord . . . ."

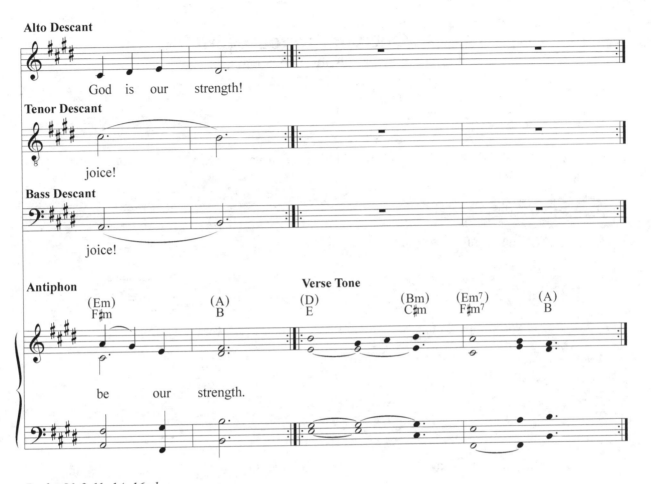

Alto Descant

God is our strength!

Tenor Descant

joice!

Bass Descant

joice!

Antiphon   **Verse Tone**

be our strength.

Psalm 81:2-11, 14, 16cd

1. Ring out your joy to God our strength,
shout in triumph to the God of Jacob.
Raise a song and sound the timbrel,
the sweet-sounding harp and the lute.

2. Ring out your joy, to God our strength,
shout in triumph to the God of Jacob.
Blow the trumpet at the new moon,
when the moon is full, on our feast.

3. For this is Israel's law,
a command of the God of Jacob,
imposed as a law on Joseph's people,
when they went out against the land of Egypt.

4. A voice I did not know said to me:
"I freed your shoulder from the burden;
your hands were freed from the load.
You called in distress and I saved you.

5. "I answered, concealed in the storm cloud;
at the waters of Meribah I tested you.
Listen, my people, to my warning.
O Israel, if only you would heed!

6. "Let there be no foreign god among you,
no worship of an alien god.
I am the LORD your God,
who brought you from the land of Egypt.
Open wide your mouth and I will fill it.

7. "O that my people would heed me,
that Israel would walk in my ways!
But Israel I would feed with finest wheat
and fill them with honey from the rock."

C-102 ➝ Third Sunday in Ordinary Time, Song for the Word, *same as C-64*

C-103

As One Body in Your Spirit

Third Sunday in Ordinary Time, Song for the Table

Verse Tone

Psalm 33:2-21

1. Give thanks to the LORD upon the harp,
   with a ten-stringed lute play your songs.
   Sing to the LORD a song that is new,
   play loudly, with all your skill.

2. For the word of the LORD is faithful
   and all his works done in truth.
   The LORD loves justice and right
   and fills the earth with love.

3. By God's word the heavens were made,
   by the breath of his mouth all the stars.
   God collects the waves of the ocean;
   and stores up the depths of the sea.

4. Let all the earth fear the LORD,
   all who live in the world stand in awe.
   For God spoke; it came to be.
   God commanded; it sprang into being.

5. The LORD foils the designs of the nations,
   and defeats the plans of the peoples.
   The counsel of the LORD stands forever,
   the plans of God's heart from age to age.

6. They are happy, whose God is the LORD,
   the people who are chosen as his own.
   From the heavens the LORD looks forth
   and sees all the peoples of the earth.

7. From the heavenly dwelling God gazes
   on all the dwellers on the earth;
   God who shapes the hearts of them all
   and considers all their deeds.

8. A king is not saved by his army,
   nor a warrior preserved by his strength.
   A vain hope for safety is the horse;
   despite its power it cannot save.

9. The LORD looks on those who fear him,
   on those who hope in his love,
   to rescue their souls from death,
   to keep them alive in famine.

10. Our soul is waiting for the LORD.
    The LORD is our help and our shield.
    Our hearts find joy in the LORD.
    We trust in God's holy name.

My Lips Will Tell of Your Justice

C-105

Fourth Sunday in Ordinary Time, Song for the Word

Psalm 71:1-4a, 5-6b, 15ab, 17

1. In you, O LORD, I take refuge; let me <u>never be</u> put to shame. *My lips will tell . . .*
   In your justice rescue me, free me; pay <u>heed to</u> me and save me. *my mouth will sing . . .*

2. Be a rock where I can take refuge, a mighty <u>strong</u>hold to save me. *(simile)*
   For you are my rock, my stronghold. Free me from the <u>hand</u> of the wicked.

3. It is you, O LORD, who are my hope, my trust, O <u>LORD</u>, since my youth.
   On you I have leaned from my birth; from my mother's womb <u>you have</u> been my help.

4. My lips will tell of your justice and day by <u>day</u> of your help.
   O God, you have taught me from my youth and I pro<u>claim your</u> wonders still.

Performance Notes
When more than one syllable is underlined, all the underlined syllables are sung to the high D.

Love Bears All Things

Fourth Sunday in Ordinary Time, Song for the Table

Verse Tone

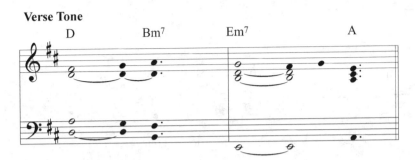

John 15:16-17; 1 Corinthians 13:4-5a, 13, 8a; 14:1a

1. You did not <u>choose</u> me
   but <u>I</u> chose you.

2. And I appointed you to go and <u>bear</u> fruit,
   fruit <u>that</u> will last,

3. so that the Father <u>will</u> give you
   whatever you ask him <u>in</u> my name.

4. I am giving you these <u>commands</u>
   so that you may love <u>one</u> another.

5. Love is patient; love <u>is</u> kind;
   love is not envious or boastful or <u>arrogant</u> or rude.

6. Love does not rejoice <u>in</u> wrongdoing,
   but rejoices <u>in</u> the truth.

7. Faith, hope and love abide, <u>these</u> three;
   and the greatest of <u>these</u> is love.

8. Love ne<u>ver</u> ends.
   Pursue love and strive for the spi<u>rit</u>ual gifts.

Here I Am

Fifth Sunday in Ordinary Time, Song for the Week

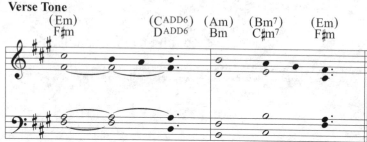

Psalm 40:2, 4ab, 7-11

1. I waited, I waited for the LORD
   who stooped down to me, and heard my cry.

2. God put a new song into my mouth,
   praise of our God.

3. You do not ask for sacrifice and offerings,
   but an open ear.

4. You do not ask for holocaust and victim.
   Instead, here am I.

5. In the scroll of the book it stands written
   that I should do your will.

6. My God, I delight in your law
   in the depth of my heart.

7. Your justice I have proclaimed
   in the great assembly.

8. My lips I have not sealed;
   you know it, O LORD.

9. I have not hidden your justice in my heart
   but declared your faithful help.

10. I have not hidden your love and your truth
    from the great assembly.

Performance Notes
The Antiphon may be sung twice each time if desired.
The descants are intended for equal voices.

In the Presence of the Angels

Fifth Sunday in Ordinary Time, Song for the Word
Seventeenth Sunday in Ordinary Time, Song for the Word

Verses *Psalm 138*
Superimposed tone

1. I thank you with all my heart, you have
2. I thank you: you are faith - ful, and I
*3. All the ru - lers of the earth shall thank you when they
*4. The LORD looks kind - ly on the low - ly but the
5. You stretch out your hand to save me, your
6. *Al - le - lu - ia, al - le - lu - ia, al - le -*

Alto Descant *Vocalize to 'oo' except for last phrase. See Performance Notes for the italic text.*

Al - le -

Bass Descant

In the pre - sence of the an - gels I de -
Al - le - lu - ia, al - le - lu - ia, al - le -

Antiphon ♩ = 76
Capo 3: (D⁷) (G) (Bm⁷)
F⁷ B♭ Dm⁷

In the pre - sence of the an - gels I de -
Al - le - lu - ia, al - le - lu - ia, al - le -

Verses Superimposed tone

1. I am poor and need-y.
2. ser - vant who trusts in you long.
3. cry to you all the day long.
4. you I lift up my soul.
5. love to all who call.
6. tend to the sound of my voice.
7. sure - ly you will re - ply.
8. glo - ri - fy your name, O LORD.
9. you who a - lone are God.
10. I may walk in your truth.
11. glo - ri - fy your name, for ev - er.
12. saved me from the depths of the grave.

Soprano/Alto Descant

to the Lord.

Tenor/Alto Descant

sing, to the Lord.

Bass Descant

sing to the Lord.

Antiphon

(Dm⁷)
Gm⁷   (Em⁷)   (A)
Am⁷   D

sing of the good - ness of the Lord.

Performance Notes

The Antiphon and descant parts are hummed when the Verse is superimposed.
The psalm text has been slightly adapted for performance purposes.

Look on My Toil

Ninth Sunday in Ordinary Time, Song for the Week

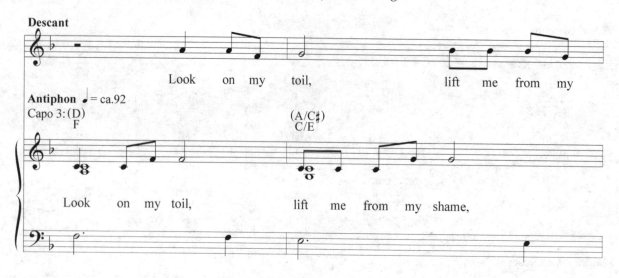

Look on my toil, lift me from my shame,

shame, let me walk your way.

teach me how to walk your way.

Verse Tone

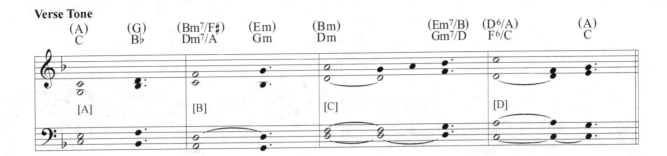

Psalm 25:2-21

1. My God, I trust in you, let me not be disap<u>poin</u>ted;
   do not let my enemies <u>tri</u>umph.
   Those who hope in you shall not be disap<u>poin</u>ted,
   but only those who wantonly <u>break</u> faith.

2. LORD, make me know your <u>ways</u>.
   LORD, teach me your <u>paths</u>.
   Make me walk in your <u>truth</u>, and teach me,
   for you are God <u>my</u> savior.

3. In you I hope all the day <u>long</u>
   because of your goodness, O <u>LORD</u>.
   Remember your <u>mer</u>cy, LORD,
   and the love you have shown from <u>of</u> old.
   [repeat C-D]
   Do not remember the sins <u>of</u> my youth.
   In your love <u>re</u>member me.

4. The LORD is good and <u>up</u>right,
   showing the path to those who <u>stray</u>,
   guiding the humble <u>in</u> the right path,
   and teaching the way to <u>the</u> poor.

5. God's ways are steadfastness and <u>truth</u>
   for those faithful to the covenant de<u>crees</u>.
   LORD, for the sake <u>of</u> your name
   forgive my guilt, for it <u>is</u> great.

6. Those who revere the <u>LORD</u>
   will be shown the path they should <u>choose</u>.
   Their souls will <u>live</u> in happiness
   and their children will possess <u>the</u> land.
   [repeat C-D]
   The LORD's friendship is <u>for</u> the God-fearing;
   and the covenant is revealed <u>to</u> them.

7. My eyes are always on the <u>LORD</u>,
   who will rescue my feet from the <u>snare</u>.
   Turn to me <u>and</u> have mercy
   for I am lonely <u>and</u> poor.

8. Relieve the anguish of my <u>heart</u>
   and set me free from my dis<u>tress</u>.
   See my affliction <u>and</u> my toil
   and take all my sins <u>away</u>.

9. See how many are my <u>foes</u>,
   how violent their hatred for <u>me</u>.
   Preserve my <u>life</u> and rescue me.
   Do not disappoint me, you are <u>my</u> refuge.
   [repeat C-D]
   May innocence and upright<u>ness</u> protect me,
   for my hope is in you, <u>O</u> LORD.

Go to the Ends of the Earth

Ninth Sunday in Ordinary Time, Song for the Word
Twenty-first Sunday in Ordinary Time, Song for the Word

Antiphon ♩. = 63-69

Go to the ends of the earth, al - le - lu - ia, al - le - lu - ia, pro -

claim the Good News to the world, al - le - lu - ia, al - le - lu - ia.

Verse Tone with Response

al - le - lu - ia!

al - le - lu - ia!

Psalm 117

1. O praise the Lord, all you nations, *alleluia!*
   acclaim God, all you peoples! *alleluia!*

2. Strong is his love for us; *alleluia!*
   the Lord is faithful for ever. *alleluia!*

Speak Your Word, O Lord

Ninth Sunday in Ordinary Time, Song for the Table

C-121

Verse Tone

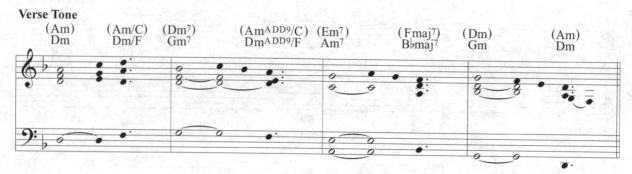

Isaiah 55:1, 5, 6-7ac, 10ab, 11ab; 56:6a, 7abd, 8; Psalm 86:1-10

1. Everyone who thirsts, come to the waters;
   and you that have no money, come, buy and eat!
   Come, buy wine and milk
   without money and without price.

2. See, you shall call nations that you do not know,
   and nations that do not know you shall run to you,
   because of the LORD your God, the Holy One of Israel,
   for he has glorified you.

3. Seek the LORD while he may be found,
   call upon him while he is near;
   let the wicked forsake their way;
   let them return to the LORD, that he may
      have mercy on them.

4. For as the rain and the snow come down from heaven,
   and do not return there until they have watered the earth,
   so shall my word be that goes out from my mouth;
   it shall not return to me empty.

5. And the foreigners who join themselves to the LORD,
   these I will bring to my holy mountain,
   and make them joyful in my house of prayer;
   for my house shall be called a house of prayer
      for all peoples.

6. Thus says the Lord GOD,
   who gathers the outcasts of Israel,
   I will gather others to them
   besides those already gathered.

7. Turn your ear, O LORD, and give answer
   for I am poor and needy.
   Preserve my life, for I am faithful;
   save the servant who trusts in you.

8. You are my God, have mercy on me, LORD,
   for I cry to you all the day long.
   Give joy to your servant, O LORD,
   for to you I lift up my soul.

9. O LORD, you are good and forgiving,
   full of love to all who call.
   Give heed, O LORD, to my prayer
   and attend to the sound of my voice.

10. In the day of distress I will call
    and surely you will reply.
    Among the gods there is none like you,
       O LORD,
    nor work to compare with yours.

11. All the nations shall come to adore you
    and glorify your name, O LORD,
    for you are great and do marvelous deeds,
    you who alone are God.

Performance Notes

The psalm text in the right-hand column is for use only when necessary for reasons of time.

The Lord Is My Light

Tenth Sunday in Ordinary Time, Song for the Week

Psalm 27:1, 3-5, 7-14

1. The LORD is my light and my <u>help</u>;
   whom shall I <u>fear</u>?
   The LORD is the stronghold <u>of</u> my life;
   before whom <u>shall</u> I shrink?

2. Though an army encamp <u>against</u> me
   my heart would not <u>fear</u>.
   Though war break <u>out</u> against me
   even then <u>would</u> I trust.

3. There is one thing I ask of the LORD, for this I <u>long</u>,
   to live in the house of the LORD all the days of my <u>life</u>,
   to savor the sweetness <u>of</u> the LORD,
   to be<u>hold</u> his temple.

4. For God makes me safe in his <u>tent</u>
   in the day of <u>evil</u>.
   God hides me in the shelter <u>of</u> his tent,
   on a rock I <u>am</u> secure.

5. O LORD, hear my voice when I <u>call</u>;
   have mercy and <u>answer</u>.
   Of you my <u>heart</u> has spoken:
   "<u>Seek</u> God's face."

6. It is your face, O LORD, that I <u>seek</u>;
   hide not your <u>face</u>.
   Dismiss not your ser<u>vant</u> in anger;
   you have <u>been</u> my help.

7. Do not abandon or for<u>sake</u> me,
   O God my <u>help</u>!
   Though father and mo<u>ther</u> forsake me,
   the LORD <u>will</u> receive me.

8. Instruct me, LORD, in your <u>way</u>;
   on an even path <u>lead</u> me.
   When they lie in ambush, protect me
   from my <u>enemies'</u> greed.
   False witnesses rise against me,
   <u>breathing</u> out fury.

9. I am sure I shall see the LORD's <u>goodness</u>
   in the land of the <u>living</u>.
   In the LORD, hold firm <u>and</u> take heart.
   Hope <u>in</u> the LORD!

C-123 → Tenth Sunday in Ordinary Time, Song for the Word, *same as C-62*

C-124

Our Shelter and Our Help

Tenth Sunday in Ordinary Time, Song for the Table

Luke 1:68-79

1. Blessed be the Lord <u>God</u> of Israel,
   for he has looked favorably on his people <u>and</u> redeemed them. *God has visited his people.*
   He has raised up a mighty sav<u>ior</u> for us
   in the house of his <u>ser</u>vant David. *God has visited his people.*

2. As he spoke through the mouth of his holy prophets <u>from</u> of old,
   that we would be saved from our enemies and from the hand of <u>all</u> who hate us, *God has visited . . .*
   thus he has shown the mercy promised <u>to</u> our ancestors,
   and has remembered his <u>ho</u>ly covenant, *(simile)*

3. the oath that he swore to our an<u>ces</u>tor Abraham,
   to grant us that we, being rescued from the hands <u>of</u> our enemies,
   might serve him without fear, in holi<u>ness</u> and righteousness
   before him <u>all</u> our days.

4. And you, child, will be called the prophet of <u>the</u> Most High;
   for you will go before the Lord to pre<u>pare</u> his ways,
   to give knowledge of salvation <u>to</u> his people
   by the forgiveness <u>of</u> their sins.

5. By the tender mercy <u>of</u> our God,
   the dawn from on high will <u>break</u> upon us,
   to give light to those who sit in darkness and in the sha<u>dow</u> of death,
   to guide our feet into the <u>way</u> of peace.

One Thing I Seek
Eleventh Sunday in Ordinary Time, Song for the Week

Antiphon ♩ = 72

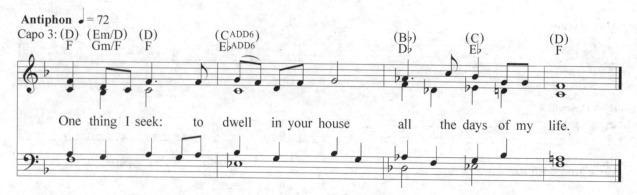

One thing I seek: to dwell in your house all the days of my life.

Verse Tone

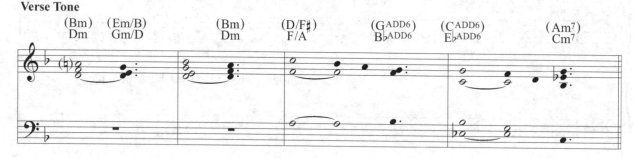

Psalm 27:1, 3-5, 7-14

1. The LORD is my light and my help;
   whom shall I fear?
   The LORD is the stronghold of my life;
   before whom shall I shrink?

2. Though an army encamp against me
   my heart would not fear.
   Though war break out against me
   even then would I trust.

3. There is one thing I ask of the LORD, for this I long,
   to live in the house of the LORD all the days of my life,
   to savor the sweetness of the LORD,
   to behold his temple.

4. For God makes me safe in his tent
   in the day of evil.
   God hides me in the shelter of his tent,
   on a rock I am secure.

5. O LORD, hear my voice when I call;
   have mercy and answer.
   Of you my heart has spoken:
   "Seek God's face."

6. It is your face, O LORD, that I seek;
   hide not your face.
   Dismiss not your servant in anger;
   you have been my help.

7. Do not abandon or forsake me,
   O God my help!
   Though father and mother forsake me,
   the LORD will receive me.

8. Instruct me, LORD, in your way;
   on an even path lead me.
   When they lie in ambush, protect me
       from my enemies' greed.
   False witnesses rise against me,
       breathing out fury.

9. I am sure I shall see the LORD's goodness
   in the land of the living.
   In the LORD, hold firm and take heart.
   Hope in the LORD!

Turn to the Lord

C-126

Eleventh Sunday in Ordinary Time, Song for the Word

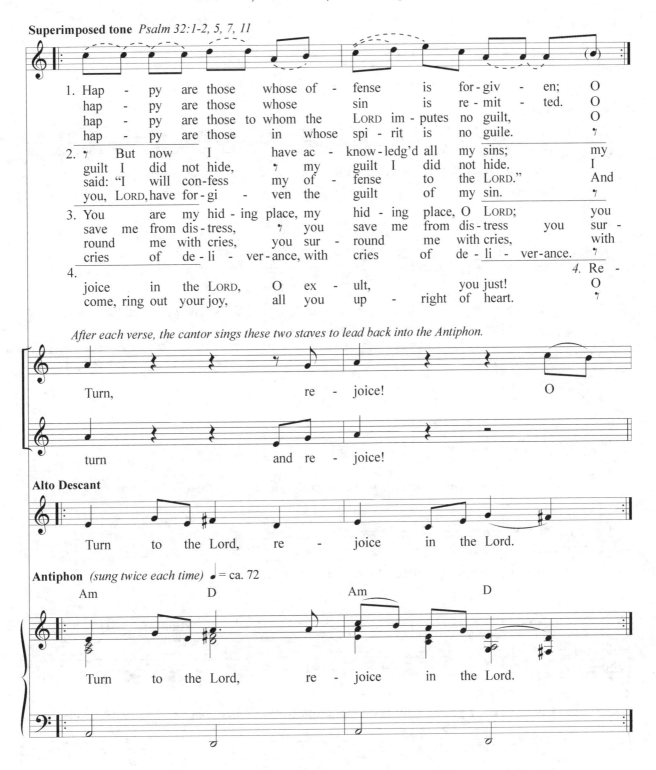

Superimposed tone *Psalm 32:1-2, 5, 7, 11*

1. Hap - py are those whose of - fense is for - giv - en; O
   hap - py are those whose sin is re - mit - ted. O
   hap - py are those to whom the LORD im - putes no guilt,
   hap - py are those in whose spi - rit is no guile.

2. But now I have ac - know - ledg'd all my sins; my
   guilt I did not hide, my guilt I did not hide. I
   said: "I will con - fess my of - fense to the LORD." And
   you, LORD, have for - gi - ven the guilt of my sin.

3. You are my hid - ing place, my hid - ing place, O LORD; you
   save me from dis - tress, you save me from dis - tress you sur -
   round me with cries, you sur - round me with cries, with
   cries of de - li - ver - ance, with cries of de - li - ver - ance.

4. joice in the LORD, O ex - ult, you just! O
   come, ring out your joy, all you up - right of heart.

After each verse, the cantor sings these two staves to lead back into the Antiphon.

Turn, re - joice! O

turn and re - joice!

Alto Descant

Turn to the Lord, re - joice in the Lord.

Antiphon *(sung twice each time)* ♩ = ca. 72

Am   D   Am   D

Turn to the Lord, re - joice in the Lord.

All Your Sins Have Been Forgiven

Eleventh Sunday in Ordinary Time, Song for the Table

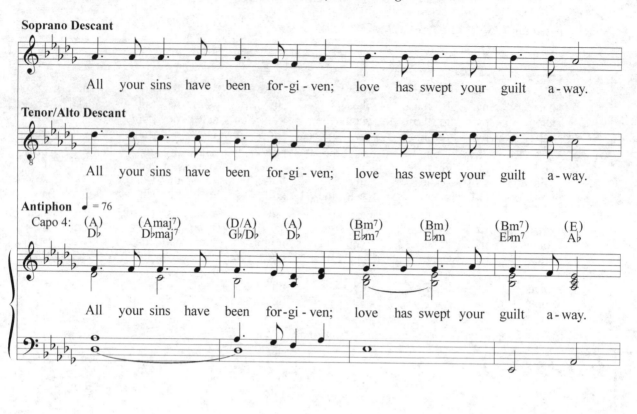

Soprano Descant

All your sins have been for-gi-ven; love has swept your guilt a-way.

Tenor/Alto Descant

All your sins have been for-gi-ven; love has swept your guilt a-way.

Antiphon ♩ = 76

Capo 4:
(A)/Db · (Amaj7)/Dbmaj7 · (D/A)/Gb/Db · (A)/Db · (Bm7)/Ebm7 · (Bm)/Ebm · (Bm7)/Ebm7 · (E)/Ab

All your sins have been for-gi-ven; love has swept your guilt a-way.

Go in peace: your faith has saved you; love has come to you to-day.

Go in peace: your faith has saved you; love has come to you to-day.

(A/C#)/Db/F · (DADD6)/GbADD6 · (E)/Ab · (F#m7)/Bbm7 · (A/E)/Db/Ab · (D)/Gb · (Bm7)/Ebm7 · (ESUS4)/AbSUS4 · (E)/Ab · (A)/Db

Go in peace: your faith has saved you; love has come to you to-day.

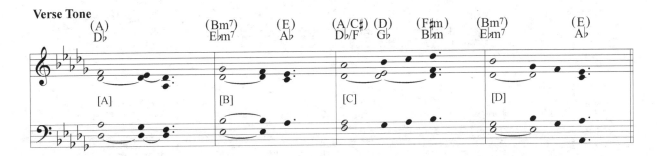

Verse Tone

Psalm 84:3-13

1. My soul is longing <u>and</u> yearning,
   is yearning for the courts of <u>the</u> LORD.
   My heart and my soul ring <u>out</u> their joy
   to God, the <u>living</u> God.

2. The sparrow herself finds <u>a</u> home
   and the swallow a nest for <u>her</u> brood;
   she lays her young <u>by</u> your altars,
   LORD of hosts, my king <u>and</u> my God.

3. They are happy, who dwell in <u>your</u> house,
   for ever singing <u>your</u> praise.
   They are happy, whose strength <u>is</u> in you,
   in whose hearts are the <u>roads</u> to Zion.

4. As they go through the <u>Bitter</u> Valley
   they make it a place of springs,
     (the autumn rain covers it <u>with</u> blessings).
   They walk with ever-<u>growing</u> strength,
   they will see the God of <u>gods</u> in Zion.

5. O LORD God of hosts, hear <u>my</u> prayer,
   give ear, O God <u>of</u> Jacob.
   Turn your eyes, O <u>God</u>, our shield,
   look on the face of <u>your</u> anointed.

6. One day within <u>your</u> courts
   is better than a thousand <u>elsewhere</u>.
   The threshold of the <u>house</u> of God
   I prefer to the dwellings <u>of</u> the wicked.

7. For the LORD God is a rampart, <u>a</u> shield.
   The LORD will give us favor <u>and</u> glory.
   The LORD will not refuse <u>any</u> good
   to those who walk <u>without</u> blame.

8. *[Omit A-B]*
   LORD, <u>God</u> of hosts,
   happy are those who <u>trust</u> in you!

C-128

Save Us, Lord
Twelfth Sunday in Ordinary Time, Song for the Week

Psalm 29

1. O give the LORD, you children of God,
   give the LORD glory <u>and</u> power;
   give the LORD the glory <u>of</u> his name.
   *Adore the LORD, resplendent <u>and</u> holy.

2. The LORD's voice resounding <u>on</u> the waters,
   *the LORD on the immensity <u>of</u> waters;
   the voice of the LORD, <u>full</u> of power,
   *the voice of the LORD, full <u>of</u> splendor.

3. The LORD's voice shatter<u>ing</u> the cedars,
   *the LORD shatters the cedars <u>of</u> Lebanon,
   makes Lebanon leap <u>like</u> a calf
   and Sirion like a young <u>wild</u> ox.

4. The LORD's voice flashes <u>flames</u> of fire,
   the LORD's voice flashes flames <u>of</u> fire.

5. The LORD's voice shak<u>ing</u> the wilderness,
   *the LORD shakes the wilderness <u>of</u> Kadesh;
   the LORD's voice rend<u>ing</u> the oak tree
   and stripping the for<u>est</u> bare.

6. The God of <u>glory</u> thunders.
   *In his temple they all <u>cry</u>: "Glory!"
   The LORD sat enthroned <u>over</u> the flood;
   *the LORD sits as king <u>for</u> ever.

7. The LORD will give strength <u>to</u> his people,
   the LORD will bless his people <u>with</u> peace.

Performance Notes
Use the small cue-size notes (last measure of verse tone) on the verse lines marked with an asterisk.

For You My Soul Is Thirsting

C-129

Twelfth Sunday in Ordinary Time, Song for the Word

Psalm 63:2-6, 8-9

1. O God, you are my God, for <u>you</u> I long;
   for you my <u>soul</u> is thirsting.
   My body <u>pines</u> for you
   like a dry, weary land <u>without</u> water.

2. So I gaze on you in the <u>sanctuary</u>
   to see your strength <u>and</u> your glory.
   For your love is <u>better</u> than life,
   my lips will <u>speak</u> your praise.

3. So I will bless you <u>all</u> my life,
   in your name I will lift <u>up</u> my hands.
   My soul shall be filled as with <u>a</u> banquet,
   my mouth shall praise <u>you</u> with joy.

4. For you have <u>been</u> my help;
   in the shadow of your wings <u>I</u> rejoice.
   My soul <u>clings</u> to you;
   your right hand <u>holds</u> me fast.

C-130

Lose Your Life and Save It

Twelfth Sunday in Ordinary Time, Song for the Table
Exaltation of the Holy Cross, Song for the Table

Psalm 116:1-9 (10-19)

1. I love the LORD, for the LORD has heard
   the cry of <u>my</u> appeal.
   The LORD was atten<u>tive</u> to me
   in the day <u>when</u> I called.

2. They surrounded me, the <u>snares</u> of death,
   with the anguish <u>of</u> the tomb;
   they caught me, sorrow <u>and</u> distress.
   I called on the LORD's name.
   O LORD my <u>God</u>, deliver me!

3. How gracious is the <u>LORD</u>, and just;
   our God <u>has</u> compassion.
   The LORD protects the <u>simple</u> hearts;
   I was helpless <u>so</u> God saved me.

4. Turn back, my soul, <u>to</u> your rest
   for the LORD <u>has</u> been good,
   and has kept my <u>soul</u> from death,
   my eyes from tears, my <u>feet</u> from stumbling.

5. I will walk in the presence <u>of</u> the LORD
   [omit B-C]
   in the land <u>of</u> the living.

Verse Tone

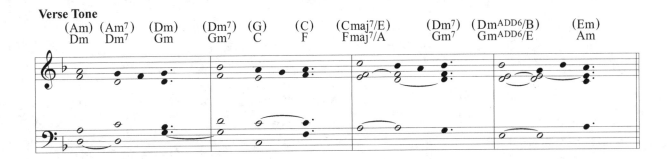

Additional verses if required (Psalm 116:10-19)

6. I trusted, even <u>when</u> I said:
   "I am sore<u>ly</u> afflicted,"
   and when I said in <u>my</u> alarm:
   "There is no one <u>I</u> can trust."

7. How can I re<u>pay</u> the LORD
   for his good<u>ness</u> to me?
   The cup of salvation <u>I</u> will raise;
   I will call <u>on</u> the LORD's name.

8. My vows to the LORD I <u>will</u> fulfill
   before <u>all</u> the people.
   O precious in the eyes <u>of</u> the LORD
   is the death <u>of</u> the faithful.

9. Your servant, LORD, your ser<u>vant</u> am I;
   you have loos<u>ened</u> my bonds.
   A thanksgiving sacri<u>fice</u> I make;
   I will call <u>on</u> the LORD's name.

10. My vows to the LORD I <u>will</u> fulfill
    before <u>all</u> the people,
    in the courts of the house <u>of</u> the LORD,
    in your midst, <u>O</u> Jerusalem.

All You Nations

Thirteenth Sunday in Ordinary Time, Song for the Week
Twenty-second Sunday in Ordinary Time, Song for the Week: Option I

Alto Descant

All you na - tions, all you peo - ples, clap your hands, O clap your hands.
Shout to God with cries of glad - ness: clap your hands, O clap your hands.

Tenor Descant

All you na - tions, all you peo - ples, clap your hands, O clap your hands.
Shout to God with cries of glad - ness: clap your hands, O clap your hands.

Bass Descant

All you na - tions, all you peo - ples, clap your hands, O clap your hands.
Shout to God with cries of glad - ness: clap your hands, O clap your hands.

Antiphon ♩ = 138-144

All you na - tions, all you peo - ples, clap your hands, O clap your hands.
Shout to God with cries of glad - ness: clap your hands, O clap your hands.

Alto Descant

Hum to 'Nn...' (lips open)

Bass Descant

Hum to 'Nn...' (lips open)

Verse Tone *(in approximately the same tempo as the Antiphon)*

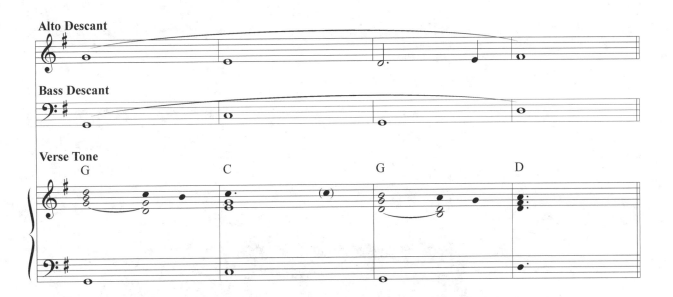

Psalm 47

1. All peoples, <u>clap</u> your hands,
   cry to God with <u>shouts</u> of joy!
   For the Lord, the Most High, <u>we</u> must fear,
   great king over <u>all</u> the earth.

2. God subdues <u>peoples</u> under us
   and | nations un<u>der</u> our feet.
   Our inheritance, our glory, <u>is</u> from God,
   given to Jacob <u>out</u> of love.

3. God goes up with <u>shouts</u> of joy;
   the | Lord goes up with <u>trump</u>et blast.
   Sing praise to <u>God</u>, sing praise,
   sing | praise to our <u>king</u>, sing praise.

4. God is king of <u>all</u> the earth,
   sing praise with <u>all</u> your skill.
   God is king o<u>ver</u> the nations;
   God reigns en<u>throned</u> in holiness.

5. The leaders of the people <u>are</u> assembled
   with the | people of A<u>braham's</u> God.
   The rulers of the earth be<u>long</u> to God,
   to | God who reigns <u>over</u> all.

Performance Notes
The pick-up notes in measures 2 & 6 of the verse tone are used only on lines marked with the symbol |
Light percussion instruments may easily be added to the Antiphon.

My Portion and My Cup

C-132

Thirteenth Sunday in Ordinary Time, Song for the Word

Psalm 16:1-2a, 5, 7-11

1. Preserve me, God, I take refuge <u>in</u> you.
   I say to you, LORD: "You <u>are</u> my God."
   O LORD, is it you who are my portion <u>and</u> cup,
   it is you yourself who <u>are</u> my prize.

2. I will bless the LORD who gives <u>me</u> counsel,
   who even at night di<u>rects</u> my heart.
   I keep you, LORD, ever in <u>my</u> sight;
   since you are at my right hand, I <u>shall</u> stand firm.

3. And so my heart re- † <u>joic</u>es,
   my soul <u>is</u> glad;
   even my body shall <u>rest</u> in safety.
   For you will not leave my soul among <u>the</u> dead,
   nor let your beloved <u>know</u> decay.

4. You will show me the path of † <u>life</u>,
   the fullness of joy in <u>your</u> presence,
   at your right hand happ<u>iness</u> for ever.

Performance Notes

The Verse Tone is sung through twice for each stanza, except for stanza 4.

We Will Follow You, Lord

Thirteenth Sunday in Ordinary Time, Song for the Table

Within Your Temple

Fourteenth Sunday in Ordinary Time, Song for the Week
Anniversary of the Dedication of a Church, Song for the Day

Antiphon ♩ = 76

With - in your tem - ple, your ho - ly dwel - ling,

we re - call your lov - ing - kind - ness, O Lord our God.

Verse Tone

Psalm 48

1. The LORD | is great and worthy to be praised in the city of <u>our</u> God,
   whose holy mountain rises in beauty, the joy of <u>all</u> the earth.

2. Mount Zi- | on, true pole of the earth, the Great <u>King's</u> city!
   God, in the midst of its citadels, is known to <u>be</u> its stronghold.

3. For the | kings assembled together, together they <u>advanced.</u>
   They saw; at once they were astounded; dismayed, they <u>fled</u> in fear.

4. A trem- | bling seized them there, like the pangs <u>of</u> birth.
   By the east wind you have destroyed the <u>ships</u> of Tarshish.

5. As we | have heard, so we have seen in the city of <u>our</u> God,
   in the city of the LORD of hosts, which God up<u>holds</u> for ever.

Verse Tone

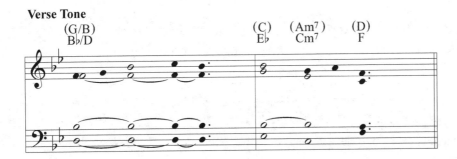

6. God, we | ponder your love within <u>your</u> temple.
   Your praise, O God, like your name reaches the ends <u>of</u> the earth.

7. With just- | ice your right hand is filled. Mount Zion re<u>joi</u>ces;
   the people of Judah rejoice at the sight <u>of</u> your judgements.

8. Walk through | Zion, walk all around it; count the number of <u>its</u> towers.
   Review all its ramparts, exa<u>mine</u> its castles,

9. that you | may tell the next generation that such is <u>our</u> God,
   our God for ever and ever will <u>al</u>ways lead us.

C-135 ➡ Fourteenth Sunday In Ordinary Time, Song for the Word, *same as C-77*

C-136   Rejoice, Your Names Are Written in Heaven

Fourteenth Sunday in Ordinary Time, Song for the Table

Psalm 40:2-12, 14-15b, 17-18

1. I waited, I waited for the L<small>ORD</small>
   who stooped down to me, and <u>heard</u> my cry.   *the kingdom of God is at hand.*

2. God drew me from the deadly pit, from the miry <u>clay</u>,
   and set my feet upon a rock and made my <u>foot</u>steps firm.   *the kingdom of God is at hand.*

3. God put a new song into my mouth, praise of our <u>God</u>.
   Many shall see and fear and shall trust <u>in</u> the L<small>ORD</small>.   *(simile)*

4. Happy those who have placed their trust in the L<small>ORD</small>
   and have not gone over to the rebels who <u>follow</u> false gods.

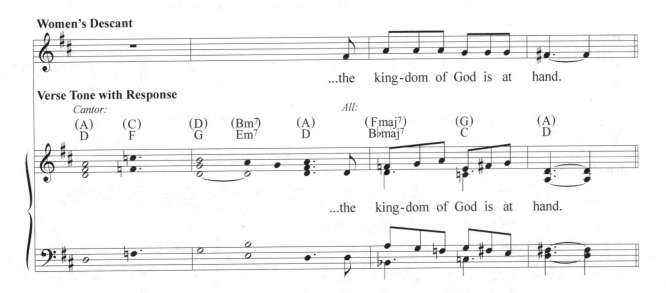

5. How many, O LORD my God, are the wonders and designs that you have <u>worked</u> for us;
   you <u>have</u> no equal.

6. Should I proclaim and speak of <u>them</u>,
   they are more than <u>I</u> can tell!

7. You do not ask for sacrifice and offerings, but an open <u>ear</u>.
   You do not ask for holocaust and victim. Instead, <u>here</u> am I.

8. In the scroll of the book it stands written that I should do your <u>will</u>.
   My God, I delight in your law in the depth <u>of</u> my heart.

9. Your justice I have proclaimed in the great as<u>sem</u>bly.
   My lips I have not sealed; you know <u>it</u>, O LORD.

10. I have not hidden your justice in my heart but declared your faithful <u>help</u>.
    I have not hidden your love and your truth from the <u>great</u> assembly.

11. O LORD, you will not withhold your com<u>pass</u>ion from me.
    Your merciful love and your truth will <u>always</u> guard me.

12. O LORD, come to my rescue; LORD, come to my <u>aid</u>.
    O let there be shame and confusion on those who <u>seek</u> my life.

13. O let there be rejoicing and gladness for all who <u>seek</u> you.
    Let them ever say: "The LORD is great," who love your <u>saving</u> help.

14. As for me, wretched and poor, the LORD thinks of <u>me</u>.
    You are my rescuer, my help, O God, do <u>not</u> delay.

To Gaze on Your Glory

C-137

Fifteenth Sunday in Ordinary Time, Song for the Week: Option I
Thirty-second Sunday in Ordinary Time, Song for the Word

Psalm 17   [*The Lectionary selections for the Thirty-second Sunday in Ordinary Time are indicated by an asterisk.*]

1. * LORD, hear a cause that is just, pay <u>heed</u> <u>to</u> my <u>cry</u>.
2. * Turn your ear to my prayer, no de<u>ceit</u> is <u>on</u> my <u>lips</u>.
3. From | you may my judgement come forth. Your <u>eyes</u> dis<u>cern</u> the <u>truth</u>.
4. You | search my heart, you <u>visit</u> <u>me</u> by <u>night</u>.
5. You | test me and you find in me no wrong. My <u>words</u> <u>are</u> not <u>sinful</u>.
6. I kept from | violence because of your word,
   * I <u>kept</u> my feet <u>firmly</u> in your <u>paths</u>;
7. * there was no faltering <u>in</u> <u>my</u> <u>steps</u>.
8. * I am | here and I call, you will hear me, O God. Turn your <u>ear</u> to <u>me</u>; hear my <u>words</u>.
9. Dis- | play your great love, whose right hand saves your <u>friends</u> from <u>all</u> their <u>enemies</u>.
10. * Guard me as the apple of your eye. <u>Hide</u> me in the <u>shadow</u> of your <u>wings</u>,
11. from the | violent attack of the wicked. My foes en<u>circle</u> me with <u>deadly</u> <u>intent</u>.
12. Their | hearts tight shut, their mouths speak proudly.
    They ad<u>vance</u> against me, <u>now</u> they sur<u>round</u> me.
13. Their eyes are watching to <u>strike</u> me <u>to</u> the <u>ground</u>,
14. like | lions ready to claw, or some young <u>lion</u> <u>crouched</u> in <u>hiding</u>.
15. LORD, a- | rise, confront them, strike them down! Let your <u>sword</u> rescue <u>me</u> from the <u>wicked</u>;
16. let your | hand, O LORD, rescue me from <u>those</u> <u>whose</u> <u>reward</u>
17. is | in this present life. You <u>give</u> them their <u>fill</u> of your <u>treasures</u>;
18. they re- | joice in abundance of offspring and <u>leave</u> their <u>wealth</u> to their <u>children</u>.
19. * As for me, in my justice, <u>I</u> shall <u>see</u> your <u>face</u>
20. * and be | filled, when I awake, with the <u>sight</u> <u>of</u> your <u>glory</u>.

Fifteenth Sunday in Ordinary Time, Song for the Week: Option II, *same as C-22* ← **C-138**

Fifteenth Sunday in Ordinary Time, Song for the Word, *same as C-64* ← **C-139**

C-140

Love the Lord Your God

Fifteenth Sunday in Ordinary Time, Song for the Table

Psalm 119:1-8

1. They are happy whose <u>life</u> is blameless,
   who fol<u>low</u> God's law! *Do this . . .*

2. They are happy who <u>do</u> God's will,
   seeking God with <u>all</u> their hearts. *Do this . . .*

3. They never do <u>any</u>thing evil
   but walk <u>in</u> God's ways. *(simile)*

4. You have laid <u>down</u> your precepts
   to be o<u>bey</u>ed with care.

5. May my foot<u>steps</u> be firm
   to o<u>bey</u> your statutes.

6. Then I shall not be <u>put</u> to shame
   as I heed <u>your</u> commands.

7. I will thank you with an <u>up</u>right heart
   as I learn <u>your</u> decrees.

8. I will o<u>bey</u> your statutes;
   do <u>not</u> forsake me.

C-141

You Alone Are My Help

Sixteenth Sunday in Ordinary Time, Song for the Week

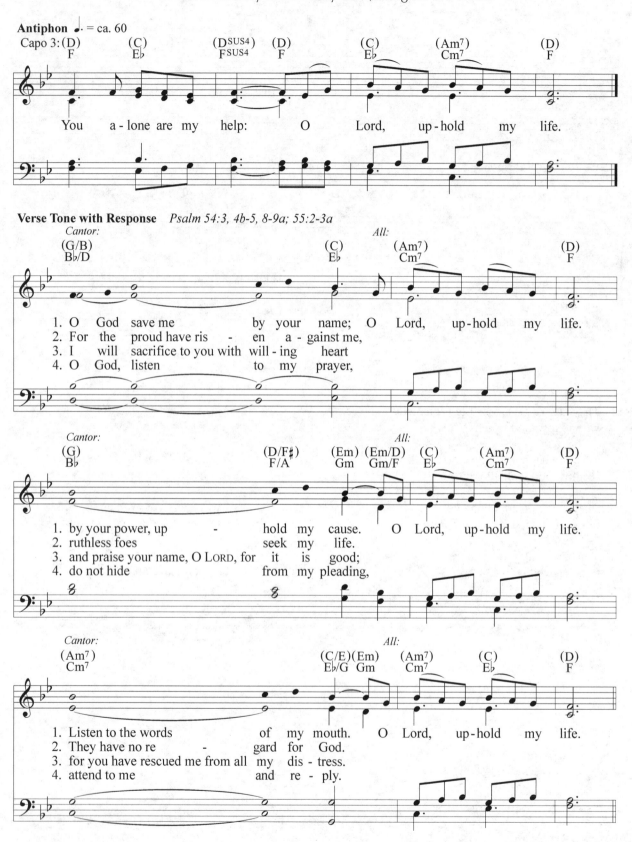

Antiphon ♩. = ca. 60

You a-lone are my help: O Lord, up-hold my life.

Verse Tone with Response *Psalm 54:3, 4b-5, 8-9a; 55:2-3a*

Cantor: / *All:*

1. O God save me by your name; O Lord, up-hold my life.
2. For the proud have ris - en a - gainst me,
3. I will sacrifice to you with will - ing heart
4. O God, listen to my prayer,

Cantor: / *All:*

1. by your power, up - hold my cause. O Lord, up-hold my life.
2. ruthless foes seek my life.
3. and praise your name, O LORD, for it is good;
4. do not hide from my pleading,

Cantor: / *All:*

1. Listen to the words of my mouth. O Lord, up-hold my life.
2. They have no re - gard for God.
3. for you have rescued me from all my dis - tress.
4. attend to me and re - ply.

Those Who Do Justice

Sixteenth Sunday in Ordinary Time, Song for the Word

Psalm 15:2-5b

1. Those who act without <u>fault</u>,
   those who act with <u>justice</u>   *shall dwell . . .*
   those who speak the truth from their <u>hearts</u>,
   who do not slander with their <u>tongue</u>,   *shall dwell . . .*

2. those who do no wrong to their <u>kin</u>dred,
   those who cast no slur on their <u>neigh</u>bors   *(simile)*
   those who hold the godless in dis<u>dain</u>,
   but honor those who fear the <u>LORD</u>;

3. those who keep their word, come what <u>may</u>,
   those who take no interest on a <u>loan</u>
   those who accept no <u>bribes</u>
   against the <u>innocent</u>.

Performance Notes
The bass line of the keyboard accompaniment can be used as a bass descant if desired.

C-143

Listen: I Stand at the Door and Knock

Sixteenth Sunday in Ordinary Time, Song for the Table

Verses *Sirach 14:20-26*

Superimposed tone

1. Happy are you who meditate on wisdom,
2. Happy you who reflect in your heart on wis - dom's ways,
3. Happy are you who pursue wisdom like a hunter,
4. Happy are you who peer through wis - dom's windows,
5. Happy are you who camp near wis - dom's house,
6. Happy are you who pitch your tent near wisdom,
7. Happy you who place your children under wis - dom's shelter,

Soprano / Alto Descants

Lis - ten: I stand at the door and knock.

Bass Descant

Antiphon ♩ = ca. 78

Capo 3: (D) (G) (D)
F Bb F

Lis - ten: I stand at the door and knock.

O - pen, and we shall feast.

(A)
C

O - pen, and we shall feast.

Verses Superimposed tone

1. happy are you who   reason with   in - tel - li gence.
2. happy are you who   ponder   her se - crets.
3. happy are you who lie in   wait on   her paths.
4. happy are you who   listen at   her doors.
5. you who fasten your   tent peg to   her walls.
6. who so occupy an   excel - lent lodg - ing place.
7. happy are you who lodge   under wis - dom's boughs.

Soprano / Alto Descants

Lis - ten: I stand at the door and knock.

Bass Descant

Antiphon

Lis - ten: I stand at the door and knock.

O - pen, and we shall feast.

O - pen, and we shall feast.

Performance Notes

When the Antiphon is sung alone, sing all the text; when the verse is superimposed, vocalize to 'oo' in measures 1–2 and 5–6 while the cantor sings the verse text.

Home for the Lonely

Seventeenth Sunday in Ordinary Time, Song for the Week

Verse Tone

Psalm 68:4-5a, 5c-7b, 10-11, 20, 36bc

1. The just shall rejoice at the pre<u>sence</u> of God,
   they shall exult and <u>dance</u> for joy.

2. Sing to the LORD, make music <u>to</u> God's name;
   rejoice in the LORD, exult <u>be</u>fore God.

3. Father of the orphan, defender <u>of</u> the widow,
   such is God in the <u>holy</u> place.

4. God gives the lonely a <u>home</u> to live in;
   and leads the prisoners forth <u>into</u> freedom.

5. You poured down, O God, a <u>gen</u>erous rain;
   when your people were starved you gave <u>them</u> new life.

6. It was there that your people <u>found</u> a home,
   prepared in your goodness, O God, <u>for</u> the poor.

7. May the LORD be blessed day <u>after</u> day.
   God our savior <u>bears</u> our burdens.

8. This is the LORD, <u>Israel's</u> God,
   who gives strength and power <u>to</u> the people.

Seventeenth Sunday In Ordinary Time, Song for the Word, *same as C-108* ← **C-145**

Ask and Receive

Seventeenth Sunday in Ordinary Time, Song for the Table

Psalm 73:1-2, 25-26, 28; 33:12-15, 18-21

1. How good is God to Israel,
   to those who are pure of heart.
   Yet my feet came close to stumbling,
   my steps had almost slipped.

2. What else have I in heaven but you?
   Apart from you I want nothing on earth.
   My body and my heart faint for joy;
   God is my possession for ever.

3. To be near God is my happiness.
   I have made the Lord God my refuge.
   I will tell of all your works
   at the gates of the city of Zion.

4. They are happy, whose God is the Lord,
   the people who are chosen as his own.

From the heavens the Lord looks forth
and sees all the peoples of the earth.

5. From the heavenly dwelling God gazes
   on all the dwellers on the earth;
   God who shapes the hearts of them all
   and considers all their deeds.

6. The Lord looks on those who fear him,
   on those who hope in his love,
   to rescue their souls from death,
   to keep them alive in famine.

7. Our soul is waiting for the Lord.
   The Lord is our help and our shield.
   Our hearts find joy in the Lord.
   We trust in God's holy name.

God, Come to My Aid

C-147

Eighteenth Sunday in Ordinary Time, Song for the Week

God, come to my aid. O Lord, make haste to help me!

You are the one who sus-tains me: O Lord, do not de-lay!

Verse Tone with Response

...O Lord, make haste to help me!

...O Lord, do not de-lay!

Psalm 70

1. O God, make haste to <u>my</u> rescue,   *O Lord, make haste . . .*
   LORD, come to <u>my</u> aid.   *O Lord, do not : . .*

2. Let there be shame and <u>confusion</u>,   *(simile)*
   on those who seek <u>my</u> life.

3. O let them turn back in <u>confusion</u>,
   who delight in <u>my</u> harm.

4. Let them retreat, covered <u>with</u> shame,
   who jeer at <u>my</u> lot.

5. Let there be rejoicing <u>and</u> gladness
   for all <u>who</u> seek you.

6. Let them say for ever: "God <u>is</u> great,"
   who love your sav<u>ing</u> help.

7. As for me, wretched <u>and</u> poor,
   come to me, <u>O</u> God.

8. You are my rescuer, <u>my</u> help,
   O LORD, do not <u>delay</u>.

C-148

When You Fill Us with Your Word

Eighteenth Sunday in Ordinary Time, Song for the Word

Antiphon ♩ = 88

When you fill us with your Word, we shall sing and be hap-py all our days!

Verse Tone

Psalm 90:3-6, 12-14, 17

1. You turn us back into dust
   and say: "Go back, children of the earth."
   To your eyes a thousand years
      are like yesterday, come and gone,
   no more than a watch in the night.

2. You sweep us away like a dream,
   like grass which springs up in the morning.
   In the morning it springs up and flowers;
   by evening it withers and fades.

3. Make us know the shortness of our life
   that we may gain wisdom of heart.
   LORD, relent! Is your anger for ever?
   Show pity to your servants.

4. In the morning, fill us with your love;
   we shall exult and rejoice all our days.
   Let the favor of the LORD be upon us:
   give success to the work of our hands.

Psalm 95:1-2, 6-9 (alternate text)

1. Come, ring out our joy to the LORD;
   hail the rock who saves us.
   Let us come before God, giving thanks,
   with songs let us hail the LORD.

2. Come in, let us bow and bend low;
   let us kneel before the God who made us
   for this is our God
      and we the people who belong to his pasture,
   the flock that is led by his hand.

3. O that today you would listen to God's voice!
   "Harden not your hearts as at Meribah,
   as on that day at Massah in the desert
   when your ancestors put me to the test;
   when they tried me,
   though they saw my work."

Performance Notes

The Verse Tone is sung through twice for each verse except verse 3 of Psalm 95 where it is sung through three times.

Do Not Store Up Earthly Treasures

C-149

Eighteenth Sunday in Ordinary Time, Song for the Table

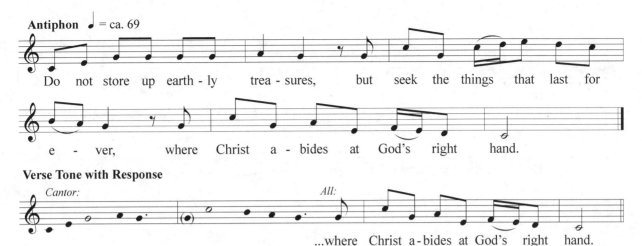

Antiphon ♩ = ca. 69

Do not store up earth-ly trea-sures, but seek the things that last for
e - ver, where Christ a-bides at God's right hand.

Verse Tone with Response

Cantor: *All:*

...where Christ a-bides at God's right hand.

Psalm 36:6-11; 63:2-6, 8-9

1. Your love, LORD, reaches to heaven,
   your truth to the skies,   *where Christ abides . . .*
   Your justice is like God's mountain,
   your judgements like the deep,   *where Christ abides . . .*

2. To mortals and beasts you give protection.
   O LORD, how precious is your love. *(simile)*
   My God, the children of the earth
   find refuge in the shelter of your wings.

3. They feast on the riches of your house;
   they drink from the stream of your delight.
   In you is the source of life
   and in your light we see light.

4. Keep on loving those who know you,
   doing justice for upright hearts.

5. O God, you are my God, for you I long;
   for you my soul is thirsting.
   My body pines for you
   like a dry, weary land without water.

6. So I gaze on you in the sanctuary
   to see your strength and your glory.
   For your love is better than life,
   my lips will speak your praise.

7. So I will bless you all my life,
   in your name I will lift up my hands.
   My soul shall be filled as with a banquet,
   my mouth shall praise you with joy.

8. For you have been my help;
   in the shadow of your wings I rejoice.
   My soul clings to you;
   your right hand holds me fast.

Performance Notes

This setting is designed for unaccompanied singing in neo-plainsong style, the recommended option, keeping the music flowing, as indicated by the metronome marking. It would of course be possible to sing the Wachet auf *chorale tune to the slower J. S. Bach harmonization found in many hymn books.*
The tone is sung twice through for each stanza except in stanza 4.

Yours Is the Day

Nineteenth Sunday in Ordinary Time, Song for the Week

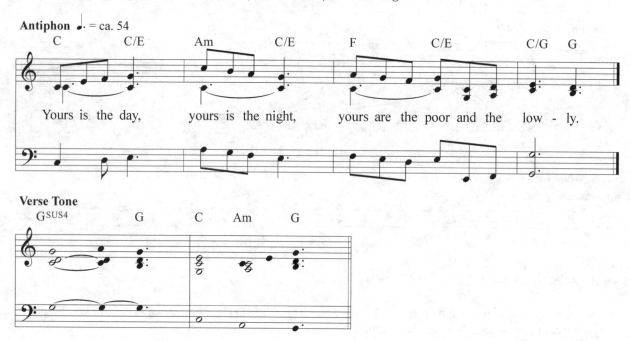

Antiphon ♩. = ca. 54

Yours is the day, yours is the night, yours are the poor and the low-ly.

Verse Tone

Psalm 74:12, 15-17, 19-21; 80:9-12

1. God is our king from <u>time</u> past,
   the giver of help through <u>all</u> the land.

2. It was you who opened springs <u>and</u> torrents;
   it was you who dried up ever-<u>flow</u>ing rivers.

3. Yours is the day and yours is <u>the</u> night.
   It was you who appointed the light <u>and</u> the sun.

4. It was you who fixed the bounds of <u>the</u> earth;
   you who made both sum<u>mer</u> and winter.

5. Do not give Israel, your dove, to <u>the</u> hawk
   nor forget the life of your poor <u>ones</u> for ever.

6. Remember your covenant; every cave in <u>the</u> land
   is a place where violence <u>makes</u> its home.

7. Do not let the oppressed return dis<u>app</u>ointed;
   let the poor and the needy <u>bless</u> your name.

8. You brought a vine out <u>of</u> Egypt;
   to plant it you drove <u>out</u> the nations.

9. Before it you cleared <u>the</u> ground;
   it took root and spread <u>through</u> the land.

10. The mountains were covered with <u>its</u> shadow,
    the cedars of God <u>with</u> its boughs.

11. It stretched out its branches to <u>the</u> sea,
    to the Great River it stretched <u>out</u> its shoots.

Happy Are They Whose God Is the Lord

C-151

Nineteenth Sunday in Ordinary Time, Song for the Word

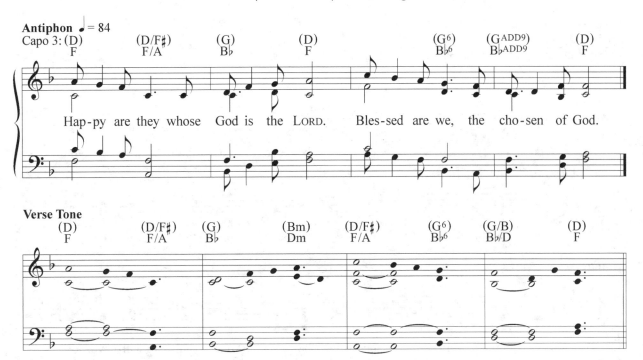

Psalm 33:1, 12, 18-20, 22

1. Ring out your joy to the LORD, O you just;
   for praise is fitting for loyal hearts.
   They are happy, whose God is the LORD,
   the people who are chosen as his own.

2. The LORD looks on those who fear him,
   on those who hope in his love,
   to rescue their souls from death,
   to keep them alive in famine.

3. Our soul is waiting for the LORD.
   The LORD is our help and our shield.
   May your love be upon us, O LORD,
   as we place all our hope in you.

Don't Be Afraid

Nineteenth Sunday in Ordinary Time, Song for the Table

Verses Superimposed tone

The following and similar psalm extracts may be used over the ostinato:

Psalm 31:2-4, 15-17, 25

1. In you, O LORD, I take <u>re</u>fuge.
   Let me never be put to <u>shame</u>.
   In your justice, set me <u>free</u>,
   hear me and speedily <u>res</u>cue me.

2. Be a rock of refuge for <u>me</u>,
   a mighty stronghold to <u>save</u> me,
   for you are my rock, my <u>strong</u>hold.
   For your name's sake, lead me and <u>guide</u> me.

3. As for me, I trust in you, <u>LORD</u>;
   I say: "You are my <u>God</u>.
   My life is in your hands, de<u>liv</u>er me
   from the hands of those who <u>hate</u> me.

4. Let your face shine on your <u>serv</u>ant.
   Save me in your <u>love</u>."
   Be strong, let your heart take <u>cour</u>age,
   all who hope in the <u>LORD</u>.

Psalm 103:1-4, 8, 10-14, 17-18

5. My soul, give thanks to the <u>LORD</u>,
   all my being, bless God's holy <u>name</u>.
   My soul, give thanks to the <u>LORD</u>
   and never forget all God's <u>bless</u>ings.

6. It is God who forgives all your <u>guilt</u>,
   who heals every one of your <u>ills</u>,
   who redeems your life from the <u>grave</u>,
   who crowns you with love and com<u>pass</u>ion.

7. The LORD is compassion and <u>love</u>,
   slow to anger and rich in <u>mer</u>cy.
   God does not treat us according to our <u>sins</u>
   nor repay us according to our <u>faults</u>.

8. For as the heavens are high above the <u>earth</u>
   so strong is God's love for the <u>God</u>-fearing;
   as far as the east is from the <u>west</u>
   so far does he remove our <u>sins</u>.

9. As parents have compassion on their <u>chil</u>dren,
   the LORD has pity on those who are <u>God</u>-fearing
   for he knows of what we are <u>made</u>,
   and remembers that we are <u>dust</u>.

10. The love of the LORD is ever<u>last</u>ing
    upon those who fear the <u>LORD</u>.
    God's justice reaches out to children's <u>chil</u>dren
    when they keep his covenant in <u>truth</u>.

Performance Notes
As the cantor sings the verses, the other voices may vocalize to 'oo' under the superimposed tone instead of singing the words.

C-153 ➡ Twentieth Sunday In Ordinary Time, Song for the Week, *same as C-113*

C-154

God, Come to My Aid

Twentieth Sunday in Ordinary Time, Song for the Word

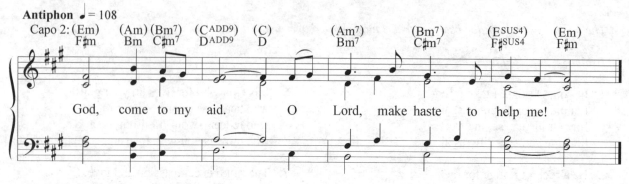

God, come to my aid. O Lord, make haste to help me!

Verse Tone with Response

...O Lord, make haste to help me!

Psalm 40:2-4, 18

1. I waited, I waited for <u>the</u> LORD, *O Lord, make haste . . .*
   who stooped down to me, and heard <u>my</u> cry. *O Lord, make haste . . .*

2. God drew me from the deadly pit, from the mi<u>ry</u> clay, *(simile)*
   and set my feet upon a rock and made my foot<u>steps</u> firm.

3. God put a new song into my mouth, praise of <u>our</u> God.
   Many shall see and fear and shall trust in <u>the</u> LORD.

4. As for me, wretched and poor, the LORD thinks <u>of</u> me.
   You are my rescuer, my help, O God, do not <u>delay</u>.

Set the Earth on Fire

Twentieth Sunday in Ordinary Time, Song for the Table

Psalm 130:1-6b, 7b-8

1. Out of the depths I cry to you, O LORD,
   LORD, hear my voice!
   O let your ears be attentive
   to the voice of my pleading.

2. If you, O LORD, should mark our guilt,
   LORD, who would survive?
   But with you is found forgiveness:
   for this we revere you.

3. My soul is waiting for the LORD,
   I | count on God's word.
   My soul is longing for the LORD
   more than those who watch for daybreak.

4. Because with the LORD there is mercy
   and fullness of redemption,
   Israel indeed God will redeem
   from all its iniquity.

Performance Notes
The Antiphon may be sung as a round, as indicated.

Turn to Me, Answer Me

Twenty-first Sunday in Ordinary Time, Song for the Week
Twenty-second Sunday in Ordinary Time, Song for the Week, Option II

Verses *Psalm 86*

Superimposed tone

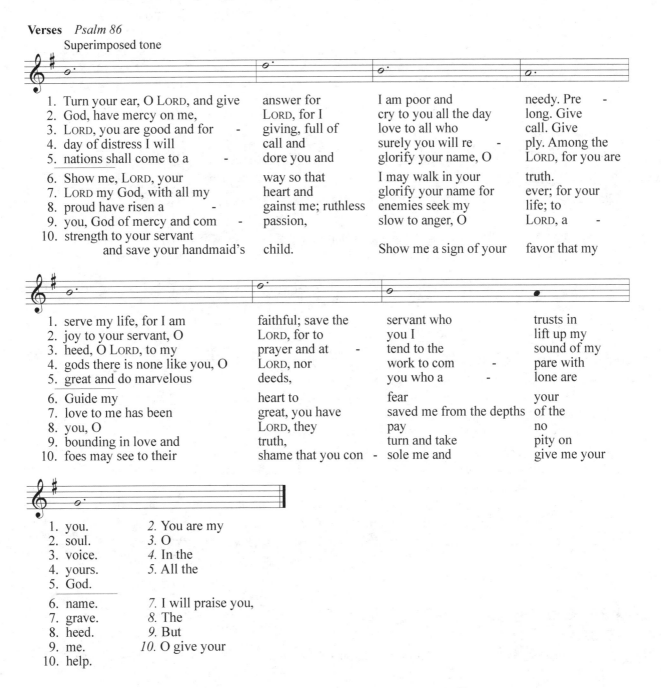

1. Turn your ear, O LORD, and give answer for I am poor and needy. Pre -
2. God, have mercy on me, LORD, for I cry to you all the day long. Give
3. LORD, you are good and for - giving, full of love to all who call. Give
4. day of distress I will call and surely you will re - ply. Among the
5. nations shall come to a - dore you and glorify your name, O LORD, for you are

6. Show me, LORD, your way so that I may walk in your truth.
7. LORD my God, with all my heart and glorify your name for ever; for your
8. proud have risen a - gainst me; ruthless enemies seek my life; to
9. you, God of mercy and com - passion, slow to anger, O LORD, a -
10. strength to your servant and save your handmaid's child. Show me a sign of your favor that my

1. serve my life, for I am faithful; save the servant who trusts in
2. joy to your servant, O LORD, for to you I lift up my
3. heed, O LORD, to my prayer and at - tend to the sound of my
4. gods there is none like you, O LORD, nor work to com - pare with
5. great and do marvelous deeds, you who a - lone are

6. Guide my heart to fear your
7. love to me has been great, you have saved me from the depths of the
8. you, O LORD, they pay no
9. bounding in love and truth, turn and take pity on
10. foes may see to their shame that you con - sole me and give me your

1. you.   *2.* You are my
2. soul.   *3.* O
3. voice.   *4.* In the
4. yours.   *5.* All the
5. God.

6. name.   *7.* I will praise you,
7. grave.   *8.* The
8. heed.   *9.* But
9. me.   *10.* O give your
10. help.

Twenty-first Sunday in Ordinary Time, *Song for the Word, same as C-120* ← **C-157**

C-158   From the East and West, from the North and South

Twenty-first Sunday in Ordinary Time, Song for the Table
Twenty-Second Sunday in Ordinary Time, Song for the Table

The Antiphon melody is adapted from the first half of the anonymous English carol tune NOEL, traditionally sung in England to "It came upon the midnight clear."

Psalm 104:10, 12-15, 27-28, 29bc-31, 33-34

1. You make springs gush forth in <u>the</u> valleys;   *we will . . .*
   they flow in between <u>the</u> hills.   *where the greatest . . .*

2. On their banks dwell the birds <u>of</u> heaven;   *(simile)*
   from the branches they sing <u>their</u> song.

3. From your dwelling you water <u>the</u> hills;
   earth drinks its fill of <u>your</u> gift.

4. You make the grass grow for <u>the</u> cattle
   and the plants to serve <u>our</u> needs,

5. that we may bring forth bread from <u>the</u> earth
   and wine to cheer <u>our</u> hearts;

6. oil, to make our fa<u>ces</u> shine
   and bread to strengthen <u>our</u> hearts.

7. All of these look <u>to</u> you
   to give them their food in <u>due</u> season.

8. You give it, they gather <u>it</u> up;
   you open your hand, they have <u>their</u> fill.

9. You take back your spirit, <u>they</u> die,
   returning to the dust from which <u>they</u> came.

10. You send forth your spirit, they are <u>created</u>;
    and you renew the face of <u>the</u> earth.

11. May the glory of the Lord last <u>for</u> ever!
    May the Lord rejoice in <u>creation</u>!

12. I will sing to the Lord all <u>my</u> life,
    make music to my God while <u>I</u> live.

13. May my thoughts be pleasing <u>to</u> God.
    I find my joy in <u>the</u> Lord.

C-159 ➡ Twenty-second Sunday In Ordinary Time, Song for the Week: Option I, *same as C-131*

C-160 ➡ Twenty-second Sunday In Ordinary Time, Song for the Week: Option II, *same as C-156*

C-161

Home for the Lonely
Twenty-second Sunday In Ordinary Time, Song for the Word

Verse Tone

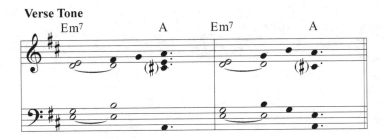

Psalm 68:4-5a, 5c-7b, 10-11

1. The just shall rejoice at the pre<u>sence</u> of God,
   they shall exult and <u>dance</u> for joy.

2. Sing to the L<small>ORD</small>, make music <u>to</u> God's name;
   rejoice in the L<small>ORD</small>, exult <u>be</u>fore God.

3. Father of the orphan, defender <u>of</u> the widow,
   such is God in the <u>ho</u>ly place.

4. God gives the lonely a <u>home</u> to live in;
   and leads the prisoners forth <u>in</u>to freedom.

5. You poured down, O God, a <u>gen</u>erous rain;
   when your people were starved you gave <u>them</u> new life.

6. It was there that your people <u>found</u> a home,
   prepared in your goodness, O God, <u>for</u> the poor.

Twenty-second Sunday in Ordinary Time, Song for the Table, *same as C-158* ← **C-162**

C-163   I Loved Wisdom More Than Health or Beauty

Twenty-third Sunday in Ordinary Time, Song for the Week

Wisdom 9:9-11, 13-14, 17

1. With you is wisdom, she who <u>knows</u> your <u>works</u>
   and was present when you <u>made</u> the <u>world</u>;
   she understands what is <u>pleasing</u> in your <u>sight</u>
   and what is right according to <u>your</u> commandments.

2. Send her forth from the <u>holy heavens</u>,
   from the throne of your <u>glory send</u> her,
   that she may <u>labor</u> at my <u>side</u>,
   that I may learn what is plea<u>sing</u> to you.

3. For she knows and under<u>stands</u> all <u>things</u>,
   she will guide me <u>wisely</u> in my <u>actions</u>

[omit C]
   and guard me <u>with</u> her glory.

4. For who can learn the <u>counsel</u> of <u>God</u>?
   Who can discern what the L<small>ORD</small> <u>wills</u>?
   For the reasoning of <u>mortals</u> is <u>worthless</u>,
   and our designs are like<u>ly</u> to fail.

5. Who has <u>learned</u> your <u>counsel</u>,
   unless you have <u>given</u> <u>wisdom</u>
[omit C]
   and sent your holy spirit <u>from</u> on high?

In Every Age, O Lord, You Have Been Our Refuge

Twenty-third Sunday in Ordinary Time, Song for the Word

Psalm 90:3-4, 5-6, 12-13, 14, 17

1. You turn us back into dust and say: "Go back, children of the earth."
   To your eyes a thousand years are like yesterday, come and gone, no more than a watch in the night.

2. You sweep us away like a dream, like grass which springs up in the morning.
   In the morning it springs up and flowers; by evening it withers and fades.

3. Make us know the shortness of our life that we may gain wisdom of heart.
   Lord, relent! Is your anger for ever? Show pity to your servants.

4. In the morning, fill us with your love; we shall exult and rejoice all our days.
   Let the favor of the Lord be upon us: give success to the work of our hands.

Performance Notes
The cantor may hold on the last note of the tone to overlap the beginning of the Antiphon.

C-165

Lose Your Life and Save It
Twenty-third Sunday in Ordinary Time, Song for the Table

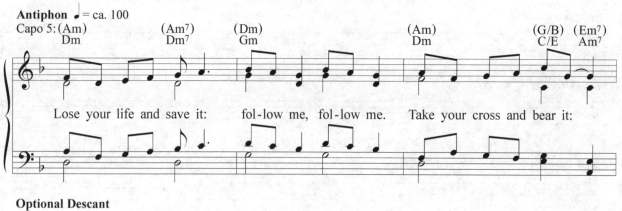

Antiphon ♩ = ca. 100

Lose your life and save it: fol-low me, fol-low me. Take your cross and bear it:

Optional Descant

fol - low me, fol - low me.

fol - low me, fol - low me.

Verse Tone

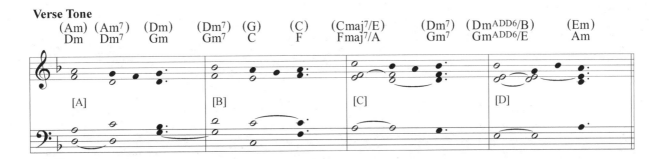

Psalm 49

1. Hear this, <u>all</u> you peoples,
   give heed, all who dwell <u>in</u> the world,
   people <u>high</u> and low,
   rich and <u>poor</u> alike!

2. My lips will speak <u>words</u> of wisdom.
   My heart is <u>full</u> of insight.
   I will turn my mind <u>to</u> a parable,
   with the harp I will <u>solve</u> my problem.

3. Why should I fear in <u>evil</u> days
   the malice of the foes <u>who</u> surround me,
   people who trust <u>in</u> their wealth,
   and boast of the vastness <u>of</u> their riches?

4. For the rich cannot buy <u>their</u> own ransom,
   nor pay a price to God <u>for</u> their lives.
   The ransom of their souls <u>is</u> beyond them.
   They cannot buy endless life,
      nor avoid coming <u>to</u> the grave.

5. They know that both wise and <u>foolish</u> perish
   and must leave their <u>wealth</u> to others.
   Their graves are their <u>homes</u> for ever,
   their dwelling place from <u>age</u> to age,
[Repeat D]
   though their names spread wide <u>through</u> the land.

6. In their riches, peo<u>ple</u> lack wisdom;
[Omit B-C]
   they are like the beasts that <u>are</u> destroyed.

7. This is the lot of those who trust <u>in</u> themselves,
   who have others at their <u>beck</u> and call.
   Like sheep they are driven <u>to</u> the grave,
   where death shall <u>be</u> their shepherd
[Repeat D]
   and the just shall be<u>come</u> their rulers.

8. With the morning their out<u>ward</u> show vanishes
   and the grave be<u>comes</u> their home.
   But God will ran<u>som</u> my soul,
   from the power of <u>death</u> will snatch me.

9. Then do not fear when o<u>thers</u> grow rich,
   when the glory of their <u>house</u> increases.
   They take nothing with them <u>when</u> they die,
   their glory does not follow <u>them</u> below.

10. Though they flattered themselves <u>while</u> they lived:
    "They will praise me for doing well <u>for</u> myself,"
    yet they will go to <u>join</u> their forebears,
    and will never see the light <u>any</u> more.

11. In their riches, peo<u>ple</u> lack wisdom;
[Omit B-C]
    they are like the beasts that <u>are</u> destroyed.

C-166

Give Peace to Those Who Wait

Twenty-fourth Sunday in Ordinary Time, Song for the Week

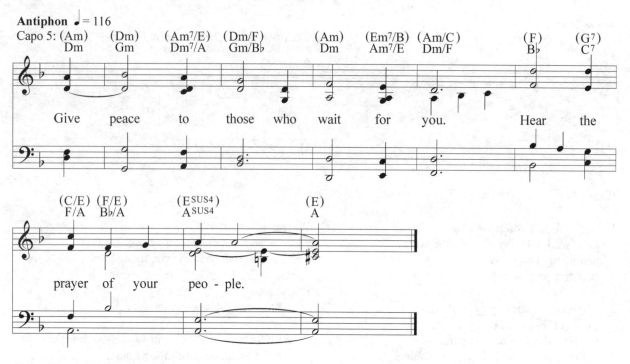

Verse Tone with Response

Sirach 36:1-7, 10, 18-22

1. Have mercy upon us, O God of all,
   and put all the nations in fear of you.
      Hear the prayer . . .

2. Lift up your hand against foreign nations
   and let them see your might.   *Hear the prayer . . .*

3. As you have used us to show your holiness to them,
   so use them to show your glory to us.   *(simile)*

4. Then they will know, as we have known
   that there is no God but you, O LORD.

5. Give new signs, and work other wonders;
   make your hand and your right arm glorious.

6. Hasten the day, and remember the appointed time,
   and let people recount your mighty deeds.

7. Have pity on the city of your sanctuary,
   Jerusalem, the place of your dwelling.

8. Fill Zion with your majesty,
   and your temple with your glory.

9. Bear witness to those whom you created
      in the beginning,
   and fulfill the prophecies spoken in your name.

10. Reward those who wait for you
    and let your prophets be found trustworthy.

11. Hear, O LORD, the prayer of your servants,
    according to your goodwill toward
       your people,

12. and all who are on the earth will know
    that you are the LORD, the God of the ages.

We Have Sinned, Lord

C-167

Twenty-fourth Sunday in Ordinary Time, Song for the Word

Verses *Psalm 51:3-6b, 12-14, 17*

Superimposed tone

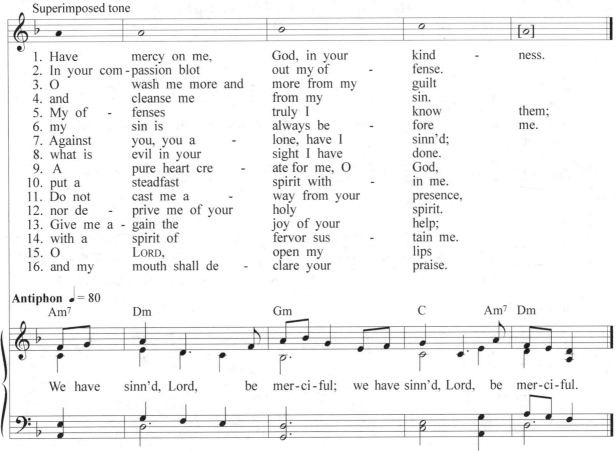

1. Have	mercy on me,	God, in your	kind - ness.
2. In your com - passion blot	out my of -	fense.	
3. O	wash me more and	more from my	guilt
4. and	cleanse me	from my	sin.
5. My of - fenses	truly I	know	them;
6. my	sin is	always be -	fore me.
7. Against	you, you a -	lone, have I	sinn'd;
8. what is	evil in your	sight I have	done.
9. A	pure heart cre -	ate for me, O	God,
10. put a	steadfast	spirit with -	in me.
11. Do not	cast me a -	way from your	presence,
12. nor de - prive me of your	holy	spirit.	
13. Give me a - gain the	joy of your	help;	
14. with a	spirit of	fervor sus -	tain me.
15. O	LORD,	open my	lips
16. and my	mouth shall de -	clare your	praise.

Antiphon ♩ = 80

Am⁷   Dm   Gm   C   Am⁷ Dm

We have   sinn'd, Lord,   be mer-ci-ful; we have sinn'd, Lord, be mer-ci-ful.

C-168 ➡ Twenty-fourth Sunday in Ordinary Time, Song for the Table, *see C-43*

C-169

I Am Your Savior, My People

Twenty-fifth Sunday in Ordinary Time, Song for the Week

Verse Tone

Psalm 56

1. Have mercy on me, God, <u>foes</u> crush me;
   they fight me all day long and <u>opp</u>ress me.
   My foes crush me all <u>day</u> long,
   for many fight proudly <u>against</u> me.

2. When I fear, I will trust <u>in</u> you,
   in God whose word <u>I</u> praise.
   In God I trust, I shall <u>not</u> fear;
   what can mere mor<u>tals</u> do to me?

3. All day long they distort <u>my</u> words,
   all their thought is <u>to</u> harm me.
   They band together <u>in</u> ambush,
   track me down and seek <u>my</u> life.

4. *A* Repay them, God, for <u>their</u> crimes;
   B in your anger, cast down <u>the</u> peoples.
   A You have kept an account of <u>my</u> wanderings;
   B you have kept a record of <u>my</u> tears;
   B (are they not written in <u>your</u> book?)
   C Then my foes will be put <u>to</u> flight
   D on the day that <u>I</u> call to you.

5. This I know, that God is on <u>my</u> side.
   In God, whose word <u>I</u> praise,
[repeat B]
      (in the LORD, whose word <u>I</u> praise,)
      in God I trust; I shall <u>not</u> fear;
      what can mere mor<u>tals</u> do to me?

6. I am bound by the vows I <u>have</u> made you.
   O God, I will offer <u>you</u> praise
[repeat A-B]
      for you rescued my soul <u>from</u> death,
      you kept my feet <u>from</u> stumbling
      that I may walk in the presence <u>of</u> God
      and enjoy the light of <u>the</u> living.

Performance Notes
The verses may be sung SATB.

Praise to God Who Lifts Up the Poor

Twenty-fifth Sunday in Ordinary Time, Song for the Word

Verses Superimposed tone

1. LORD,	praise the name	of	the
2. blessed	both	now	and	for	e - ver -
3. LORD,	a - bove the heav'ns	God's
4. God,	the	one	en - thron'd	on
5. down,	to	look	down	up - on	hea - ven and
6. lowly,	from	the	dung - heap	God	rai - ses the
7. princes,	yes,	with	the	ru - lers of

Soprano Descant

poor,   to God   who   lifts   up   the   poor.

Tenor Descant

Sing al - le - lu - ia, God   lifts   up   the   poor.

Antiphon

(Em) (A) (D)   (Bm) (G/A)   (A)   (D)
Gm   C   F   Dm   B♭/C   C   F

Sing al - le - lu - ia, God   lifts   up   the   poor.

Performance Notes

In the superimposed tone, the note values shown are approximations, modifiable by natural speech rhythm.

Do Not Store Up Earthly Treasures

Twenty-fifth Sunday in Ordinary Time, Song for the Table

Psalm 37:3-6, 18-19, 23-24, 27-29; [36:6-11]

1. If you trust in the LORD and do good,
   then you will | live in the land and be secure.
      where Christ abides . . .
   If you find your delight in the LORD,
   he will | grant you your heart's desire.
      where Christ abides . . .

2. Commit your life to the LORD,
   be confident, and God will act, *(simile)*
   so that your justice breaks forth like the light,
   your cause like the noonday sun.

3. God protects the lives of the upright,
   their heritage will last for ever.
   They shall not be put to shame in evil days,
   in time of famine their food shall not fail.

4. The LORD guards the steps of the upright
   and favors the path that they take.
   Though they stumble they shall never fall
   for the | LORD holds them by the hand.

5. Then turn away from evil and do good
   and you shall have a home for ever;
   for the LORD loves justice
   and will | never forsake the faithful.

6. The unjust shall be wiped out for ever
   and the | children of the wicked destroyed.
   The just shall inherit the land;
   | there they shall live for ever.

If further verses are needed:

7. Your love, LORD, reaches to heaven,
   your truth to the skies,
   Your justice is like God's mountain,
   your judgements like the deep.

8. To mortals and beasts you give protection.
   O LORD, how precious is your love.
   My God, the children of the earth
   find refuge in the shelter of your wings.

9. They feast on the riches of your house;
   they drink from the stream of your delight.
   In you is the source of life
   and in your | light we see light.

10. Keep on loving those who know you,
    doing | justice for upright hearts.

Performance Notes

This setting is designed for unaccompanied singing in neo-plainsong style, the recommended option, keeping the music flowing, as indicated by the metronome marking. It would of course be possible to sing the Wachet auf *chorale tune to the slower J.S. Bach harmonization found in many hymn books.*

The tone is sung twice through for each stanza except in stanza 10.

When there is more than one syllable on the pick-up note in parentheses in the second measure of the tone, the vertical stroke indicates the change to the main reciting note.

C-172 → Twenty-sixth Sunday in Ordinary Time, Song for the Week, *same as C-32*

God Heals the Broken

C-173

Twenty-sixth Sunday in Ordinary Time, Song for the Word

Psalm 146:6c-10

1. It is the LORD who keeps <u>faith</u> for ever,
   who is just to those who <u>are</u> oppressed.
   It is God who gives bread <u>to</u> the hungry,
   the LORD, who sets <u>pris</u>'ners free,

2. the LORD who gives sight <u>to</u> the blind,
   who raises up those who <u>are</u> bowed down,

   the LORD, who pro<u>tects</u> the stranger
   and upholds the wi<u>dow</u> and orphan.

3. It is the LORD who <u>loves</u> the just
   but thwarts the path <u>of</u> the wicked.
   The LORD will <u>reign</u> for ever,
   Zion's God from <u>age</u> to age.

Psalm text: The Grail (England), © 1963, 1986, 1993, 2000, The Grail, GIA Publications, Inc., agent. All rights reserved. Used with permission.
Music and antiphon text: © 2006, The Collegeville Composers Group. All rights reserved. Published and administered by the Liturgical Press, Collegeville, MN 56321.

Take Hold of Eternal Life

Twenty-sixth Sunday in Ordinary Time, Song for the Table

1 Peter 2:21-24; Philippians 2:6-11

1. Christ suffered for us, leaving us an example, so that we should follow in his steps.

2. "He committed no sin, and no deceit was found in his mouth."

3. When he was abused, he did not return abuse; when he suffered, he did not threaten.

4. Christ entrusted himself to the one who judges justly.

5. He himself bore our sins in his body on the cross, so that, free from sins, we might live for righteousness.

6. By his wounds we have been healed.

7. Though he was in the form of God, Christ Jesus did not regard equality with God
    as something to be exploited.

8. He emptied himself, taking the form of a slave; being born in human likeness, he humbled himself.

9. Christ became obedient to the point of death—even death on a cross.

10. Therefore God also highly exalted him and gave him the name that is above every name,

11. so that at the name of Jesus every knee should bend, in heaven and on earth and under the earth,

12. and every tongue confess that Jesus Christ is Lord, to the glory of God the Father.

Performance Notes

The superimposed verses should be sung in free speech rhythm on the monotone indicated during the first half of the Antiphon. The voice parts could be vocalized to 'oo' when the verses are being sung, coming back in with the text in the second half of the Antiphon.

The metronome marking indicates the solemn tread needed by this piece.

You Have Given Everything Its Place

Twenty-seventh Sunday in Ordinary Time, Song for the Week

C-175

Optional Canonic Descant

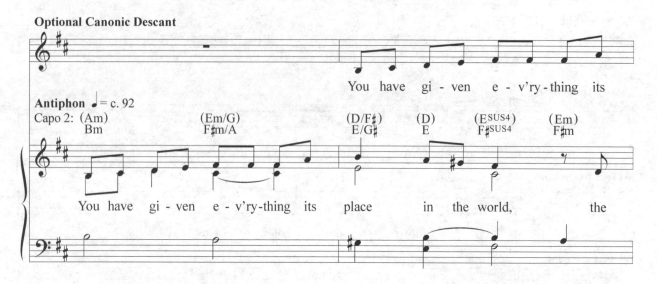

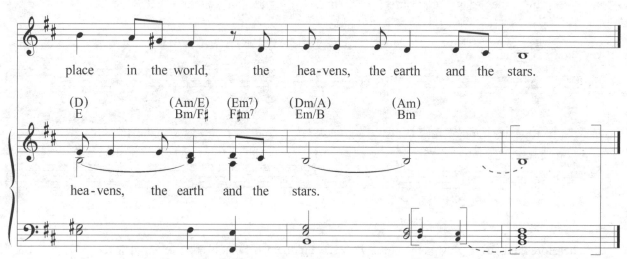

*Cue-size notes and additional measure
only if descant is used*

Verse Tone with Response

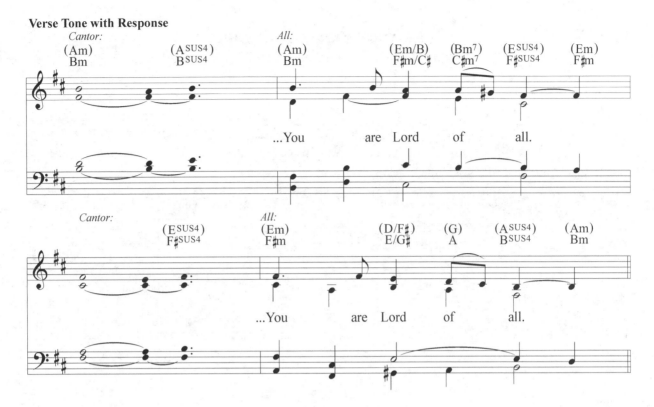

Psalm 8:2, 4-10

1. How great is your name, O LORD our God, through all the earth!   *You are Lord of all!*
   Your majesty is praised above the heavens.   *You are Lord of all!*

2. When I see the heavens, the work of your hands,   *(simile)*
   the moon and the stars which you arranged,

3. what are we that you should keep us in mind,
   mere mortals that you care for us?

4. Yet you have made us little less than gods;
   and crowned us with glory and honor.

5. You gave us power over the work of your hands,
   put all things under our feet.

6. All of them, sheep and cattle,
   yes, even the savage beasts,

7. birds of the air, and fish
   that make their way through the waters.

8. How great is your name, O LORD our God,
   through all the earth!

C-177

Take Your Place at the Table

Twenty-seventh Sunday in Ordinary Time, Song for the Table

Psalm 112:1-9

1. Happy are those who fear <u>the</u> Lᴏʀᴅ,
   who take delight in all <u>God's</u> commands.
   do this and you shall live.

2. Their descendants shall be powerful <u>on</u> earth;
   the children of the up<u>right</u> are blessed.   *(simile)*

3. Wealth and riches are in <u>their</u> homes,
   their justice stands <u>firm</u> for ever.

4. They are lights in the darkness for <u>the</u> upright;
   they are generous, mer<u>ciful</u> and just.

5. Good people take pity <u>and</u> lend,
   they conduct their af<u>fairs</u> with honor.

6. The just will ne<u>ver</u> waver,
   they will be remem<u>bered</u> for ever.

7. They have no fear of e<u>vil</u> news;
   with firm hearts they trust <u>in</u> the Lᴏʀᴅ.

8. With steadfast hearts they will <u>not</u> fear;
   they will see the downfall <u>of</u> their foes.

9. Openhanded
   they give <u>to</u> the poor.

10. Their justice stands firm <u>for</u> ever.
    Their heads will be <u>raised</u> in glory.

You Are Rich in Mercy

Twenty-eighth Sunday in Ordinary Time, Song for the Week

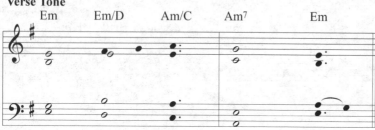

Psalm 130:1-6b, 7b-8

1. Out of the depths I cry to you, O LORD,
   LORD, hear my voice!

2. O let your ears be attentive
   to the voice of my pleading.

3. If you, O LORD, should mark our guilt,
   LORD, who would survive?

4. But with you is found forgiveness:
   for this we revere you.

5. My soul is waiting for the LORD.
   I count on God's word.

6. My soul is longing for the LORD
   more than those who watch for daybreak.

7. Because with the LORD there is mercy
   and fullness of redemption,

8. Israel indeed God will redeem
   from all its iniquity.

Performance Notes

The Antiphon may be sung twice each time. If desired, the repetition could overlap on the final note, with "You are" being sung at the same time as "God."

All the Ends of the Earth

Twenty-eighth Sunday in Ordinary Time, Song for the Word

Antiphon ♩ = ca.120

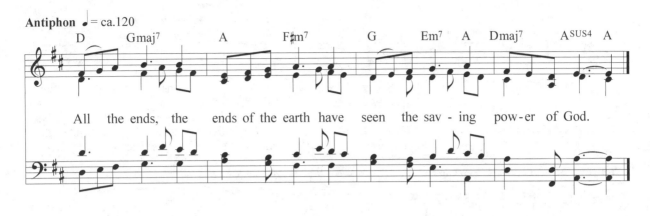

All the ends, the ends of the earth have seen the sav- ing pow-er of God.

Verse Tone

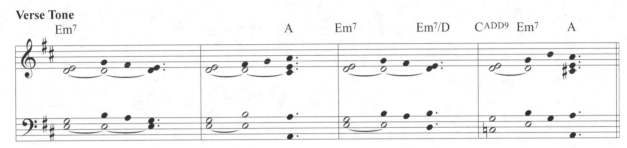

Psalm 98   *[The Lectionary selections for the day are indicated by an asterisk.]*

1. * Sing a new song <u>to</u> the L<small>ORD</small>
   * who <u>has</u> worked wonders;
   * whose right hand and <u>ho</u>ly arm
   * have <u>brought</u> salvation.

2. * The L<small>ORD</small> has made <u>known</u> salvation;
   * has shown justice <u>to</u> the nations;
   * has remembered <u>truth</u> and love
   * for the <u>house</u> of Israel.

3. * All the ends of the <u>earth</u> have seen
   * the salvation <u>of</u> our God.
   * Shout to the L<small>ORD</small>, <u>all</u> the earth,
   * ring <u>out</u> your joy.

4. Sing psalms to the L<small>ORD</small> <u>with</u> the harp,
   with the <u>sound</u> of music.
   With trumpets and the sound <u>of</u> the horn
   acclaim the <u>King</u>, the L<small>ORD</small>.

5. Let the sea and all with<u>in</u> it thunder;
   the world and <u>all</u> its peoples.
   Let the rivers <u>clap</u> their hands
   and the hills ring <u>out</u> their joy

6. at the presence of the L<small>ORD</small>, who comes,
   who comes to <u>rule</u> the earth.
   God will rule the <u>world</u> with justice
   and the peo<u>ples</u> with fairness.

Performance Notes

The Antiphon may be sung twice through each time.

C-180 I Thank You, Lord, with All My Heart

Twenty-eighth Sunday in Ordinary Time, Song for the Table

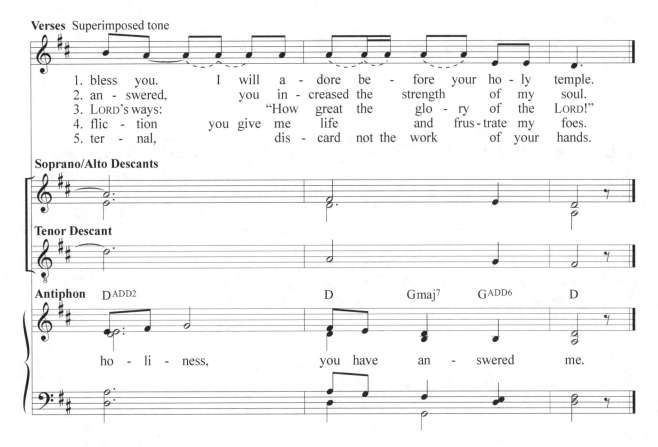

Verses Superimposed tone

1. bless you.   I will a - dore be - fore your ho - ly temple.
2. an - swered,   you in - creased the strength of my soul.
3. LORD's ways: "How great the glo - ry of the LORD!"
4. flic - tion   you give me life and frus - trate my foes.
5. ter - nal,   dis - card not the work of your hands.

Soprano/Alto Descants

Tenor Descant

Antiphon   D^ADD2   D   Gmaj^7   G^ADD6   D

ho - li - ness,   you have an - swered me.

Performance Notes

The vocal descants hum to 'n' or vocalize to 'oo'.

Whenever the tone is superimposed on the Antiphon, this tone replaces the Soprano descant.

The cue-notes in measures 2 and 3 are used with verses 3, 4 and 5.

C-181

Guard Me as the Apple of Your Eye!

Twenty-ninth Sunday in Ordinary Time, Song for the Week

Verse Tone

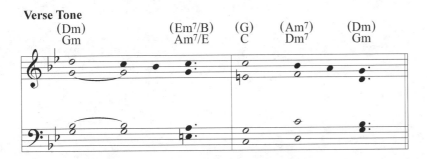

Psalm 17:1-3b, 5-7, 15

1. Lord, hear a cause <u>that</u> is just,
   pay heed <u>to</u> my cry.

2. Turn your ear <u>to</u> my prayer,
   no deceit is <u>on</u> my lips.

3. From you may my judge<u>ment</u> come forth.
   Your eyes dis<u>cern</u> the truth.

4. You search my heart, you visit <u>me</u> by night.
   You test me and you find in <u>me</u> no wrong.

5. I kept my feet firmly <u>in</u> your paths;
   there was no faltering <u>in</u> my steps.

6. I am here and I call, you will hear <u>me</u>, O God.
   Turn your ear to me; <u>hear</u> my words.

7. Display your great love, you whose <u>right</u> hand saves
   your friends from those who re<u>bel</u> against them.

8. As for me, in my justice I shall <u>see</u> your face
   and be filled, when I awake, with the sight <u>of</u> your glory.

Performance Notes
Once the Antiphon is well known by the assembly, it could be sung in two overlapping parts as shown in the alternate setting.
If two cantors are available, the assembly could be divided into two parts, with one cantor leading each section.
Or a single cantor could sing the upper line, with choir and assembly singing the lower line.
Or the upper line could be taken by male voices, the lower line taken by female voices.

Our Help Shall Come from the Lord

Twenty-ninth Sunday in Ordinary Time, Song for the Word

Antiphon ♩· = 66 *May be sung as a round*

Our help shall come from the Lord, the Lord who made hea-ven and earth. Our

Verse Tone

Psalm 121

1. I lift up my <u>eyes</u> to the mountains;
from where shall come <u>my</u> help?
My help shall <u>come</u> from the LORD
who made heaven <u>and</u> earth.

2. May God never al<u>low</u> you to stumble!
Let your guard <u>not</u> sleep.
Behold, neither <u>sleep</u>ing nor slumbering,
Is<u>rael's</u> guard.

3. The LORD is your <u>guard</u> and your shade;
and stands at <u>your</u> right.
By day the <u>sun</u> shall not smite you
nor the moon in <u>the</u> night.

4. The LORD will <u>guard</u> you from evil,
and will guard <u>your</u> soul.
The LORD will guard your <u>going</u> and coming
both now and <u>for</u> ever.

Performance Notes
When sung as a 4-part round, this piece works best divided into men - women - women - men.

God Feeds Us, God Saves Us

Twenty-ninth Sunday in Ordinary Time, Song for the Table

Alto Descant

God feeds us, saves us, eyes of the Lord are up-on us. God

Tenor Descant

God feeds us, saves us, eyes of the Lord are up-on us. God

Bass Descant

God feeds us, God saves us, the eyes of the Lord are up-on us. God

Antiphon ♩ = 46

Capo 3: (Am) (Dm7) (G) (Em7) (Am) (F) (C) (Am) (Esus4) (E) (Am)
Cm Fm7 Bb Gm7 Cm Ab Eb Cm Gsus4 G Cm

God feeds us, God saves us, the eyes of the Lord are up-on us. God

feeds us, saves us, eyes of the Lord are up-on us.

feeds us, saves us, eyes of the Lord are up-on us.

feeds us, God saves us, the eyes of the Lord are up-on us.

(Dm7) (G) (Em7) (Am) (F) (C) (Am) (Esus4) (E) (Am)
Fm7 Bb Gm7 Cm Ab Eb Cm Gsus4 G Cm

feeds us, God saves us, the eyes of the Lord are up-on us.

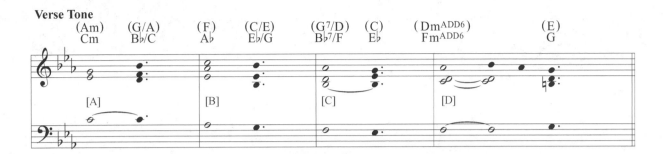

Verse Tone

Psalm 33

1. Ring out your joy to the LORD, O you just;
[Omit B-C]
    for praise is fitting for loyal hearts.

2. Give thanks to the LORD upon the harp,
    with a ten-stringed lute play your songs.
    Sing to the LORD a song that is new,
    play loudly, with all your skill.

3. For the word of the LORD is faithful
    and all his works done in truth.
    The LORD loves justice and right
    and fills the earth with his love.

4. By God's word the heavens were made,
    by the breath of his mouth all the stars.
    God collects the waves of the ocean,
    and stores up the depths of the sea.

5. Let all the earth fear the LORD,
    all who live in the world stand in awe.
    For God spoke; it came to be.
    God commanded; it sprang into being.

6. The LORD foils the designs of the nations,
    and defeats the plans of the peoples.
    The counsel of the LORD stands forever,
    the plans of God's heart from age to age.

7. They are happy, whose God is the LORD,
    the people who are chosen as his own.
    From the heavens the LORD looks forth
    and sees all the peoples of the earth.

8. From the heavenly dwelling God gazes
    on all the dwellers on the earth;
    God who shapes the hearts of them all
    and considers all their deeds.

9. A king is not saved by his army,
    nor a warrior preserved by his strength.
    A vain hope for safety is the horse;
    despite its power it cannot save.

10. The LORD looks on those who revere him,
    on those who hope in his love,
    to rescue their souls from death,
    to keep them alive in famine.

11. Our soul is waiting for the LORD.
    The LORD is our help and our shield.
    Our hearts find joy in the LORD.
    We trust in God's holy name.

12. May your love be upon us, O LORD,
[Omit B-C]
    as we place all our hope in you.

When the Poor Cry Out

Thirtieth Sunday in Ordinary Time, Song for the Word

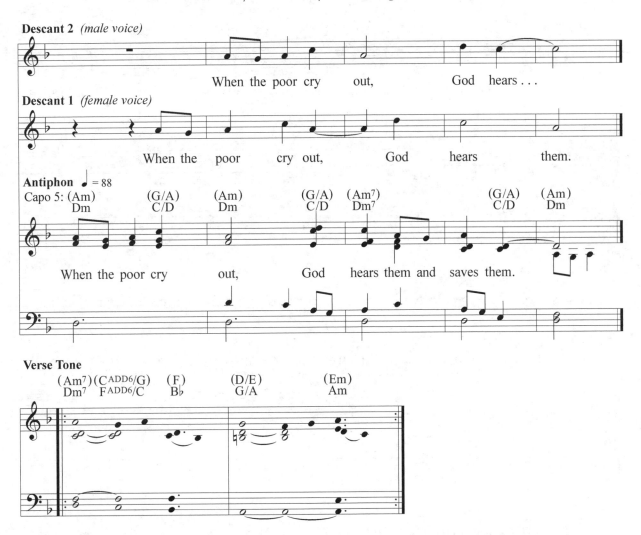

Descant 2 *(male voice)*

When the poor cry out, God hears . . .

Descant 1 *(female voice)*

When the poor cry out, God hears them.

Antiphon ♩ = 88

Capo 5: (Am) (G/A) (Am) (G/A) (Am⁷) (G/A) (Am)
Dm C/D Dm C/D Dm⁷ C/D Dm

When the poor cry out, God hears them and saves them.

Verse Tone

(Am⁷)(C^ADD6/G) (F) (D/E) (Em)
Dm⁷ F^ADD6/C B♭ G/A Am

Psalm 34:2-3,17-19, 23

1. I will bless the LORD at all times,
   God's praise always on my lips;
   in the LORD my soul shall make its boast.
   The humble shall hear and be glad.

2. The face of the LORD rebuffs the wicked
   to destroy their remembrance from the earth.
   The just call and the LORD hears
   and rescues them in all their distress.

3. The LORD is close to the broken-hearted;
   those whose spirit is crushed God will save.
   The LORD ransoms the souls of the faithful.
   None who trust in God shall be condemned.

The Prayer of Our Hearts

Thirtieth Sunday in Ordinary Time, Song for the Table

Psalms 123; 141:1-4, 8-9; 143:1-2, 7-8, 10

1. To you have I lifted up my eyes,
   you who dwell in the heavens;
   my eyes, like the eyes of slaves
   on the hand of their lords.

2. Like the eyes of a servant
   on the hand of her mistress,
   so our eyes are on the LORD our God
   till we are shown mercy.

3. Have mercy on us, LORD, have mercy.
   We are filled with contempt.
   Indeed all too full is our soul
   with the scorn of the rich,
      the disdain of the proud.

4. I have called to you, LORD; hasten to help me!
   Hear my voice when I cry to you.
   Let my prayer rise before you like incense,
   the raising of my hands like an evening oblation.

5. Set, O LORD, a guard over my mouth;
   keep watch, O LORD, at the door of my lips!
   Do not turn my heart to things that are wrong,
   to evil deeds with those who are sinners.

6. To you, LORD God, my eyes are turned;
   in you I take refuge; spare my soul!
   From the trap they have laid for me keep me safe;
   keep me from the snares of those who do evil.

Verse Tone

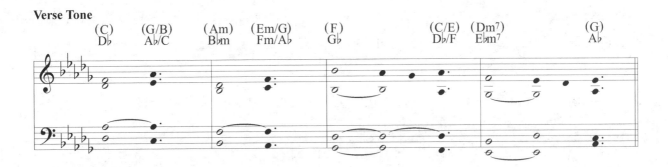

7. LORD, listen to my prayer, turn your ear to my ap<u>peal</u>.
   You are faithful, you are just; give <u>answer</u>.
   Do not call your ser<u>vant</u> to judgement
   for no one is just <u>in</u> your sight.

8. LORD, make haste and <u>answer</u>;
   for my spirit fails with<u>in</u> me.
   Do not <u>hide</u> your face
   lest I become like those <u>in</u> the grave.

9. In the morning let me know your <u>love</u>
   for I put my trust in <u>you</u>.
   Make me know the way <u>I</u> should walk;
   to you I lift <u>up</u> my soul.

10. Teach me to do your <u>will</u>
    for you, O LORD, are my <u>God</u>.
    Let your good <u>spirit</u> guide me
    in ways that are le<u>vel</u> and smooth.

Performance Notes

As indicated, the Antiphon may be sung as a two-part round, the second part entering halfway through, or as a four-part round.

Merciful and Tender

Thirty-first Sunday in Ordinary Time, Song for the Week: Option I

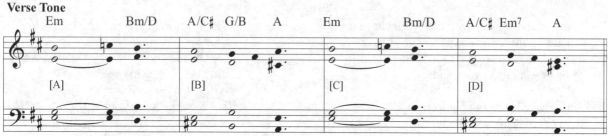

Psalm 103 [The Lectionary selections for the day are indicated by an asterisk.]

1. * My soul, give thanks to the LORD,
   * all my being, bless God's holy name.
   * My soul, give thanks to the LORD
   * and never forget all God's blessings.

2. * It is God who forgives all your guilt,
   * who heals every one of your ills,
   * who redeems your life from the grave,
   * who crowns you with love and compassion,
   [repeat C-D]
   who fills your life with good things,
   renewing your youth like an eagle's.

3. The LORD does deeds of justice,
   gives judgement for all who are oppressed.
   The LORD's ways were made known to Moses;
   the LORD's deeds to Israel's children.

4. * The LORD is compassion and love,
   * slow to anger and rich in mercy.
   The LORD will not always chide,
   will not be angry forever.
   [repeat C-D]
   * God does not treat us according to our sins
   * nor repay us according to our faults.

5. For as the heavens are high above the earth
   so strong is God's love for the God-fearing;
   * as far as the east is from the west
   * so far does he remove our sins.

6. * As parents have compassion on their children,
   * the LORD has pity on those who are God-fearing
   for he knows of what we are made,
   and remembers that we are dust.

7. As for us, our days are like grass;
   we flower like the flower of the field;
   the wind blows and we are gone
   and our place never sees us again.

8. *A* But the love of the LORD is everlasting
   B upon those who fear the LORD.
   A God's justice reaches out to children's children
   B when they keep his covenant in truth,
   D when they keep his will in their mind.

9. *A* The LORD has set his throne in heaven
   B and his kingdom rules over all.
   A Give thanks to the LORD, all you angels,
   B mighty in power, fulfilling God's word,
   D who heed the voice of that word.

10. *A* Give thanks to the LORD, all you hosts,
    B you servants who do God's will.
    A Give thanks to the LORD, all his works,
    B in every place where God rules.
    D My soul, give thanks to the LORD!

Do Not Abandon Me, Lord

Thirty-first Sunday in Ordinary Time, Song for the Week: Option II

Psalm 38

1. O | LORD, do not rebuke me in your anger;
   do not | punish me, LORD, in your rage.
   Your | arrows have sunk deep in me;
   your | hand has come down upon me.
   Through your | anger all my body is sick;
   through my | sin, there is no health in my limbs.

2. My | guilt towers high above my head;
   it is a | weight too heavy to bear.
   My | wounds are foul and festering,
   the | result of my own folly.
   I am | bowed and brought to my knees.
   I go | mourning all the day long.

3. All my | frame burns with fever;
   all my body is sick.
   Spent and utterly crushed,
   I cry a- | loud in anguish of heart.

4. O | LORD, you know all my longing;
   my | groans are not hidden from you.
   My | heart throbs, my strength is spent;
   the very | light has gone from my eyes.

5. My | friends avoid me like a leper;
   those | closest to me stand afar off.
   Those who | plot against my life lay snares;

those who | seek my ruin speak of harm,
| planning treachery
| all the day long.

6. But | I am like the deaf who cannot hear,
   like the | mute I cannot open my mouth.
   I am like one who hears nothing,
   in whose | mouth is no defense.

7. | I count on you, O LORD;
   it is | you, LORD God, who will answer.
   I | pray: "Do not let them mock me,
   those who | triumph if my foot should slip."

8. For | I am on the point of falling
   and my | pain is always before me.
   I con- | fess that I am guilty
   and my | sin fills me with dismay.

9. My | wanton enemies are numberless
   and my | lying foes are many.
   They re- | pay me evil for good
   and at- | tack me for seeking what is right.

10. O | LORD, do not forsake me!
    My | God, do not stay afar off!
    Make | haste and come to my help,
    O | LORD, my God, my savior!

C-189

I Will Praise Your Name For Ever

Thirty-first Sunday in Ordinary Time, Song for the Word

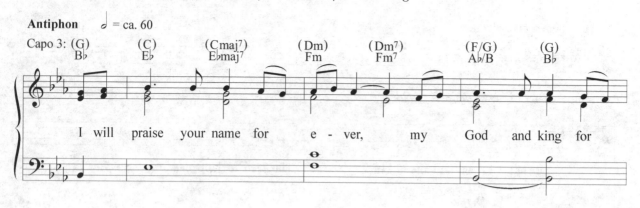

Antiphon ♩ = ca. 60

I will praise your name for e - ver, my God and king for

Descants

Al - le - lu - ia, al - le - lu - ia, al - le - lu - ia.

Antiphon

e - ver. Al - le - lu - ia, al - le - lu - ia, al - le - lu - ia.

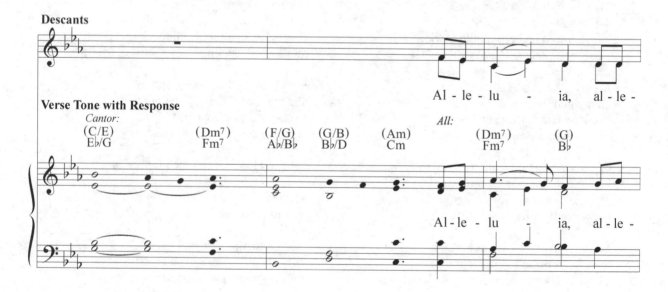

Descants

Al - le - lu - ia, al - le -

Verse Tone with Response

Cantor: *All:*

Al - le - lu - ia, al - le -

Descants

lu - ia, al - le - lu - ia.

Verse Tone with Response

lu - ia, al - le - lu - ia.

Psalm 145:1-2, 8-11, 13c-14

1. I will give you glory, O God my king,
   I will bless your name for ever. *Alleluia . . .*

2. I will bless you day after day
   and praise your name for ever. *Alleluia . . .*

3. You are kind and full of compassion,
   slow to anger, abounding in love. *(simile)*

4. How good you are, LORD, to all,
   compassionate to all your creatures.

5. All your creatures shall thank you, O LORD,
   and your friends shall repeat their blessing.

6. They shall speak of the glory of your reign
   and declare your might, O God.

7. You are faithful in all your words
   and loving in all your deeds.

8. You support all those who are falling
   and raise up all who are bowed down.

Salvation Has Come to This House

Thirty-first Sunday in Ordinary Time, Song for the Table

C-190

Verse Tone

Psalm 16:1-2, 5-11

1. Preserve me, God, I take <u>refuge</u> in you.
   I say to you, LORD: "You <u>are</u> my God.
   [Omit C]
   My happiness lies in <u>you</u> alone."

2. O LORD, it is you who are my <u>portion</u> and cup,
   it is you yourself who <u>are</u> my prize.
   The lot marked out for me is <u>my</u> delight,
   welcome indeed the her<u>itage</u> that falls to me!

3. I will bless you, LORD, you <u>give</u> me counsel,
   and even at night di<u>rect</u> my heart.
   I keep you, LORD, ever <u>in</u> my sight;
   since you are at my right hand, I <u>shall</u> stand firm.

4. And so my heart rejoices, my <u>soul</u> is glad;
   even my body shall <u>rest</u> in safety.
   For you will not leave my soul a<u>mong</u> the dead,
   nor let your beloved <u>know</u> decay.

5. You will show me the <u>path</u> of life,
   the fullness of joy <u>in</u> your presence,
   [Omit C]
   at your right hand happ<u>iness</u> for ever.

Let My Prayer Come Before You, Lord

Thirty-second Sunday in Ordinary Time, Song for the Week

Descant *(hum)*

Alto Descant *(hum)*

Bass Descant *(hum)*

Antiphon ♩ = 88

Capo 5: (C)

Let my prayer come be - fore you, Lord: lis - ten and an - swer.
Hear me, Lord, when I cry to you: lis - ten and an - swer.

Lis - ten and an - swer.

Lis - ten and an - swer.

Lis - ten and an - swer.

Verse Tone with Response

Cantor: All:

...lis - ten and an - swer.

Verse Tone with Response

Psalm 88:2-5, 7-19

1. LORD my God, I call for <u>help</u> by day,
   Listen and answer.
   I cry at <u>night</u> before you.
   Listen and answer.
   Let my prayer come in<u>to</u> your presence.
   Listen and answer.
   O turn your ear <u>to</u> my cry.
   Listen and answer.

2. For my soul is <u>filled</u> with evils;   *(simile)*
   my life is on the brink <u>of</u> the grave.
   I am reckoned as one <u>in</u> the tomb;
   I have reached the end <u>of</u> my strength.

3. You have laid me in the depths <u>of</u> the tomb,
   in places that are dark, <u>in</u> the depths.
   Your anger weighs <u>down</u> upon me;
   I am drowned be<u>neath</u> your waves.

4. You have taken a<u>way</u> my friends
   and made me hateful <u>in</u> your sight.
   Imprisoned, I ca<u>nnot</u> escape;
   my eyes are sun<u>ken</u> with grief.

5. I call to you, LORD, all <u>the</u> day long;
   to you I stretch <u>out</u> my hands.
   Will you work your wonders <u>for</u> the dead?
   Will the shades <u>stand</u> and praise you?

6. Will your love be told <u>in</u> the grave
   or your faithfulness a<u>mong</u> the dead?
   Will your wonders be known <u>in</u> the dark
   or your justice in the land <u>of</u> oblivion?

7. As for me, LORD, I call to <u>you</u> for help;
   in the morning my prayer <u>comes</u> before you.
   LORD, why do <u>you</u> reject me?
   Why do you <u>hide</u> your face?

8. Wretched, close to death <u>from</u> my youth,
   I have borne your trials; <u>I</u> am numb.
   Your fury has swept <u>down</u> upon me;
   your terrors have utter<u>ly</u> destroyed me.

9. They surround me all the day <u>like</u> a flood,
   they assail me <u>all</u> together.
   Friend and neighbor you have ta<u>ken</u> away;
   my one compan<u>ion</u> is darkness.

C-193

God of Life, God of Hope

Thirty-second Sunday in Ordinary Time, Song for the Table

Verses Superimposed tone (Tenor)

Psalm 105:2-11, 40-45

1. O | sing to the Lord, sing | praise;
   | tell all his wonderful | works!
   Be | proud of God's holy | name,
   let the | hearts that seek the Lord re- | joice.

2. Con- | sider the Lord who is | strong;
   | constantly seek his | face.
   Re- | member the wonders of the | Lord,
   the | miracles and judgements pro- | nounced.

3. O | children of Abraham, God's | servant,
   O | children of Jacob, the | chosen,
   | this is the Lord, our | God;
   whose | judgements prevail in all the | earth.

4. God re- | members the covenant for | ever,
   the | promise for a thousand gene- | rations,
   the | covenant made with | Abraham,
   the | oath that was sworn to | Isaac.

5. God con- | firmed it for Jacob as a | law,
   for | Israel as a covenant for | ever;
   and said: | "I am giving you a | land,
   | Canaan, your appointed | heritage."

6. When they | asked for food God sent | quails;
   and | filled them with bread from | heaven.
   The | Lord pierced the rock; water | gushed;
   it | flowed in the desert like a | river.

7. For God re- | membered the holy | promise,
   which was | given to Abraham, his | servant.
   God | brought out the people with | joy,
   the | chosen ones with shouts of re- | joicing.

8. God | gave them the land of the | nations.
   They took the | fruit of the labor of | others,
   that | thus they might keep God's | precepts,
   that | thus they might observe God's | laws.

C-194

My Plans for You Are Peace
Thirty-third Sunday in Ordinary Time, Song for the Week

Soprano & Alto Descants

My plans are peace.

Antiphon ♩ = ca. 88

My plans for you are peace, not af - flic - tion, says the Lord.

On - ly cry and I will bring you home.

On - ly cry to me, and I will bring you home.

Verse Tone

Psalm 126

1. When the LORD delivered Zion from bondage,
   it seemed like a dream.
   Then was our mouth filled with laughter,
   on our lips there were songs.

2. The heathens themselves said: "What marvels
   the LORD worked for them!"
   What marvels the Lord worked for us!
   Indeed we were glad.

3. Deliver us, O LORD, from our bondage
   as streams in dry land.
   Those who are sowing in tears
   will sing when they reap.

4. They go out, they go out, full of tears,
   carrying seed for the sowing;
   they come back, they come back, full of song,
   carrying their sheaves.

Don't Be Afraid

Thirty-third Sunday in Ordinary Time, Song for the Table

Verses Superimposed tone

Alto Descant

Don't be a-fraid, on - ly be-lieve. Your faith will save you:

Tenor Descant

Don't be a-fraid, on - ly be-lieve. Your faith will save you:

Antiphon ♩ = 54

Don't be a-fraid, on - ly be-lieve. Your faith will save you:

on - ly be - lieve.

on - ly be - lieve.

on - ly be - lieve.

Verses Superimposed tone

The following and similar psalm extracts may be used over the ostinato:

Psalm 31:2-4, 15-17, 20-22b, 24ab, 25

1. In you, O LORD, I take <u>refuge</u>.
   Let me never be put to <u>shame</u>.
   In your justice, set me <u>free</u>,
   hear me and speedily <u>rescue</u> me.

2. Be a rock of refuge for <u>me</u>,
   a mighty stronghold to <u>save</u> me,
   for you are my rock, my <u>strong</u>hold.
   For your name's sake, lead me and <u>guide</u> me.

3. As for me, I trust in you, <u>LORD</u>;
   I say: "You are my <u>God</u>.
   My life is in your hands, de<u>liv</u>er me
   from the hands of those who <u>hate</u> me.

4. Let your face shine on your <u>servant</u>.
   Save me in your <u>love</u>."
   Blessed be the LORD who has <u>shown</u> me
   such a steadfast <u>love</u>.

5. How great is the goodness, <u>LORD</u>,
   that you keep for those who <u>fear</u> you,
   that you show to those who <u>trust</u> you
   in the sight of <u>all</u>.

6. You hide them in the shelter of your <u>presence</u>
   from human <u>plots</u>;
   you keep them safe within your <u>tent</u>
   from disputing <u>tongues</u>.

7. Love the LORD, all you <u>saints</u>.
   The LORD guards the <u>faithful</u>.
   Be strong, let your heart take <u>courage</u>,
   all who hope in the <u>LORD</u>.

Psalm 73:1-2, 23-26

8. How good is God to <u>Israel</u>,
   to those who are pure of <u>heart</u>.
   Yet my feet came close to <u>stumbling</u>,
   my steps had almost <u>slipped</u>.

9. Yet I was always in your <u>presence</u>;
   you were holding me by my right <u>hand</u>.
   You will guide me by your <u>counsel</u>
   and so you will lead me to <u>glory</u>.

10. What else have I in heaven but <u>you</u>?
    Apart from you I want nothing on <u>earth</u>.
    My body and my heart faint for <u>joy</u>;
    God is my possession for <u>ever</u>.

Performance Notes
As the cantor sings the verses, the other voices may vocalize to 'oo' under the superimposed tone instead of singing the words.

Worthy Is the Lamb Who Was Slain

Christ the King, Song for the Week

Descant

Worth-y is the Lamb, worth-y, worth-y of glo-ry.

Antiphon ♩. = ca. 72

Capo 5: (G) (Gmaj7/B) (C) (Gmaj7/B) (Am7) (G/B) (C) (D)
C Cmaj7/E F Cmaj7/E Dm7 C/E F G

Worth-y is the Lamb who was slain, worth-y of power, worth-y of glo-ry.

Worth-y is the Lamb, worth-y of wis-dom and might.

(G) (Gmaj7/B) (C) (Gmaj7/B) (C) (Dm7/G) (G)
C Cmaj7/E F Cmaj7/E F Gm7/C C

Worth-y is the Lamb who was slain, worth-y of wis-dom and might.

Verse Tone with Response *Psalm 24:7; 72:5-6, 8, 18-19*

Cantor: *All:*

(G) (Gmaj7/B) (C) (Gmaj7/B) (Am7) (G/B) (C) (D)
C Cmaj7/E F Cmaj7/E Dm7 C/E F G

1. Lift your heads, O an - cient doors: *worth-y of power, worth-y of glo-ry.*
2. May he live as long as the sun:
3. May he be like rain on the grass:
4. May he rule from sea to sea:
5. Bless the God of Is - ra - el:
6. Bles - sed be God's glo - ri - ous name:

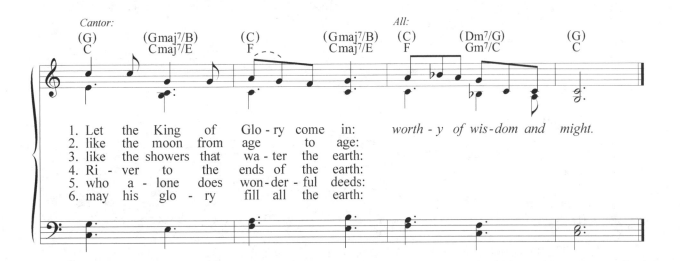

1. Let the King of Glory come in: *worth-y of wis-dom and might.*
2. like the moon from age to age:
3. like the showers that wa-ter the earth:
4. Ri-ver to the ends of the earth:
5. who a-lone does won-der-ful deeds:
6. may his glo-ry fill all the earth:

Additional verses if required:

Psalm 72:1, 9-12, 14, 15bc, 17

7. To the king give judgement, O God:
   worthy of power, worthy of glory.
   justice to the son of the king:
   worthy of wisdom and might.

8. All his foes before him shall fall: *(simile)*
   all his foes shall lick the dust:

9. All the kings pay tribute to him:
   all the kings shall bring him their gifts:

10. In his presence rulers shall bow:
    every land shall serve his will:

11. He shall save the poor when they cry:
    save the needy asking for help:

12. He will rescue all the oppressed:
    precious is their blood in his sight:

13. They will pray for him without end:
    they will bless him all the day long:

14. May his name for ever be blessed:
    may his name endure like the sun:

15. Every land be blessed in him:
    every nation bless his name.

C-198

Let Us Go Rejoicing

Christ the King, Song for the Word
Anniversary of the Dedication of a Church, Song for the Word: Option III

Verse Tone

Psalm 122   *[The Lectionary selections for the Anniversary of the Dedication of a Church*
            are indicated by an asterisk.]

1. * I rejoiced when I <u>heard</u> them say:
   * "Let us go <u>to</u> God's house."
   * And now our <u>feet</u> are standing
   * within your <u>gates</u>, O Jerusalem.

2. * Jerusalem is built <u>as</u> a city
   * strong<u>ly</u> compact.
   * It is there that the <u>tribes</u> go up,
   * the tribes of <u>the</u> LORD.

3. For Israel's <u>law</u> it is,
   there to praise <u>the</u> LORD's name.
   There were set the <u>thrones</u> of judgement
   of the house <u>of</u> David.

4. For the peace of Jeru<u>salem</u> pray:
   "Peace be <u>to</u> your homes!
   May peace reign <u>in</u> your walls,
   in your pal<u>aces</u>, peace!"

5. * For love of my fam'<u>ly</u> and friends
   * I say: "Peace u<u>pon</u> you."
   * For love of the house <u>of</u> the LORD
   * I will ask for <u>your</u> good.

C-199 ➡ Christ the King, Song for the Table, *same as C-22*

C-200

You Have Shown You Love Us
The Most Holy Trinity, Song for the Week

Antiphon ♩ = 92-96

You have shown you love us, Fa-ther, Son and Spi-rit.

Bless'd are you, O God, the God of faith-ful love.

Verse Tone

Omit for doxology

Psalm 113

1. Praise, O servants of the Lord,
   praise the name of the Lord!
   May the name of the Lord be blessed
   both now and for evermore!
   From the rising of the sun to its setting
   praised be the name of the Lord!

2. High above all nations is the Lord,
   above the heavens God's glory.
   Who is like the Lord, our God,
   the one enthroned on high,
   who stoops from the heights to look down,
   to look down upon heaven and earth?

3. From the dust God lifts up the lowly,
   from the dungheap God raises the poor
   to set them in the company of rulers,
   yes, with the rulers of the people.
   To the childless wife God gives a home
   and gladdens her heart with children.

Trinitarian doxology (for Trinity Sunday):

Sing praise to the Abba of Jesus,
through the Spirit poured into our hearts.
By the Spirit, the Water and the Blood
we are saved and share in their love.

How Wonderful Your Name, O Lord

The Most Holy Trinity, Song for the Word

Psalm 8:4-9

1. When I see the heavens, the work of <u>your</u> hands,
   the moon and the stars which <u>you</u> arranged,
   what are we that you should keep us <u>in</u> mind,
   mere mortals <u>that</u> you care for us?

2. Yet you have made us little less <u>than</u> gods;
   and crowned us with <u>glory</u> and honor,
   you gave us power over the work of <u>your</u> hands,
   put all things un<u>der</u> our feet.

3. All of them, sheep <u>and</u> cattle,
   yes, even the <u>savage</u> beasts,
   birds of the air, <u>and</u> fish
   that make their way <u>through</u> the waters.

C-203

With Finest Wheat and Finest Wine

The Most Holy Body and Blood of Christ, Song for the Week

Psalm 147:1-11

1. Sing praise to the Lord who is good;
[omit B]
> sing to our God who is loving:
> to God our praise is due.

2. The Lord builds up Jerusalem
and brings back Israel's exiles,
[repeat A-B]
> God heals the broken-hearted,
> and binds up all their wounds.
> God fixes the number of the stars;
> and calls each one by its name.

3. Our Lord is great and almighty;
God's wisdom can never be measured.
[repeat A-B]
> The Lord raises the lowly,
> and humbles the wicked to the dust.
> O sing to the Lord, giving thanks;
> sing psalms to our God with the harp.

4. God covers the heavens with clouds,
and prepares the rain for the earth;
[repeat A-B]
> making mountains sprout with grass
> and with plants to serve our needs.
> God provides the beasts with their food
> and the young ravens when they cry.

5. God takes no delight in horses' power
nor pleasure in warriors' strength.
> The Lord delights in those who revere him,
> in those who wait for his love.

The Most Holy Body and Blood of Christ, Song for the Word

Psalm 110:1-4

1. The LORD's revelation to my Master: "Sit on my right;   *a priest for ever,*
   your foes I will put beneath your feet."   *like Melchizedek of old.*

2. The LORD will wield from Zion your scepter of power;   *(simile)*
   rule in the midst of all your foes.

3. A prince from the day of your birth on the holy mountains;
   from the womb before the dawn I begot you.

4. The LORD has sworn an oath and will not change. "You are a priest for ever,
   a priest like Melchizedek of old."

C-206

All Who Labor, Come to Me
The Most Sacred Heart of Jesus, Song for the Day

Psalm 33:1, 12-13, 18-22

1. *[Omit A-B]*
   Ring out your joy to the LORD, O you just,
   for praise is fitting for loyal hearts.

2. They are happy whose God is the LORD,
   the people who are chosen as his own.
   From the heavens the LORD looks forth
   and sees all the peoples of the earth.

3. The LORD looks on those who fear him,
   on those who hope in his love,

   to rescue their souls from death,
   to keep them alive in famine.

4. Our soul is waiting for the LORD.
   The LORD is our help and our shield.
   Our hearts find joy in the LORD.
   We trust in God's holy name.

5. *[Omit A-B]*
   May your love be upon us, O LORD,
   as we place all our hope in you.

Performance Notes *The Antiphon may be sung SATB.*

My Shepherd Is the Lord

C-207

The Most Sacred Heart of Jesus, Song for the Word

Psalm 23

1. Fresh and green are <u>the</u> pastures   *there is . . .*
   where you give me re<u>pose</u>.   *my God . . .*
   Near restful waters <u>you</u> lead me   *there is . . .*
   to revive my droop<u>ing</u> spirit.   *my God . . .*

2. You guide me along the <u>right</u> path;   *(simile)*
   you are true to <u>your</u> name.
   If I should walk in the valley <u>of</u> darkness
   no evil would <u>I</u> fear.
   You are there with your crook and <u>your</u> staff;
   with these you give <u>me</u> comfort.

3. You have prepared a banquet <u>for</u> me
   in the sight of <u>my</u> foes.
   My head you have anointed <u>with</u> oil;
   my cup is o<u>ver</u>flowing.

4. Surely goodness and kindness <u>shall</u> follow me
   all the days of <u>my</u> life.
   In the LORD's own house shall <u>I</u> dwell
   for ever <u>and</u> ever.

My Sheep I Will Pasture

The Most Sacred Heart of Jesus, Song for the Table

Canonic Descant

Canon

the lost I will seek and bring back the stray. My

Antiphon ♩ = 42-44

Capo 5: (G) (C) (G/B) (C) (C/E) (G)
C F C/E F F/A C

My sheep I will pas-ture and lead them to rest; the

sheep I will pas-ture and lead them to rest;

(C) (G/B) (G) (C/E) (C) (G)
F C/E C F/A F C

lost I will seek and bring back the stray.

Verse Tone

1st ending for tone **Alternate ending for tone*

(C) (G/B) (F/A) (G) (F/A) (G)
F C/E B♭/D C B♭/D C

Ezekiel 36:24-28; 34:11-16

1. I will take you from the nations, and gather you from <u>all</u> the countries,
   and bring you into <u>your</u> own land.

2. I will sprinkle clean water upon you, and you shall be clean from all <u>your</u> uncleannesses,
   *and from all your idols <u>I</u> will cleanse you.

3. A new heart <u>I</u> will give you,
   *and a new spirit I will <u>put</u> within you.

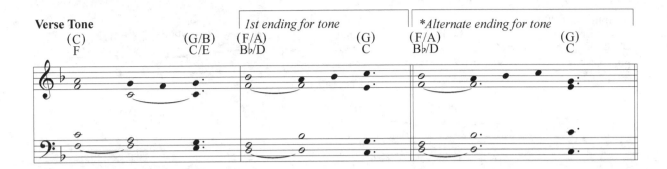

4. And I will remove from your body the <u>heart</u> of stone
   and give you a <u>heart</u> of flesh.

5. I will put my sp<u>ir</u>it within you,
   and make you follow my statutes and be careful to ob<u>serve</u> my ordinances.

6. Then you shall live in the land that I gave <u>to</u> your ancestors;
   and you shall be my people, and I will <u>be</u> your God.

7. I myself will search <u>for</u> my sheep,
   and will <u>seek</u> them out.

8. As shepherds seek out their flocks when they are among their <u>scat</u>tered sheep,
   *so I will <u>seek</u> out my sheep.

9. I will rescue them from all the places to which they <u>have</u> been scattered
   *on a day of <u>clouds</u> and thick darkness.

10. I will bring them out from the peoples and gather them <u>from</u> the countries,
    and will bring them into <u>their</u> own land.

11. And I will feed them on the moun<u>tains</u> of Israel,
    *by the watercourses, and in all the inhabited <u>parts</u> of the land.

12. I will feed them <u>with</u> good pasture,
    and the mountain heights of Israel shall <u>be</u> their pasture.

13. There they shall lie down in good <u>graz</u>ing land,
    *and they shall feed on rich pasture on the <u>moun</u>tains of Israel.

14. I myself will be the shepherd <u>of</u> my sheep,
    *and I will make them lie down, <u>says</u> the Lord GOD.

15. I will seek the lost, and I will bring <u>back</u> the strayed,
    *and I will bind up the injured, and I will <u>streng</u>then the weak.

16. The fat and the strong I <u>will</u> destroy.
    *I will <u>feed</u> them with justice.

Performance Notes
Use the alternate ending of the psalm tone for the lines marked with an asterisk.

You Are Rich in Mercy

Ash Wednesday, Song for the Day

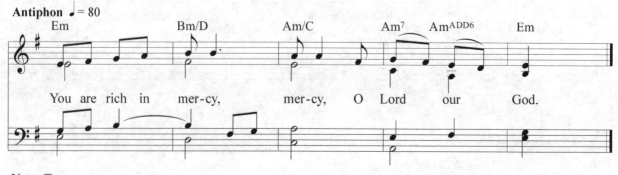

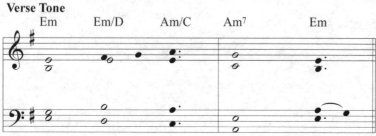

Wisdom 11:21–12:2

1. O LORD, it is always in your power to <u>show</u> great strength,
   and who can withstand the might of your <u>arm</u>?

2. Because the whole world before you is like a speck that <u>tips</u> the scales,
   and like a drop of morning dew that falls on the <u>ground</u>.

3. But you are merciful to all, for you can <u>do</u> all things,
   and you overlook people's sins, so that they may re<u>pent</u>.

4. For you love all things that exist, and detest none of the things that <u>you</u> have made,
   for you would not have made anything if you had <u>hated</u> it.

5. How would anything have endured if you <u>had</u> not willed it?
   Or how would anything not called forth by you have been pre<u>served</u>?

6. You spare all things for they are yours, O LORD, you who <u>love</u> the living.
   For your immortal spirit is in <u>all</u> things.

7. Therefore you correct little by little those who trespass,
       and you remind and warn them of the things through <u>which</u> they sin,
   so that they may be freed from wickedness, and put their trust in you, O <u>LORD</u>.

Performance Notes

The Antiphon may be sung twice each time. If desired, the repetition could overlap on the final note, with "You are" being sung at the same time as "God."

C-210 → Ash Wednesday, Song for the Word, *same as C-167*

Give: Your Father Sees

C-211

Ash Wednesday, Song for the Table

Matthew 5:3-10

1. Blessed are the <u>poor</u> in spirit,
   for theirs is the king<u>dom</u> of heaven.
   Blessed are <u>those</u> who mourn,
   for they <u>will</u> be comforted.

2. Blessed <u>are</u> the meek,
   for they will in<u>her</u>it the earth.
   Blessed are those who hunger
       and <u>thirst</u> for righteousness,
   for they <u>will</u> be filled.

3. Blessed <u>are</u> the merciful,
   for they will re<u>ceive</u> mercy.
   Blessed are the <u>pure</u> in heart,
   for they <u>will</u> see God.

4. Blessed <u>are</u> the peacemakers,
   for they will be called chil<u>dren</u> of God.
   Blessed are those who are persecuted
       for right<u>eous</u>ness' sake,
   for theirs is the king<u>dom</u> of heaven.

Christ Is the Light

Presentation of the Lord (February 2), Introductory Rites

Alto Descant

Christ is the light, light of the na-tions, glo-ry of Is-rael, glo-ry for all.

Tenor Descant

Christ is the light, light of the na-tions, glo-ry of Is-ra-el, glo-ry for all.

Antiphon ♩. = 65

Capo 2: (D) (A) (G) (A⁷/E)(D) (Bm) (Em) (G)(A)
E B A B⁷/F♯ E C♯m F♯m A B

Christ is the light, light of the na-tions, glo-ry of Is-ra-el, glo-ry for all.

...glo-ry of Is-ra-el, glo-ry for all.

...glo-ry of Is-ra-el, glo-ry for all.

Verse Tone with Response

Cantor: *All:*
(D) (A) (G) (A⁷/E)(D) (Bm) (Em) (G)(A)
E B A B⁷/F♯ E C♯m F♯m A B

...glo-ry of Is-ra-el, glo-ry for all.

Verse Tone with Response

...glo-ry of Is-ra-el, glo-ry for all.

Verses for the Gathering and Kindling of Candles

Luke 2:29-32

1. At last, all-powerful <u>Mas</u>ter,
   you give leave to <u>your</u> servant   *glory of Israel . . .*
   to go in <u>peace</u>,
   according to <u>your</u> promise.   *glory of Israel . . .*

2. For my eyes have seen your sal<u>va</u>tion
   which you have prepared for <u>all</u> nations,   *(simile)*
   the light to enlighten the <u>Gen</u>tiles,
   and give glory to Israel, <u>your</u> people.

Verses for the Entrance Procession of Candles

Psalm 122

1. I rejoiced when I heard them <u>say</u>:
   "Let us go to <u>God</u>'s house."   *glory of Israel . . .*
   And now our feet are <u>stand</u>ing
   within your gates, O <u>Je</u>rusalem.   *glory of Israel . . .*

2. Jerusalem is built as a <u>ci</u>ty
   strongly <u>com</u>pact.   *(simile)*
   It is there that the tribes go <u>up</u>,
   the tribes of <u>the</u> LORD.

3. For Israel's law it <u>is</u>,
   there to praise the LORD's name.
   There were set the thrones of <u>judge</u>ment
   of the house <u>of</u> David.

4. For the peace of Jerusalem <u>pray</u>:
   "Peace be to <u>your</u> homes!
   May peace reign in your <u>walls</u>,
   in your pal<u>ac</u>es, peace!"

5. For love of my family and <u>friends</u>
   I say: "Peace up<u>on</u> you."
   For love of the house of the LORD
   I will ask for <u>your</u> good.

Let the King of Glory Come In

C-213

Presentation of the Lord (February 2), Song for the Word

Verse Tone

Cantor:

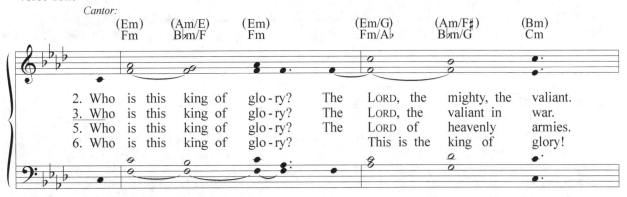

2. Who is this king of glo-ry? The LORD, the mighty, the valiant.
3. Who is this king of glo-ry? The LORD, the valiant in war.
5. Who is this king of glo-ry? The LORD of heavenly armies.
6. Who is this king of glo-ry? This is the king of glory!

Alto Descant

Let the king of glo-ry come in.

Tenor/Alto Descant

Let the king of glo-ry come in.

Response *All:*

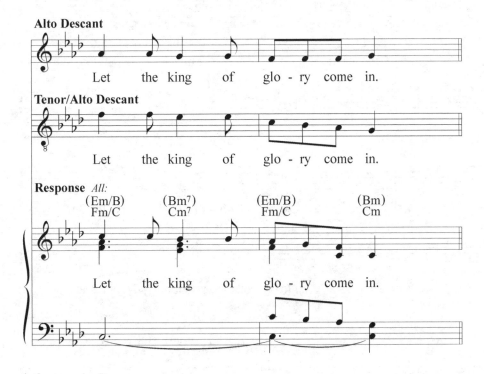

Let the king of glo-ry come in.

Christ Is the Light

Presentation of the Lord (February 2), Song for the Table

Alto Descant

Christ is the light, light of the na-tions, glo-ry of Is-ra-el, glo-ry for all.

Tenor Descant

Christ is the light, light of the na-tions, glo-ry of Is-ra-el, glo-ry for all.

Antiphon ♩. = 65

Christ is the light, light of the na-tions, glo-ry of Is-ra-el, glo-ry for all.

...glo-ry of Is-ra-el, glo-ry for all.

...glo-ry of Is-ra-el, glo-ry for all.

Verse Tone with Response

...glo-ry of Is-ra-el, glo-ry for all.

Verse Tone with Response

...glo-ry of Is - ra - el, glo-ry for all.

Psalm 145

1. *[For this verse only, omit the tone repeat.]*
   I will give you glory, O God my <u>king</u>,
   I will bless your name <u>for</u> ever. *glory of Israel . . .*

2. I will bless you day after <u>day</u>
   and praise your name <u>for</u> ever. *glory of Israel . . .*
   You are great, LORD, highly to be <u>praised</u>,
   your greatness cannot <u>be</u> measured. *glory of Israel . . .*

3. Age to age shall proclaim your <u>works</u>,
   shall declare your mighty <u>deeds</u>, *(simile)*
   shall speak of your splendor and <u>glory</u>,
   tell the tale of your wonder<u>ful</u> works.

4. They will speak of your terrible <u>deeds</u>,
   recount your greatness <u>and</u> might.
   They will recall your abundant <u>goodness</u>;
   age to age shall ring out <u>your</u> justice.

5. You are kind and full of com<u>passion</u>,
   slow to anger, abounding <u>in</u> love.
   How good you are, LORD, to <u>all</u>,
   compassionate to all <u>your</u> creatures.

6. All your creatures shall thank you, O <u>LORD</u>,
   and your friends shall repeat <u>their</u> blessing.
   They shall speak of the glory of your <u>reign</u>
   and declare your might, <u>O</u> God,

7. to make known to all your mighty <u>deeds</u>
   and the glorious splendor of <u>your</u> reign.
   Yours is an everlasting <u>kingdom</u>;
   your rule lasts from age <u>to</u> age.

8. You are faithful in all your <u>words</u>
   and loving in all <u>your</u> deeds.
   You support all those who are <u>falling</u>
   and raise up all who are <u>bowed</u> down.

9. The eyes of all creatures look to <u>you</u>
   and you give them their food in <u>due</u> season.
   You open wide your <u>hand</u>,
   grant the desires of all <u>who</u> live.

10. You are just in all your <u>ways</u>
    and loving in all <u>your</u> deeds.
    You are close to all who <u>call</u> you,
    who call on you from <u>their</u> hearts.

11. You grant the desires of those who <u>fear</u> you,
    you hear their cry and <u>you</u> save them.
    LORD, you protect all who <u>love</u> you;
    but the wicked you will utterly <u>destroy</u>.

12. Let me speak your praise, O <u>LORD</u>,
    let all peoples bless your ho<u>ly</u> name,
    for <u>ever</u>,
    for ages <u>unending</u>.

John Was Sent from God

The Nativity of Saint John the Baptist (June 24), Song for the Day

Verses   Superimposed tone

Antiphon ♩ = 65

John was sent from God, a wit-ness to the light, cho-sen to pre-pare a

Drone E⁻³

peo - ple for the Lord.

Psalm 119:105-112

1. Your word is a lamp for <u>my</u> steps
   and a light <u>for</u> my path.
   I have sworn and have made up <u>my</u> mind
   to obey your <u>decrees</u>.

2. LORD, I am deeply <u>afflicted</u>;
   by your word <u>give</u> me life.
   Accept, LORD, the homage of <u>my</u> lips
   and teach me your <u>decrees</u>.

3. Though I carry my life in <u>your</u> hands,
   I remem<u>ber</u> your law.
   Though the wicked try to <u>ensnare</u> me,
   I do not stray from <u>your</u> precepts.

4. Your will is my heritage <u>for</u> ever,
   the joy <u>of</u> my heart.
   I set myself to carry out <u>your</u> statutes
   in fullness, <u>for</u> ever.

Performance Notes

The drone is preferably hummed (to an 'n' sound rather than an 'm' sound), but may also be sustained on the organ or played by guitars strumming an E chord without the 3rd on the first beat of every measure only.

I Will Praise You, I Will Thank You

The Nativity of Saint John the Baptist (June 24), Song for the Word

Psalm 139:1-3, 13-15

1. O Lord, you search me <u>and</u> you know me,
   you know my resting and my rising,
     you discern my purpose <u>from</u> afar.
   You mark when I walk <u>or</u> lie down,
   all my ways lie <u>open</u> to you.

2. For it was you who cre<u>ated</u> my being,
   knit me together in my <u>mother's</u> womb.

I thank you for the wonder <u>of</u> my being,
for the wonders of all <u>your</u> creation.

3. Already you <u>knew</u> my soul,
   my body held no se<u>cret</u> from you
   when I was being <u>fashioned</u> in secret
   and molded in the depths <u>of</u> the earth.

Performance Notes

In the first two full measures of the Antiphon, the accompaniment bass clef and alto/bass descant rhythms could be sung and played as two dotted quarter notes (as in the third full measure) instead of half note followed by quarter note.

C-217

God's Tender Mercy
The Nativity of Saint John the Baptist (June 24), Song for the Table

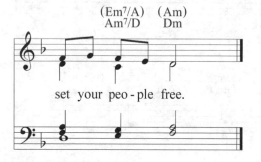

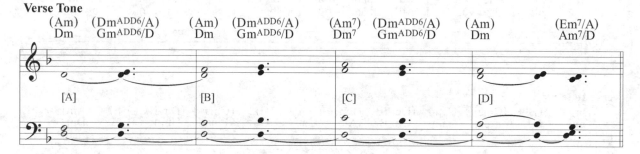

Psalm 92:2-6, 13-16

1. It is good to give thanks to the LORD,
   to make music to your name, O Most High,
   to proclaim your love in the morning
   and your truth in the watches of the night,
   [Repeat C-D]
   on the ten-stringed lyre and the lute,
   with the murmuring sound of the harp.

2. Your deeds, O LORD, have made me glad;
   for the work of your hands I shout with joy.
   O LORD, how great are your works!
   How deep are your designs!

3. The just will flourish like the palm tree
   and grow like a Lebanon cedar.
   Planted in the house of the LORD
   they will flourish in the courts of our God,

4. still bearing fruit when they are old,
   still full of sap, still green,
   to proclaim that the LORD is just,
   my rock, in whom there is no wrong.

Performance Notes
The Antiphon could be sung as a four-part round, if desired.

You Are Peter

Saints Peter and Paul, Apostles (June 29), Song for the Day

Verse Tone

Psalm 116:10-19

1. I trusted, even when I said:
   "I am sorely <u>af</u>flicted,"
   and when I said in my <u>a</u>larm:
   "There is no one <u>I</u> can trust."

2. How can I repay <u>the</u> LORD
   for his goodness <u>to</u> me?
   The cup of salvation I <u>will</u> raise;
   I will call <u>on</u> the LORD's name.

3. My vows to the LORD I will <u>ful</u>fill
   before all <u>the</u> people.
   O precious in the eyes of <u>the</u> LORD
   is the death <u>of</u> the faithful.

4. Your servant, LORD, your servant <u>am</u> I;
   you have loosened <u>my</u> bonds.
   A thanksgiving sacrifice <u>I</u> make;
   I will call <u>on</u> the LORD's name.

5. My vows to the LORD I will <u>ful</u>fill
   before all <u>the</u> people,
   in the courts of the house of <u>the</u> LORD,
   in your midst, <u>O</u> Jerusalem.

Performance Notes

In the Antiphon, the assembly sings the full-size notes, imitating the cantor's melody, while choir members may add the descant part in cue-size notes. If by chance the assembly becomes confused and sings the descant part instead of the main melody at any point, this does not matter: a built-in congregational mistake that still fits! It would even be possible for the assembly to sing all their sections of the Antiphon to the same melody.

I Called in My Distress

C-219

Saints Peter and Paul, Apostles (June 29), Song for the Word

Psalm 34:2-9

1. I will bless the LORD at all times,
   God's praise always on my lips;
   God set me free.
   In the LORD my soul shall make its boast.
   The humble shall hear and be glad.
   God set me free.

2. Glorify the LORD with me.
   Together let us praise God's name.
   God set me free.
   I sought the LORD and was heard;
   from all my terrors set free.
   God set me free.

3. Look towards God and be radiant;
   let your faces not be abashed.
   God set me free.
   When the poor cry out the LORD hears them
   and rescues them from all their distress.
   God set me free.

4. The angel of the LORD is encamped
   around those who fear God, to rescue them.
   God set me free.
   Taste and see that the LORD is good.
   They are happy who seek refuge in God.
   God set me free.

C-220

If You Love Me, Feed My Lamb

Saints Peter and Paul, Apostles (June 29), Song for the Table

Psalm 80:2ac, 3bc, 9-12, 15-16, 18-19

1. O shepherd of Israel, hear us,
   shine forth from your cherubim throne.
   O Lord, rouse up your might,
   O Lord, come to our help.

2. You brought a vine out of Egypt;
   to plant it you drove out the nations.
   Before it you cleared the ground;
   it took root and spread through the land.

3. The mountains were covered with its shadow,
   the cedars of God with its boughs.

It stretched out its branches to the sea,
to the Great River it stretched out its shoots.

4. God of hosts, turn again, we implore,
   look down from heaven and see.
   Visit this vine and protect it,
   the vine your right hand has planted.

5. May your hand be on the one you have chosen,
   the one you have given your strength.
   And we shall never forsake you again;
   give us life that we may call upon your name.

Performance Notes   *The Antiphon may be sung SATB.*

The Transfiguration of the Lord (August 6), Song for the Day, *same as C-26* ← **C-221**

The Transfiguration of the Lord (August 6), Song for the Word, *see C-93* ← **C-222**

We Shall Be Like You

C-223

The Transfiguration of the Lord (August 6), Song for the Table

Verses *Psalm 27:1, 4, 7-14*
Superimposed tone

1. The LORD is my light and my help; whom shall I fear?
2. The LORD is the stronghold of my life; before whom shall I shrink?
3. There is one thing I ask of the LORD, for this I long,
4. to live in the house of the LORD, all the days of my life,
5. to savor the sweetness of the LORD, to be - hold his temple.
6. O LORD, hear my voice when I call; have mer - cy and answer.
7. Of you my heart has spoken: "Seek God's face."
8. It is your face, O LORD, that I seek; hide not your face.
9. Dis - miss not your servant in anger; you have been my help.
10. Do not abandon or forsake me, O God my help!
11. Though father and mother forsake me, the LORD will re - ceive me.
12. In - struct me, LORD, in your way; on an e - ven path lead me.
13. When they lie in ambush, protect me from my e - nemies' greed.
14. False witnesses rise against me, breath - ing out fury.
15. I am sure I shall see the LORD's goodness in the land of the living.
16. In the LORD, hold firm and take heart. Hope in the LORD!

Descant
Canon

you are re-vealed. We shall be like you when

Bass Descant

We shall be like you when you are re-vealed.

Antiphon ♩ = ca. 63
Capo 4: (Dm) (DmADD6/F) (Am) (F) (Dm) (Fmaj7) (ASUS4) (Am)
F#m F#mADD6/A C#m A F#m Amaj7 C#SUS4 C#m

We shall be like you when you are re-vealed.

C-224

A Woman Clothed with the Sun

Assumption of the Blessed Virgin Mary (August 15), Song for the Day

Song of Songs 2:13b-14; 4:8ab; 5:9; 6:1; 7:6

1. Arise, my love, my fair one, and <u>come</u> away.
   O my dove, in the clefts of the rock, in the covert <u>of</u> the cliff.

2. Let me see your face, let me <u>hear</u> your voice;
   for your voice is sweet, and your <u>face</u> is lovely.

3. Come with me from Leba<u>non</u>, my bride;
   come with <u>me</u> from Lebanon.

4. What is your beloved more than <u>another</u> beloved,
   O fair<u>est</u> of women?

5. Where has your beloved gone, O fair<u>est</u> of women?
   Which way has your beloved turned, that we may seek <u>him</u> with you?

6. How fair and <u>pleas</u>ant you are,
   O loved one, delect<u>able</u> maiden!

Rise Up, O Lord

Assumption of the Blessed Virgin Mary (August 15), Song for the Word

Antiphon $\quad$ = 50

Rise up, O Lord, to the place of your rest,

you and the ark of your ho - li - ness.

Verse Tone

Psalm 132:6-7, 9-10, 13-14

1. At Ephrata we heard of the ark;
   we found it in the plains of Yearim.
   "Let us go to the place of God's dwelling;
   let us go to kneel at God's footstool."

2. Your priests shall be clothed with holiness;
   your faithful shall ring out their joy.
   For the sake of David your servant
   do not reject your anointed.

3. For the LORD has chosen Zion;
   has desired it for a dwelling:
   "This is my resting-place for ever,
   here have I chosen to live."

C-226

My Soul Rejoices in God

Assumption of the Blessed Virgin Mary (August 15), Song for the Table

Antiphon ♩= 104

My soul re-joi-ces in God, all my be-ing bles-ses God's name.

Verse Tone with Response

...My soul re-joi-ces in God,

...all my be-ing bles-ses God's name.

Luke 1:46-55

1. My soul glorifies <u>the</u> Lord, *My soul rejoices . . .*
   my spirit rejoices in <u>God</u>, my Savior. *All my being . . .*

2. He looks on his servant in <u>her</u> lowliness; *(simile)*
   henceforth all generations will <u>call</u> me blessed.

3. The Almighty works marvels <u>for</u> me.
   Ho<u>ly</u> his name!

4. His mercy is from age <u>to</u> age
   on <u>those</u> who fear him.

5. He puts forth his arm <u>in</u> strength
   and scat<u>ters</u> the proud-hearted.

6. He casts the mighty from <u>their</u> thrones
   and rai<u>ses</u> the lowly.

7. He fills the starving with <u>good</u> things,
   sends the rich <u>away</u> empty.

8. He protects Israel <u>his</u> servant,
   remember<u>ing</u> his mercy,

9. the mercy promised to <u>our</u> fathers,
   for Abraham and his chil<u>dren</u> for ever.

Our Glory and Pride Is the Cross of Jesus Christ

Exaltation of the Holy Cross (September 14), Song for the Day

Antiphon ♩ = 88

Our glo - ry and pride is the cross of Je - sus Christ; re - deemed by him, we have life, raised from the dead.

Verse Tone

Let the peoples praise you, O God; let all the peo - ples praise you.

Psalm 67

1. O God, be gracious <u>and</u> bless us
   and let your face shed <u>its</u> light upon us.
   So will your ways be known up<u>on</u> earth
   and all nations learn your sav<u>ing</u> help.
   Let the peoples . . .

2. Let the nations be glad and <u>exult</u>
   for you rule the world <u>with</u> justice.

With fairness you rule <u>the</u> peoples,
you guide the nations <u>on</u> earth.
(simile)

3. The earth has yielded <u>its</u> fruit
   for God, our God, <u>has</u> blessed us.
   May God still give <u>us</u> blessing
   till the ends of the earth stand <u>in</u> awe.

C-228

Rise Up and Tell All Your Children

Exaltation of the Holy Cross (September 14), Song for the Word

Psalm 78:1-2, 34-38

1. Give heed, my people, <u>to</u> my teaching;
   turn your ear to the words <u>of</u> my mouth.
       Do not forget . . .
   I will open my mouth <u>in</u> a parable
   and reveal hidden lessons <u>of</u> the past.
       Do not forget . . .

2. When God slew them <u>they</u> would seek him,
   return and seek <u>him</u> in earnest.   *(simile)*
   They remembered that God <u>was</u> their rock,
   God, the Most High, <u>their</u> redeemer.

3. But the words they spoke <u>were</u> mere flattery;
   they lied to God <u>with</u> their lips.
   For their hearts were not tru<u>ly</u> sincere;
   they were not faithful <u>to</u> the covenant.

4. Yet the one who is full <u>of</u> compassion
   forgave them their <u>sin</u> and spared them.
   So often God held <u>back</u> the anger
   that might have been stirred <u>up</u> in rage.

C-230 Rejoice in the Lord on This Feast of the Saints

All Saints (November 1), Song for the Day

Psalm 33

1. | Ring out your joy to the | LORD, O you just;
   for | praise is fitting for | loyal hearts.

2. Give | thanks to the LORD upon the | harp,
   with a | ten-stringed lute play your | songs.

3. | Sing to the LORD a | song that is new,
   play | loudly with all your | skill.

4. | For the word of the | LORD is faithful
   and | all his works done in | truth.

5. | The LORD loves | justice and right
   and | fills the earth with his | love.

6. | By God's word the | heavens were made,
   by the | breath of his mouth all the | stars.

7. | God collects the | waves of the ocean,
   and | stores up the depths of the | sea.

8. | Let all the earth fear the | LORD,
   all who | live in the world stand in | awe.

9. For God | spoke; it came to | be.
   God com- | manded; it sprang into | being.

10. The | LORD foils the designs of the | nations,
    and de- | feats the plans of the | peoples.

11. The | counsel of the LORD stands for- | ever,
    the | plans of God's heart from age to | age.

12. | They are happy, whose | God is the LORD,
    the | people who are chosen as his | own.

13. From the | heavens the LORD looks | forth
    and | sees all the peoples of the | earth.

14. From the | heavenly dwelling God | gazes
    on | all the dwellers on the | earth;

15. | God who shapes the | hearts of them all
and con- | siders all their | deeds.

16. A | king is not saved by his | army,
nor a | warrior preserved by his | strength.

17. A | vain hope for safety is the | horse;
despite its | power it cannot | save.

18. The | Lord looks on those who re- | vere him,
on | those who hope in his | love,

19. to | rescue their souls from | death,
to | keep them alive in | famine.

20. | Our soul is | waiting for the Lord.
The | Lord is our help and our | shield.

21. | Our hearts find | joy in the Lord.
We | trust in God's holy | name.

22. May your | love be upon us, O | Lord,
as we | place all our hope in | you.

Lord, This Is the People

All Saints (November 1), Song for the Word

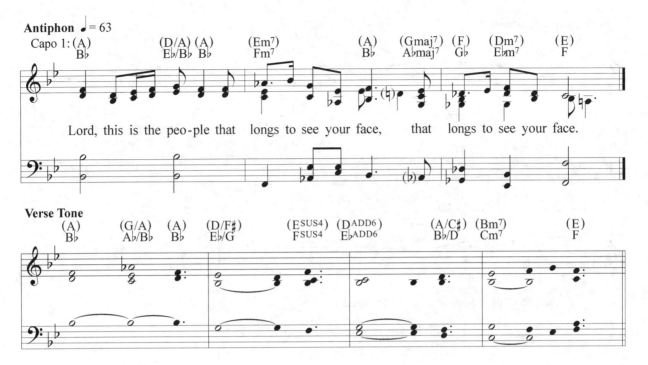

Psalm 24:1-6

1. The LORD's is the <u>earth</u> and its <u>full</u>ness,
   the world and all <u>its</u> peoples.
   It is God who set it on <u>the</u> seas,
   who made it firm <u>on</u> the waters.

2. Who shall climb the <u>moun</u>tain of the <u>LORD</u>?
   Who shall stand in God's ho<u>ly</u> place?
   Those with clean hands and <u>pure</u> hearts,
   who desire not <u>worth</u>less things.

3. They shall receive <u>bless</u>ings from the <u>LORD</u>
   and reward from the God <u>who</u> saves them.
   These are the ones <u>who</u> seek,
   seek the face of the <u>God</u> of Jacob.

The Spirit and the Bride Say "Come!"

All Saints (November 1), Song for the Table

Antiphon *Very flexibly* ♩ = ca. 80

The Spi - rit and the Bride say "Come!" Hap - py are they in -

vi - ted to the wed - ding of the Lamb.

Verse Tone

Matthew 5:3-10; Isaiah 66:10-14a

1. Blessed are the poor in spirit,
   for theirs is the kingdom of heaven.
   Blessed are those who mourn,
   for they will be comforted.

2. Blessed are the meek,
   for they will inherit the earth.
   Blessed are those who hunger and
      thirst for righteousness,
   for they will be filled.

3. Blessed are the merciful,
   for they will receive mercy.
   Blessed are the pure in heart,
   for they will see God.

4. Blessed are the peacemakers,
   for they will be called children of God.
   Blessed are those who are persecuted for
      righteousness' sake,
   for theirs is the kingdom of heaven.

5. Rejoice with Jerusalem,
   and be glad for her, all you who love her;
   rejoice with her in joy,
   all you who mourn over her—

6. that you may nurse and be satisfied
   from her consoling breast;
   that you may drink deeply with delight
   from her glorious bosom.

Verse Tone

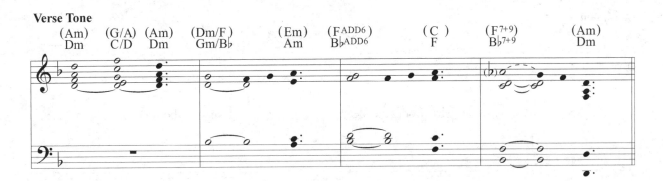

7. For thus <u>says</u> the L<small>ORD</small>:
   I will extend prosperity to her <u>like</u> a river,
   and the wealth <u>of</u> the nations
   like an over<u>flow</u>ing stream;

8. and you shall nurse and be <u>carried</u> on her <u>arm</u>,
   and dandled <u>on</u> her knees.
   As a mother com<u>forts</u> her child,
   so I will <u>comfort</u> you.

9. You shall be <u>comforted</u> in Jeru<u>salem</u>.
   You shall see, and your heart <u>shall</u> rejoice;
   your bo<u>dies</u> shall flourish
   <u>like</u> the grass.

10. And it <u>shall</u> be <u>known</u>
    that the hand of the L<small>ORD</small> is <u>with</u> his servants,
    and his <u>indignation</u>
    is a<u>gainst</u> his enemies.

Alternate Verse Tone

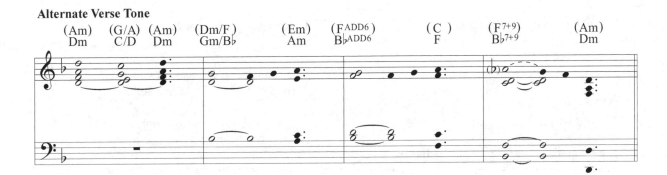

Performance Notes

In both Antiphon and tone, the A-naturals with flats in parentheses indicate optional "blue notes."
The double underlined word "like" in verse nine is sung over the slurred notes.

C-233
God, Who Raised Jesus from the Dead
All Souls (November 2), Song for the Day

Psalm 16:1-2, 5-11

1. Preserve me, God, I take <u>ref</u>uge in <u>you</u>.
[Repeat A]
   I say to you, L<small>ORD</small>: "You are my <u>God</u>.
   My happiness lies in <u>you</u> alone."

2. O L<small>ORD</small>, it is you who are my <u>por</u>tion and <u>cup</u>,
   it is you yourself who <u>are</u> my prize.

3. The lot marked out for <u>me</u> is my de<u>light</u>,
   welcome indeed the her<u>it</u>age that falls to me!

4. I will bless you, L<small>ORD</small>, you give me <u>coun</u>sel,
   and even at night di<u>rect</u> my heart.

5. I keep you, L<small>ORD</small>, ever in my <u>sight</u>;
   since you are at my right hand, I <u>shall</u> stand firm.

6. And so my heart re<u>joic</u>es, my soul is <u>glad</u>;
   even my body shall <u>rest</u> in safety.

7. For you will not leave my <u>soul</u> among the <u>dead</u>,
   nor let your beloved <u>know</u> decay.

8. You will show me the <u>path</u> of <u>life</u>,
   the fullness of joy <u>in</u> your presence,
[Repeat B]
   at your right hand happ<u>iness</u> for ever.

My Shepherd Is the Lord

All Souls (November 2), Song for the Word: First Mass

Psalm 23

1. Fresh and green are the pastures   *there is . . .*
   where you give me repose.   *my God . . .*
   Near restful waters you lead me   *there is . . .*
   to revive my drooping spirit.   *my God . . .*

2. You guide me along the right path;   *(simile)*
   you are true to your name.
   If I should walk in the valley of darkness
   no evil would I fear.
   You are there with your crook and your staff;
   with these you give me comfort.

3. You have prepared a banquet for me
   in the sight of my foes.
   My head you have anointed with oil;
   my cup is overflowing.

4. Surely goodness and kindness shall follow me
   all the days of my life.
   In the LORD's own house shall I dwell
   for ever and ever.

Lord, Listen to My Prayer

All Souls (November 2), Song for the Word: Second Mass

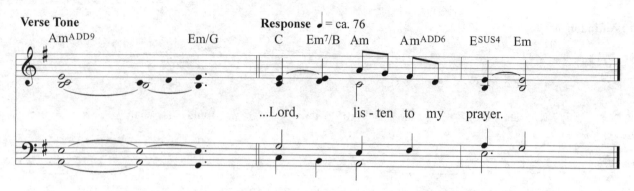

Psalm 143 *[The Lectionary selections for the day are indicated by an asterisk.]*

1. * LORD, turn your ear to <u>my</u> appeal: *Lord, listen . . .*
2. * You are faithful, you are <u>just</u>; give answer: *(simile)*
3. Do not call your ser<u>vant</u> to judgement:
4. No one is just <u>in</u> your sight:
5. The enemy pur<u>sues</u> my soul:
6. The enemy has crushed my life <u>to</u> the ground:
7. The enemy has made me <u>dwell</u> in darkness:
8. The enemy has made me like the dead, <u>long</u>-forgotten:
9. Therefore my <u>spirit</u> fails:
10. My heart is <u>numb</u> within me:
11. * I remember the days <u>that</u> are past:
12. * I ponder <u>all</u> your works:
13. * I muse on what your <u>hand</u> has wrought:
14. * To you I stretch <u>out</u> my hands:
15. * Like a parched land my soul <u>thirsts</u> for you:
16. * LORD, make <u>haste</u> and answer:
17. * My spirit <u>fails</u> within me:
18. Do not <u>hide</u> your face:
19. Do not let me become like those <u>in</u> the grave:
20. * In the morning let me <u>know</u> your love:
21. * I put my <u>trust</u> in you:
22. Make me know the way <u>I</u> should walk:
23. To you I lift <u>up</u> my soul:
24. Rescue me, LORD, <u>from</u> my enemies;
25. I have fled to <u>you</u> for refuge:
26. * Teach me to <u>do</u> your will:
27. * You, O LORD, <u>are</u> my God:
28. * Let your good <u>spirit</u> guide me:
29. * Lead me in ways that are <u>level</u> and smooth:
30. For your name's sake, LORD, <u>save</u> my life:
31. In your justice save my soul <u>from</u> distress:
32. In your love make an end <u>of</u> my foes:
33. Destroy all those <u>who</u> oppress me:
34. I am your <u>servant</u>, LORD:

How I Thirst for You

All Souls (November 2), Song for the Word: Third Mass

Psalm 42:2-3, 5cdef; 43:3-5

1. Like the deer that yearns for <u>running</u> streams   *How I thirst . . .*
   so my soul is yearning for <u>you</u>, my God.   *When shall I see . . .*

2. My soul is thirsting for God, the God <u>of</u> my life;   *(simile)*
   when can I enter and see the <u>face</u> of God?

3. I would lead the rejoicing crowd into the <u>house</u> of God,
   amid cries of gladness and thanksgiving, the throng <u>wild</u> with joy.

4. O send forth your light and your truth; let these <u>be</u> my guide.
   Let them bring me to your holy mountain, to the place <u>where</u> you dwell.

5. And I will come to your altar, O God, the God <u>of</u> my joy.
   My redeemer, I will thank you on the harp, O <u>God</u>, my God.

6. Why are you cast down, my soul, why <u>groan</u> within me?
   Hope in God; I will praise yet again my savior <u>and</u> my God.

Eat My Flesh and Drink My Blood

All Souls (November 2), Song for the Table

Verses Superimposed tone

cf. John 11:25-26; 2 Esdras 2:35, 34; Psalm 27:1, 4, 6c-10, 13-14

1. Believe in me and <u>you</u> shall live,
   even though <u>you</u> die.
   Live and be<u>lieve</u> in me,
   and you will never <u>die</u>.

2. Let eternal <u>light</u>, O Lord,
   for ever shine up<u>on</u> them.
   Set them with your <u>saints</u>, O Lord,
   give them eternal <u>rest</u>.

3. The Lord is my light <u>and</u> my help;
   whom shall <u>I</u> fear?
   The Lord is the stronghold <u>of</u> my life;
   before whom shall I <u>shrink</u>?

4. There is one thing I ask <u>of</u> the Lord,
   for this <u>I</u> long,
   to live in the house <u>of</u> the Lord
   all the days of my <u>life</u>,

5. to savor the sweetness <u>of</u> the Lord,
   to behold <u>his</u> temple;
   and I shall offer with<u>in</u> God's tent
   a sacrifice of <u>joy</u>.

6. O Lord, hear my voice <u>when</u> I call;
   have mercy <u>and</u> answer.
   Of you my <u>heart</u> has spoken:
   "Seek God's <u>face</u>."

7. It is your face, O Lord, <u>that</u> I seek;
   hide not <u>your</u> face.
   Dismiss not your ser<u>vant</u> in anger;
   you have been my <u>help</u>.

8. Do not abandon <u>or</u> forsake me,
   O God <u>my</u> help!
   Though father and mo<u>ther</u> forsake me,
   the Lord will re<u>ceive</u> me.

9. I am sure I shall see <u>the</u> Lord's goodness
   in the land of <u>the</u> living.
   In the Lord, hold firm <u>and</u> take heart.
   Hope in the <u>Lord</u>!

I Will Dwell with You

Dedication of the Lateran Basilica (November 9), Song for the Day

Verse Tone

Antiphon ♩ = 65

I will dwell with you, my house a house of prayer: you shall be my peo-ple,

Drone E⁻³

I will be your God.

Revelation 21:1a, 2-5ab, 6; 22:17

1. I saw a new heaven and a new earth
   and I saw the holy city,
   the new Jerusalem,
   coming down out of heaven
   prepared as a bride
   adorned for her husband.
   And I heard a loud voice
   from the throne saying:

2. "See, the home of God is among mortals.
   He will dwell with them as their God;
   they will be his peoples,
   and God himself will be with them;
   he will wipe every tear from their eyes.
   Death will be no more:
   mourning and crying and pain will be no more,
   for the first things have passed away."

3. And the one who was seated on the throne said,
   "See, I am making all things new."
   Then he said to me:
   "It is done!
   I am the Alpha and the Omega,
   the beginning and the end.
   To the thirsty I will give water
   from the spring of the water of life."

4. The Spirit and the bride say, "Come."
   And let everyone who hears say, "Come."
   And let everyone who is thirsty come,
   take the water of life as a gift.

Performance Notes

The drone is preferably hummed (to an 'n' sound rather than an 'm' sound), but may also be sustained on the organ or played by guitars strumming an E chord without the 3rd on the first beat of every measure only.
Note the correct accentuation of "Omega" in verse 3, with the stress on the first and not the second syllable.

A River Flows

Dedication of the Lateran Basilica (November 9), Song for the Word

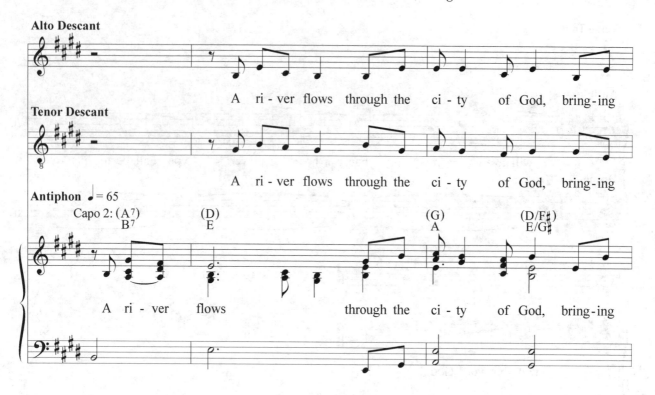

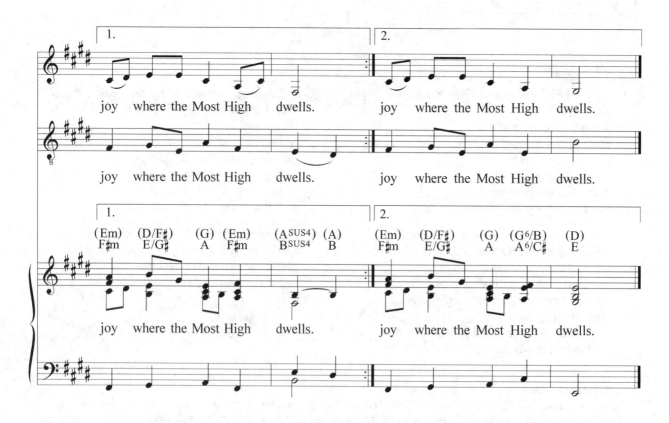

Verse Tone

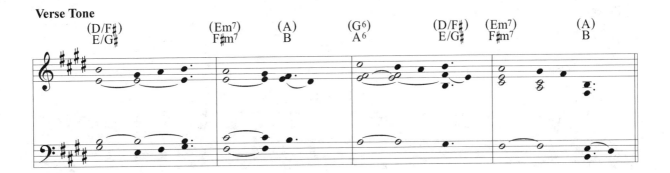

Psalm 46:2-3, 5-6, 11-12

1. God is for us a refuge and strength,
   a helper close at hand, in time of distress,
   so we shall not fear though the earth should rock,
   though the mountains fall into the depths of the sea.

2. The waters of a river give joy to God's city,
   the holy place where the Most High dwells.
   God is within, it cannot be shaken;
   God will help it at the dawning of the day.

3. "Be still and know that I am God,
   supreme among the nations, supreme on the earth!"
   The LORD of hosts is with us;
   the God of Jacob is our stronghold.

C-240

Ask and Receive

Dedication of the Lateran Basilica (November 9), Song for the Table

Psalms 133, 134, 135:1-4, 13-14

1. How good and how pleasant it <u>is</u>,
[omit B-C]
   when people <u>live</u> in unity.

2. It is like precious oil upon the <u>head</u>,
   running down upon the <u>beard</u>,
   running down upon <u>Aaron's</u> beard,
   upon the collar <u>of</u> his robes.

3. It is like the dew of <u>Hermon</u>
   which falls on the heights of <u>Zion</u>.
   For there the Lord gives blessing,
   <u>life</u> for ever.

4. O come, bless the Lord,
   all you who serve the Lord,
   who stand in the house <u>of</u> the Lord,
   in the courts of the house <u>of</u> our God.

5. Lift up your hands to the <u>holy</u> place
   and bless the Lord through the <u>night</u>.
   May the Lord bless <u>you</u> from Zion,
   God who made both hea<u>ven</u> and earth.

6. Alleluia! Praise the name of the Lord,
   praise, you servants of the Lord,
   who stand in the house <u>of</u> the Lord,
   in the courts of the house <u>of</u> our God.

7. Praise the Lord, for the Lord is <u>good</u>.
   Praise God's name; God is <u>gracious</u>.
   For Jacob has been chosen <u>by</u> the Lord;
   Israel for God's <u>own</u> possession.

8. Lord, your name stands for <u>ever</u>,
   unforgotten from age to <u>age</u>,
   for the Lord does justice <u>for</u> his people;
   the Lord takes pity <u>on</u> his servants.

The Immaculate Conception of the Blessed Virgin Mary (December 8), Song for the Day, same as C-100 ← **C-241**

The Immaculate Conception of the Blessed Virgin Mary (December 8), Song for the Word, same as C-83 ← **C-242**

The Immaculate Conception of the Blessed Virgin Mary (December 8), Song for the Table, same as C-12 ← **C-243**

Anniversary of the Dedication of a Church, Song for the Day, *same as C-134* ← **C-244**

Anniversary of the Dedication of a Church, Song for the Word: Option I, *same as C-18* ← **C-245**

Venite, adoremus

Anniversary of the Dedication of a Church, Song for the Word: Option II

Psalm 95:1-9   [The Lectionary selections for the day are indicated by an asterisk.]

1. * Come, ring out our joy to the LORD;
   * <u>hail</u> the rock who saves us.

2. * Let us come before God, giving thanks,
   * with <u>songs</u> let us hail the LORD.

3. * A mighty God is the LORD,
   * a <u>great</u> king above all gods,

4. * in God's hands are the depths of the earth;
   * the <u>heights</u> of the mountains as well.

5. * The sea belongs to God, who made it
   * and the <u>dry</u> land shaped by his hands.

6. * Come in; let us bow and bend low;
   * let us <u>kneel</u> before the God who made us

7. * for this is our God and we
   * the <u>people</u> who belong to his pasture,

8. * we are the flock
   * that is <u>led</u> by God's hand.

9. O that today you would
   <u>listen</u> to God's voice!

10. "Harden not your hearts as at Meribah,
    as on that <u>day</u> at Massah in the desert;

11. harden not your hearts
    as when your <u>ancestors</u> put me to the test;

12. harden not your hearts
    as when your <u>ancestors</u> tried me,
    though they saw my work."

Performance Notes

The Antiphon can be used as an ostinato chant, or with psalm verses. When using the psalm, the Antiphon should be established before the cantor begins to chant lines of the psalm on a high C over the first half of the Antiphon, (pickup and measure one with first line of psalm verse; the underlined syllable in the second line of the verse coincides with the beginning of measure two). Meanwhile, the first half of the Antiphon can be sung quietly underneath with its text, or simply hummed. The second half of the Antiphon (with its text) then becomes a refrain at the end of each verse.

You Are God's Temple

Anniversary of the Dedication of a Church, Song for the Table

Verses *Psalms 133; 134; and 135:1-2*

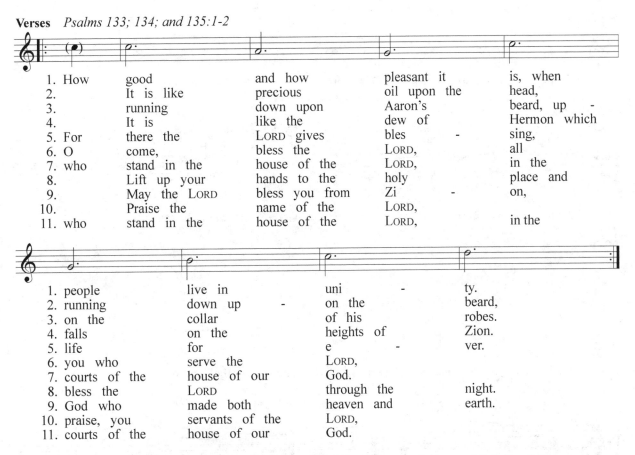

1. How good and how pleasant it is, when
2. It is like precious oil upon the head,
3. running down upon Aaron's beard, up -
4. It is like the dew of Hermon which
5. For there the LORD gives bles - sing,
6. O come, bless the LORD, all
7. who stand in the house of the LORD, in the
8. Lift up your hands to the holy place and
9. May the LORD bless you from Zi - on,
10. Praise the name of the LORD,
11. who stand in the house of the LORD, in the

1. people live in uni - ty.
2. running down up - on the beard,
3. on the collar of his robes.
4. falls on the heights of Zion.
5. life for e - ver.
6. you who serve the LORD,
7. courts of the house of our God.
8. bless the LORD through the night.
9. God who made both heaven and earth.
10. praise, you servants of the LORD,
11. courts of the house of our God.

C-249

Sing and Make Music
Thanksgiving Day, Song for the Day

Descant

Sing and make mu - sic to God in your hearts.

Antiphon ♩ = 120

Capo 3: (Em) (Bm) (A⁷) (Bm)
Gm Dm C⁷ Dm

Sing and make mu - sic to God in your hearts.

Al - ways give thanks in the name of the Lord.

(C) (G) (Am) (D)
E♭ B♭ Cm⁷ F

Al - ways give thanks in the name of the Lord.

Verse Tone

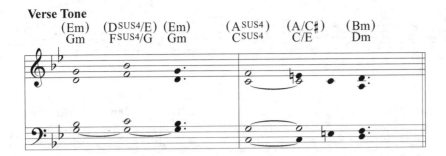

Psalm 147

1. Alleluia, alleluia!
   Sing praise to the LORD who is good.

2. Sing to our God who is loving:
   to God our praise is due.

3. The LORD builds up Jerusalem
   and brings back Israel's exiles.

4. God heals the broken-hearted,
   and binds up all their wounds.

5. God fixes the number of the stars;
   and calls each one by its name.

6. Our LORD is great and almighty;
   God's wisdom can never be measured.

7. The LORD raises the lowly;
   and humbles the wicked to the dust.

8. O sing to the LORD, giving thanks;
   sing psalms to our God with the harp.

9. God covers the heavens with clouds,
   and prepares the rain for the earth.

10. God makes mountains sprout with grass
    and with plants to serve our needs.

11. God provides the beasts with their food
    and the young ravens when they cry.

12. God takes no delight in horses' power
    nor pleasure in warriors' strength.

13. The LORD delights in those who revere him,
    in those who wait for his love.

14. O praise the LORD, Jerusalem!
    Zion, praise your God!

15. God has strengthened the bars of your gates,
    and has blessed the children within you.

16. God has established peace on your borders,
    and feeds you with finest wheat.

17. God sends out word to the earth
    and swiftly runs the command.

18. God showers down snow white as wool,
    and scatters hoarfrost like ashes.

19. God hurls down hailstones like crumbs,
    and causes the waters to freeze.

20. God sends forth a word and it melts them:
    at the breath of God's mouth the waters flow.

21. God makes his word known to Jacob,
    to Israel his laws and decrees.

22. God has not dealt thus with other nations;
    has not taught them divine decrees. Alleluia!

C-250

Our God Has Blessed Us
Thanksgiving Day, Song for the Word

Descant

God, our God has bless'd us.

Antiphon ♩ = 88

C   Cmaj7   AmADD9   F   Em/G   Dm7   Am

God, our God has bless'd us and the earth brings forth her fruit.

Verse Tone

C   G/C   F/C   C   Am   Em/G   F   Dm7   Em7   F

Psalm 67

1. O God, be gracious <u>and</u> bless us
   and let your face shed its light <u>upon</u> us.
   So will your ways be known <u>upon</u> earth
   and all nations learn your <u>saving</u> help.

2. Let the nations be glad and <u>exult</u>
   for you rule the world <u>with</u> justice.
   With fairness you <u>rule</u> the peoples,
   you guide the <u>nations</u> on earth.

3. The earth has yielded <u>its</u> fruit
   for God, our God, <u>has</u> blessed us.
   May God still <u>give</u> us blessing
   till the ends of the earth <u>stand</u> in awe.

4. Let the peoples praise you, <u>O</u> God;
   let all the <u>peoples</u> praise you.
   Let the peoples praise <u>you</u>, O God,
   let all the <u>peoples</u> praise you.

May God Grant Us Joy of Heart

Thanksgiving Day, Song for the Table

Verses *Psalm 138*

Superimposed tone

1. I thank you with all my heart, you have
2. I thank you: you are faith - ful, and I
3. All the ru - lers of the earth shall thank you when they
4. The LORD looks kind - ly on the low - ly but the
5. You stretch out your hand to save me, your
6. *Al - le - lu - ia, al - le - lu - ia, al - le -*

Alto Descant *(hummed except for last two measures)*

Al - le -

Bass Descant

May God grant us joy of heart, and may
Al - le - lu - ia, al - le - lu - ia, al - le -

Antiphon ♩ = 76

Capo 3: (D⁷) (G) (Bm⁷)
F⁷ B♭ Dm⁷

May God grant us joy of heart, and may
Al - le - lu - ia, al - le - lu - ia, al - le -

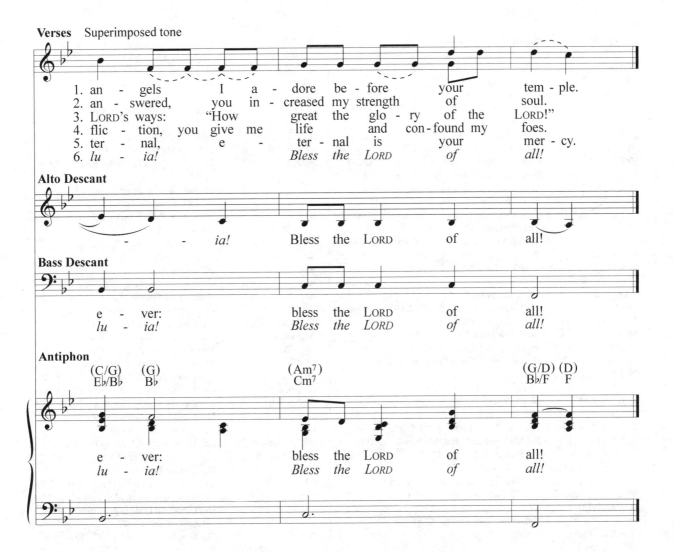

Verses Superimposed tone

1. an - gels I a - dore be - fore your tem - ple.
2. an - swered, you in - creased my strength of soul.
3. LORD's ways: "How great the glo - ry of the LORD!"
4. flic - tion, you give me life and con - found my foes.
5. ter - nal, e - ter - nal is your mer - cy.
6. *lu - ia!* *Bless the LORD of all!*

Alto Descant

- - ia! Bless the LORD of all!

Bass Descant

e - ver: bless the LORD of all!
lu - ia! *Bless the LORD of all!*

Antiphon

(C/G) (G) (Am⁷) (G/D) (D)
Eb/Bb Bb Cm⁷ Bb/F F

e - ver: bless the LORD of all!
lu - ia! *Bless the LORD of all!*

Performance Notes

At the end of the piece, the Antiphon may be repeated using the Alleluias in italics instead of the usual text or humming.